HOW THE DESTINATION CONTENT WORKS

Each destination includes a short introduction, an A–Z of practical information and recommended points of interest, split into 4 different categories:

- Highlights
- Accommodation
- Eating out
- What to do

You can view the location of every point of interest and save it by adding it to your Favourites. In the 'Around Me' section you can view all the points of interest within 5km.

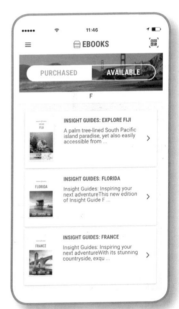

HOW THE EBOOKS WORK

The eBooks are provided in EPUB file format. Please note that you will need an eBook reader installed on your device to open the file. Many devices come with this as standard, but you may still need to install one manually from Google Play.

The eBook content is identical to the content in the printed guide.

HOW TO DOWNLOAD THE WALKING EYE APP

1. Download the Walking Eye App from the App Store or Google Play.
2. Open the app and select the scanning function from the main menu.
3. Scan the QR code on this page – you will then be asked a security question to verify ownership of the book.
4. Once this has been verified, you will see your eBook and destination content in the purchased ebook and destination sections, where you will be able to download them.

Other destination apps and eBooks are available for purchase separately or are free with the purchase of the Insight Guide book.

Contents

THE BEST OF BANGKOK: TOP ATTRACTIONS

At a glance, the attractions in and around Bangkok that you can't afford to miss, from fairy-tale temples to flea markets and ancient ruins to idyllic beaches.

◁ **Ayutthaya.** Thailand's former capital until the Burmese destroyed it in 1767, ancient Ayutthaya is now a Unesco World Heritage Site, where the ruins offer a glimpse into the city's glorious past. See page 216.

▽ **Islands of the Eastern Seaboard.** From the small islands off Pattaya to Ko Samet and Ko Chang, there are white sand beaches with diving, sailing and delicious barbecue parties with succulent fresh seafood. See page 208.

▽ **Chatuchak Market.** Join the 100,000 shoppers at "the world's largest flea market". Search hard and you'll find what you are looking for; follow your nose and you'll discover unimagined treasures. See page 180.

▽ **Wat Pho.** Bangkok's oldest temple is known as Thailand's first university, and it is still the main centre for learning Thai massage. It also holds the stunning Reclining Buddha image. See page 118.

△ **The Bridge over the River Kwai.** In one of the most scenic parts of Thailand yet close to Bangkok, Kanchanaburi draws in tourists for its natural beauty and war-time attractions. The bridge, made famous in the movie of the same name, isn't far from the town centre and is a moving experience. See page 193.

△ **The Mandarin Oriental.** The "Old Lady of Bangkok" has provided lodgings since the 19th century. Guests have included many famous writers, who are honoured in its colonial-style Author's Wing, a lovely spot for afternoon tea. See page 168.

▽ **Erawan Falls.** Climb the seven tiers to the top of this most famous of waterfalls, and you'll be rewarded with stunning views over the national park countryside towards the border with Burma (Myanmar). See page 197.

△ **Ancient City.** Leave Bangkok for the bucolic surrounds of this Thailand-shaped park with near life-size, and painstakingly accurate, replicas of important temples and palaces, including some lost centuries ago. See page 205.

▽ **Khao Yai.** You probably won't see a tiger in Thailand's first national park, but you will see macaques, and possibly bears, and the waterfall from the film *The Beach*. And then you can tour wine country. See page 224.

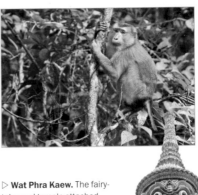

▷ **Wat Phra Kaew.** The fairy-tale royal temple attached to Bangkok's Grand Palace glitters golden in the sun. It contains several important religious buildings and the most sacred Buddha image in Thailand, over which *yaksha* (demon) statues stand guard. See page 106.

THE BEST OF BANGKOK: EDITOR'S CHOICE

Setting priorities, saving money, unique attractions... here, at a glance, are our recommendations, plus some tips and tricks even Bangkokians won't always know.

BEST FOR FAMILIES

These attractions are popular with children, though not all will suit every age group.

Dusit Zoo. Kids love the lions and tigers and monkeys swinging through the trees. Boating on the lake provides respite when they get tired. See page 144.

Crocodile Farm and Zoo. Visitors shriek as handlers wrestle with large crocodiles and stick their heads between the snapping jaws of these monstrous reptiles. See page 207.

Dream World. There are good views from the cable cars at this adventure park and stomach-churners like

the Grand Canyon water ride. They even have snow to cool you down. See page 182.

Rose Garden Riverside Resort. Traditional dancers, Thai boxing and other folk culture are performed in a garden setting outside Bangkok. See page 189.

Samphran Elephant Ground. Learn about the pachyderm's role in Thailand, with fun elephant rides and re-enactments of battles. See page 190.

Siam Ocean World. A giant aquarium with over 30,000 marine creatures and glass-bottomed boat rides will leave kids spellbound. See page 158.

Dream World roller coaster fun.

Frenetic Thai boxing, or muay thai.

ONLY IN BANGKOK

Canal Cruising. Hop aboard a longtail boat and glide along canals (khlong) for a slice of Bangkok's past. See page 130.

Extreme Makeover. On holiday, why not have a tummy tuck, nose-job, or even a gender reassignment? Bangkok is a world hub for medical tourism with 5-star care at bargain prices. See page 240.

Jumbo Queen. See a charitable beauty pageant open to only heavier women. See page 190.

Ladyboy Cabaret. Bangkok's Vegas-style shows by elaborately costumed transvestite

performers are now travelling the world. See page 88.

Motorcycle Taxis. Fast and furious, these waistcoat-wearing madmen weave through the city's grid-lock at knee-trembling speeds. Helmets optional, courage essential. See page 233.

Thai Boxing. Punishing and brutal, this ancient martial art is more than just sport, with drinking and gambling on the sidelines. See page 89.

Tuk-Tuk. An icon of the city, these noisy three-wheelers should be experienced at least once. See page 233.

BEST FESTIVALS AND EVENTS

Bangkok Film Festival. A chance to view acclaimed local- and foreign-produced flicks and mingle with stars at the film screenings. Nov. www.worldfilmbkk.com

Chinese New Year. Get into the action in Chinatown where loud firecrackers, boisterous lion and dragon dances and festival foods herald in the start of the new year for Bangkok's Chinese. Jan/Feb. See page 239.

Father's Day. On Father's Day, key streets in Bangkok are magically lit up in the colours of the national flag while fireworks pierce the night sky. 5 Dec. See page 239.

Loy Krathong. Expect a visual treat as Bangkokians honour water spirits by lighting candles and incense and setting them afloat on tiny baskets along the city's waterways. Full moon day, Nov. See page 239.

Songkran. Pack water pistols (along with a sense of humour) for a three-day soaking. The Thai Lunar New Year is the nation's largest and wettest celebration. 13–15 Apr. See page 239.

Lighting candles in honour of the water spirits during the Loy Krathong festival.

BEST WALKS

Banglamphu. A district of old shophouses, grand mansions, colourful backpacker bars and a riverbank park. See page 140.

Chinatown. This is Bangkok at its visceral best: narrow lanes awash with local colour and mercantile bustle. See page 147.

Lumphini Park. The city's favourite green lung buzzes to life at dawn and dusk with both exercise fiends and those content to just watch them. See page 161.

Rattanakosin. The capital's historic heart brims with architectural grandeur. Royal palaces and devotional tributes abound in this old neighbourhood. See page 105.

The Old City. Experience the slower, calmer side of the city with traditional crafts, Buddhist shops, amulet markets and views from the Golden Mount. See page 133.

The Temple of the Emerald Buddha (Wat Phra Kaew) in Rattanakosin.

BEST MARKETS

Chatuchak Weekend Market. The mother of all markets, pulling in nearly half a million people every weekend. An unbeatable shopping experience; it has it all and then some. See page 180.

Damnoen Saduak Floating Market. This century-old market has become a bit of a circus, with tourists clambering to photograph fruit-laden boats paddled by women in straw hats. Nevertheless, it's worth seeking out. See page 192.

Pak Khlong Talad. A 24-hour riot of colour and fragrance; this is where Bangkok gets all its floral garlands for temple offerings. See page 135.

Patpong Night Market. Surrounded by sleaze and neon, the location is as much the attraction as the piles of counterfeit watches, bags, clothes and general tourist tat. See page 171.

Damnoen Saduak Floating Market.

BEST BARS AND CLUBS

Glow. A small club with a big reputation, Glow brings in DJs from around the world, and nurtures local talent. The club is probably at the epicentre of Bangkok's club culture. 96/4-5 Sukhumvit Soi 23; tel: 02 261 4446.

Club Culture. Set in a reclaimed traditional Thai theatre, this club attracts international DJs with a funky edge. Eclectic music range. Soi Damnoen Klang Tai; tel: 089 497 8422.

Distil. This 64th-floor wine bar with heart-stopping views rises taller than any of the city's other stalwart nightspots. Part of State Tower's opulent Dome. www.lebua.com/distil.

The futuristic interior of Bed Supperclub.

Tapas Room. Located at Silom Soi 4's party strip, sit outside to ogle passers-by or head inside for the funkiest DJ-spun house grooves. Soi 4 Thanon Silom; tel: 02 234 4737.

BEST SHOPPING EXPERIENCES

MBK. Lots of fun at this old-school Thai-style mall with stalls in the corridors and everything from cameras to copies of master artworks. See page 157.

Siam Square and

Siam Paragon. A study in contrasts: the former is one of the city's last surviving low-rise street shopping enclaves (popular with pimply adolescents), while the latter, just across the road, is a luxury mall filled with designer goods and the city's high society. See page 157.

Panthip Plaza. Tech-geeks should make a beeline for Bangkok's mecca for computer gadgetry. Stocks both legitimate hard and software as well as pirated games, software, DVDs and VCDs. See page 162.

Central World. Bangkok loves big shopping and this is the biggest mall in the country, full of restaurants, beauty shops, fashion and two department stores. See page 158.

Shopping at Siam Square.

BEST SPAS AND MASSAGES

Devarana. Located at the luxury Dusit Thani hotel, ethereal Devarana is a million miles away from the frenetic city. Calming Zen mood with private treatment suites and a range of therapies that will ease away urban strain. See page 92.

Divana. A well-regarded local spa chain with the full range of treatments at reasonable prices. The Sukhumvit Soi 35 outlet is the most popular. See page 92.

The Mandarin Oriental Spa. In the historic Oriental, this atmospheric luxury spa sits in a century-old teakwood house on the banks of the Chao Phraya river. See page 92.

Wat Pho. In the city's oldest temple, this famous no-frills traditional massage school has blind masseuses giving vigorous rub downs for next to nothing. See pages 119 and 92.

BEST CULTURAL DINING

Loy Nava. Take a wooden barge dinner cruise along the Chao Phraya river, with Thai dancing and traditional music on board. www.loynava.com.

Sala Rim Nam. At the Oriental's riverside restaurant, sit around low tables on cushions and feast on Thai food while watching a condensed history of Thai dance and drama. www.mandarinoriental.com/bangkok/fine-dining/sala-rim-naam.

Siam Niramit. A visual spectacle that presents Thailand's rich history and culture in three acts. Pre-show dinner buffet is optional. www.siamniramit.com.

Thai lakhon dancer in traditional costume.

Luxury Thai spa.

MONEY-SAVING TIPS

Bargaining for Best Deals. While department stores have fixed prices, it's common to bargain at markets and at some small shops. If a shop owner offers to give the "best price", then negotiations are thrown open (see page 75). Remember to keep a sense of humour while bargaining.

Counterfeit Goods. Even the most morally upright go weak in the knees when faced with the onslaught of quality knock-offs at Bangkok's markets, from watches and bags to clothing. There have been recent efforts made to curtail the trade, without too much success. If you succumb, remember: you get what you pay for (see page 76).

Hit the Happy Hour. Afternoon and early evening drinking isn't part of the Bangkok scene, so to draw customers many bars offer incredible happy hour deals – like cheap drinks from noon till 9pm or two-drinks-for-one promotions.

Keep Your Ticket. Hold onto your Grand Palace/Wat Phra Kaew entry ticket as it also gets you into most of the Dusit Park sites (like Vimanmek Mansion and Abhisek Dusit Throne Hall, to name a few) for free.

No Invite, No Matter. Check the daily newspapers and monthly listings magazines for upcoming social events, art openings and promo parties. The city's freeloaders always turn up for free buffets, drinks and entertainment. It's a great way to rub shoulders with the city's elite and fill up for free.

VAT Refunds. Before making significant purchases, ask if the shop offers VAT refunds (7 percent) to tourists. Refunds (see page 243) can be claimed on single items of B2,000 or more, as long as your overall shopping exceeds B5,000. Allow time at the airport to process claims.

A tuk-tuk ride is a quintessential Bangkok experience.

The rewarding climb to the Golden Mount.

Drinks with a stunning view over the Bangkok skyline.

Wat Pho, the Temple of the Reclining Buddha.

WHITE HOT BANGKOK

Still sprawling and steamy hot, Bangkok is reinventing itself for the 21st century. The Asian Tiger economy brought unimagined riches and booming construction but, in old markets and golden temples, glimmers of history poke tantalisingly from behind the modern malls.

Bangkok has hurtled into the 21st century at time-travel pace; a city where it sometimes feels you can live 200 years in a single day. Downtown, booming construction leaves pockets of tradition concealed in its wake. Glass-and-steel shopping malls glint in the sun, dwarfing the wooden trestles of next-door markets; kosher Gucci and fake Rolex just a stone's throw apart. Businessmen savour Fine de Claire oysters in posh restaurants outside which office girls enjoy spicy aromatic salads at a noisy street-side diner. These days they increasingly travel by the underground Metro or elevated Skytrain, as, below, vendors weave their pedal carts between the lines of traffic, where the steamy heat envelopes you like a blanket.

A buzzing night market.

There's a noticeable change of pace in Chinatown, with thrusting commerce in narrow lanes that haven't changed much since the early 19th century. In the Old City the golden spires of fairy-tale temples overlook 100-year-old shophouses where monks search for lucky amulets and Buddha statues down tiny alleyways. Walk ten minutes north and you're in the cosmopolitan backpacker warren of the Khao San Road, a pedestrian-friendly block of guesthouses, bars and clubs, where people make new friends before heading to the islands.

Thais live for *sanuk* (fun), and after sunset there's something for everyone: rice whisky at country music halls; designer cocktails at funky dance clubs; cheap beers in a bar with no walls; or flutes of champagne served up with 200-metre (656ft) -high rooftop views of the city.

Bangkok is modern Asia, its all-too-recent traditional life breathing strong inside a thrilling new adventure.

Door detail at the Phra Nakhon Khiri Historical Park, Phetchaburi.

Fresh lime juice vendor.

PEOPLE

The furious pace of growth has caused huge disparities between Bangkok's residents. Well-heeled "hi-sos" sip champagne in nightclubs, as northeastern migrants down rice whisky at boondock barns. Both, though, buy garlands from kids on the street. And binding all is a ubiquitous sense of fun.

The Bangkokian appears in many guises. Sitting behind the darkened windows of a chauffeur-driven Mercedes is the high-society lady on her way to a VIP gala function. Hurrying up the steps of the Skytrain station is the young and smartly dressed office manager, late for a meeting. Slicing up a watermelon on his cart in front of a towering office block is the fruit vendor busy with the lunchtime crowds. Bangkok is a city of contrasts – between wealth and poverty, east and west, the old and the new. The city's inhabitants dwell on all sides of these delineations, with many creatively straddling more than one divide.

City on the move

Bangkok is forever shifting, always adapting to Western trends and outside influences. The cityscape is in a constant state of renewal, with old wooden buildings frequently demolished to make way for modern office and shopping complexes. For the most part, Bangkokians are creatures of this environment, enthusiastically embracing all things new. Trends spread through the city like wildfire, from the craze for fitness gyms to Starbucks copy-cat cafés. Clubs and restaurants open and close at a bewildering rate as they fall in and out of fashion.

Though the capital's official population hovers around 6 million, the large number of migrant workers bring most estimates closer to 12 million. Bangkok's biggest growth spurt has taken place during the economic boom years from the 1980s, during which the Bangkok dream has become a reality for many. As glass-and-chrome condos rise into the sky, Western

Friendly smile at the Flower Market.

COOL HEARTS

The essential ingredient to surviving the stresses of daily life in the hot and humid streets of Bangkok is the Thai concept of *jai yen* (literally, "cool heart"). *Jai yen* is about taking obstacles in your stride. It is the antithesis of out-of-control tempers and sudden anger. This very Thai concept ensures that an oasis of calm exists inside every Bangkokian; differences of opinion rarely escalate to fistfights, and misunderstandings are countered with a smile. The accompanying phrase that answers to all of life's vicissitudes is *mai pen rai*, or "never mind". Make use of both these concepts and Bangkok will seem a little less difficult.

A NATION DIVIDED

Thailand's recent political crisis started in 2006 with the disposing of Prime Minister Thaksin Shinawatra via a bloodless military coup d'état. Thaksin was roundly regarded as a self-serving politician who changed laws to further his business interests. But this is far from unusual in Thailand; what he did that was slightly different to the norms of political life was his introduction of policies such as affordable health care that made real changes to poor people's lives. They elected him time and again with a huge majority.

In the years following the coup the anti-Thaksin Yellow Shirts and pro-Thaksin Red Shirts infiltrated every aspect of daily life. Hundreds of thousands marched on both sides; people defined themselves as "red shirt" or "yellow shirt", dividing offices and homes; Thais discussed politics like never before.

Grass-roots movements, previously a mess of disparate causes, have united behind the Red Shirts, who by February 2010 consisted of 459 affiliated organisations from around the country. The media claimed the 2006 coup instigators were "the traditional ruling elite". The cost for them of removing Thaksin has been long-term change in the political landscape. As one Red Shirt leader said about the coup makers: "They have turned Thaksin the big capitalist into Thaksin the revolutionary." Subsequent demonstrations and counter demonstrations led to another coup in 2014. The military have taken a sterner line with decent this time around and the political landscape is changing as a result.

fast-food outlets take over the streets, along with glitzy nightclubs and swanky restaurants.

This perennial change is oiled by the generally accepting Thai nature and the Buddhist concept of non-attachment. Historically, rather than resisting outside influences, Thailand has always welcomed them, and traditionally chooses compromise over conflict. Which is why the ongoing, sometimes violent, political struggle of recent years has taken many by surprise (see box). While there are those who deride Bangkok as not representing the "real" Thailand, the city stubbornly retains a sense of Thai-ness. Beneath the yellow arches of McDonald's you'll find women threading fragrant jasmine garlands and next to every modern skyscraper is an old shrine where the spirits of the land are still appeased each day.

The traditional Thai greeting known as the wai.

Sanuk means fun

The city is infused with the Bangkokian's search for *sanuk*, a Thai word meaning fun. The quantity and quality of *sanuk*, whether in work or play, determines if something is worth pursuing. Checking out anything new – the latest movie, a recently opened restaurant or shopping mall – is a sure-fire *sanuk* activity. Gatherings of friends always have high *sanuk* value, whether it's an evening beneath the gaudy chandeliers of a karaoke club, or huddled around a tin table on the pavement quaffing whisky.

Doing anything alone is generally considered *mai sanuk* (not fun). Thailand's culture and society have traditionally been centred on agriculture, an activity that nurtures a sense of community. The shift to urban life has changed much of the countryside's ways, but it is a rare Thai who does not enjoy getting together with friends. Most are puzzled by Westerners who dine or holiday alone, as they do not understand the occasional need for solitude. The *sanuk* quota of any given event can usually be gauged by the number of people involved: the general rule

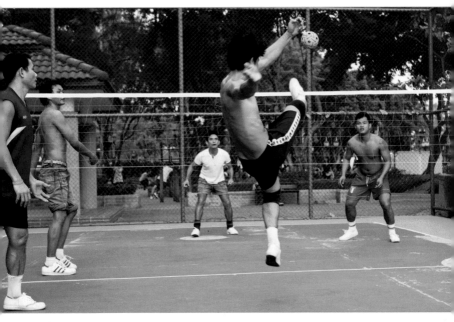

A game of takraw, or kick volleyball.

being "the more, the merrier". A Bangkokian's mobile phone is never silent for long.

Hi-So and Lo-So

Bangkok society is fiercely hierarchical. At the top of the pyramid are the "hi-so", a Thai slang abbreviation for high society. The phrase and its counterpart, "lo-so" (for low society), are used to boost or deride a person's standing: "She's *very* hi-so", or, "Oh no, he's too lo-so". The city's hi-so tribe is not limited only to aristocratic Thai families; the economic boom has created a significant *nouveau riche* class; being hi-so is as much about glamour and wealth as it is about pedigree. The hi-so are pictured in the society pages of newspapers and magazines (like the English-language *Thailand Tatler*), with the women sporting big hair and big jewels. Hi-so life is a seemingly endless whirl of lunches, cocktail parties and shopping.

Many members of the hi-so are Sino-Thai. The Chinese knack for entrepreneurial know-how has ensured that Sino-Thai families control much of Bangkok's wealth. Chinese traders have lived in the Bangkok area since the 18th

> The concept of sanuk (fun) is always close to the surface in Bangkok. Thais seemingly never crave solitude, preferring to gather in groups for drinks and laughter-filled meals of shared food.

century, and have been assimilated, to a remarkable degree, into the life of their adopted land. Chinese and Thais have intermarried freely and there is no outward anti-Chinese bias in Thailand, and racial conflicts like those found in neighbouring countries have been very rare. While some estimates state that a quarter of Bangkok's population is Chinese, it is now hard to differentiate between Chinese and Thais as most second and third generation immigrants are Thai citizens and no longer speak Chinese.

All over the city are billboards advertising the *moo bahn*, or housing estates, that litter the outskirts of Bangkok. Depicting Western-style houses complete with two children and a dog playing in the garden, they appeal to Bangkok's

Spectacular views from the Vertigo Grill – popular with the hi-so.

burgeoning middle-classes. Residing on cheaper land at the city's edge, though, means a long daily commute to work.

Mixed races and migrants

A Bangkok phenomenon of recent years is the rise of the *luk kreung*, literally "half child". *Luk kreung* are mixed-race children, mostly with one

Taxi driver.

Thai and one Caucasian parent. The *luk kreung* "look" is astoundingly popular with Bangkokians and many Bangkok celebrities are *luk kreung* TV presenters, pop stars, soap opera actors and actresses, or models. The *luk kreung* epitomises Bangkok's hybrid culture: Thai, but also a little bit Western. It is a blend that infuses everything from the mix-and-match style of pop music to the city's creative takes on fusion cuisine.

Of other minorities in the city, Indians make up the second largest group after the Chinese. There are around a million Muslim Thai-Malays who are fairly well integrated into Thai society, despite the many killings on both sides in the last decade of separatist unrest in the Muslim provinces of the Deep South. There are also significant groups of expatriates living in Bangkok, working mostly for international companies. Among them are some 25,000 Westerners, known as *farang* or foreigner in Thai, and around 50,000 Japanese, whose "Little Tokyo" is centred around Sukhumvit Soi 33/1.

Less integrated with Bangkok society are the illegal immigrants fleeing poverty in Cambodia and Burma (Myanmar). They provide the city with low-cost labour and are forced into the

Teashop in Chinatown.

seen a shift as the internet generation, many educated abroad, have found a new confidence in Thai and Asian styling, particularly in clothes fashions and interiors. Foreign influences in music and youth trends are as likely to be Japanese or Korean as Western, and bands from both these countries (J-Pop and K-Pop) have huge numbers of fans. And if Japanese manga comics are the biggest read for teenagers, when it comes to music Korean popstars and Korean culture are at the zenith amongst Bangkok's teenage population. Korean restaurants are springing up everywhere and a small Korea 'town' on Sukhumvit Road draws large numbers. Daily viewing of Korean soap-operas (dubbed into Thai) is rapidly becoming the norm for Bangkokian middle class consumption.

Bangkok as a village

The most neglected Bangkokians are the poor, hundreds of thousands of whom live in inner-city slums. The largest of these, Klong Toey, is rapidly disappearing, being replaced by high-rise towers and high-end condo projects. Slum life persists though and is fuelled by *yaa baa* (the Thai word for amphetamines, meaning, literally, "crazy medicine") and desperation forces many people into crime and prostitution. Many are migrants escaping rural poverty in Isaan, northeastern Thailand, where a tenant farmer may earn as little as B30,000 a year. Though the Bangkok dream has yet to filter into their lives, the city would surely collapse without them. Manpower from the northeast provides the city

jobs no one else wants: on construction sites, refuse collection and in factories and brothels. Of the estimated one million migrant workers in Thailand, 800,000 are from Burma.

Rising above and beyond all these social divisions is the king and the Thai royal family. The passing in October 2016 of His Majesty King Bhumibol (see page 47), much-loved and revered figurehead of the nation, was felt as a national tragedy and a year of mourning was

> The admirably named radio station "Let's Get Together and Help People" was established to do just that. People phone in with problems and the listeners rally round to help them.

declared. Portraits of the king and queen hang in almost every office, shop and restaurant. At cinemas, the audience stands while the King's anthem is played before each film. In many ways, the king acts as a moral arbiter for all Bangkokians; while the city races helter-skelter towards all that is new, the monarch stands as a symbol of Thai tradition and old-world values. This institution of the monarchy is still very much revered in Thailand with the passing of King Bhumibol and the crowning of King Vajiralongkorn.

Asian influence

Thailand, like many other countries, in the past looked to the dominant West for direction in fashion, music and film. But the last decade has

Girls at a Japanese-style costume role-play in Bangkok.

Children diving in the polluted canals in the Siam district.

with a crucial task force of taxi and tuk-tuk drivers, construction workers, cleaners and security guards. Many find work in the streets as roving vendors or rubbish-collectors.

Living away from the air-conditioned world of shopping malls and nightclubs, these rural

Little girl coming back from school to life in the slums.

migrants bring a touch of the village to the capital. The outskirts of the city especially have many barn-like halls where bands play regional music like *morlam* to hundreds of Isaanites fuelled by rice whisky.

Despite its wide variety of residents, Bangkok retains many of the traditional communal elements of Thai village life. Proof comes in the form of one of the most popular radio stations, Ruam Duay Chuay Kan, or "Let's Get Together and Help Each Other". The radio station is broadcast live, 24-hours-a-day, and its concept is simple: a person calls in with a problem and the presenters muster all the forces of good in the city to solve it. Bureaucratic tangles are untied, lost relatives are reunited and even Bangkok's steaming gridlock can be moved when drivers hear that a screaming woman in labour is trying to get to hospital. The radio show emphasises the familiar sense of community inherent in village life. Through it, Bangkokians can share practical advice, help out in times of trouble and, of course, stick their noses into other people's businesses. Most of all, though, the station is proof that the big bad city has a heart of gold.

Sin City Bangkok

Bangkok has a complex historical relationship with its sex workers: the trade is both illegal and openly tolerated, a source of shame to some, and of income to others.

Thailand made prostitution illegal in 1960, although the law is rarely enforced, and sex is openly for sale in the capital's many girlie bars, brothels and massage parlours. In part this is because it is an accepted and common practice for Thai men to patronise prostitutes or have a *mia noi*, literally "little wife" or mistress on the side. They will usually patronise more discreet brothels or, at the higher end, plush members-only clubs, while foreign tourists go for the brash red lights of Patpong and Nana Entertainment Plaza.

Sex tourism escalated with American troops taking R&R during the Vietnam War, and, by the 1980s, planeloads of men were flying in for the purpose. Most Bangkok sex workers, both male and female, come from northeast Thailand, where incomes are the lowest in the country. They regularly send money home to support their families. Many cross-cultural marriages have started in a Bangkok brothel, and government figures often cite foreign husbands in northeastern villages as being significant contributors to GDP.

NGOs estimate there are between 200,000 and 300,000 sex workers in Thailand, and, having found that few are motivated to leave the business, no longer focus their primary efforts on extricating them. Organisations such as Empower instead educate bar girls and boys about the dangers of HIV, and teach them English so they are less likely to be exploited by their clients.

The non-voluntary side of the sex trade is infinitely more grim. There are an estimated 60,000 child prostitutes in Thailand, many willingly sold by their parents, against whom convictions are very rare. Young women and girls are also trafficked from neighbouring Laos, Burma and Cambodia. Lured by promises of factory jobs or waitress work, they unwittingly sell themselves into lock-up brothels, where they must work until they have earned back the price the brothel-owner paid for them. Thailand is also an established transit point for trafficking to other countries.

The highly visible nature of sex work in Thailand is at odds with the otherwise high moral code of behaviour in the country. Women especially are expected to deport themselves modestly, and the Min-

Pole-dancing bar along Soi Cowboy in Sukhumvit.

istry of Culture (much to the outrage of many) is constantly making edicts about appropriate behaviour and dress. (Websites that criticise the ministry have been closed down). The discrepancy between the requirement for modesty and the prominent profile of sex work is often attributed to the Thais' general high tolerance for other lifestyles.

DECISIVE DATES

A French map of Siam (old Thailand), dating from 1686.

Pre-Thai Civilisation
3600–250 BC
Ban Chiang culture flourishes in northeastern Thailand.

4th–8th centuries AD
Influence of Mon and Khmer empires spreads into Thailand.

9th–13th centuries
The Khmer empire is founded in Angkor. Thai people migrate south from Yunnan Province in China into northern Thailand.

The Sukhothai Era
1238
Khmer power wanes. Kingdom of Sukhothai founded by King Intradit.

1277–1318
Reign of Ramkamhaeng, often called Thailand's "Golden Age", with flourishing arts and the first use of Thai script.

1296
Lanna kingdom founded at Chiang Mai. King Mengrai eventually controls much of northern Thailand and Laos.

The Kingdom of Ayutthaya
1350
Phya U-Thong founds the kingdom of Ayutthaya, proclaims himself Ramathibodi I, and soon rules areas belonging to Sukhothai and the Khmer empire.

1390
Ramathibodi's son King Ramesuen captures Chang Mai.

1393
Ramesuen seizes Angkor, base of the Khmer empire, in Cambodia.

1448–88
Reign of King Trailok, who finally unites the Lanna (Chiang Mai) and Ayutthaya kingdoms.

King Narai, ruler of Ayutthaya, 1656–88.

1569
Burmese seize Ayutthaya.

1584
Naresuen declares the independence of Siam.

1590
Naresuen becomes king and defeats Burmese. Ayutthaya expands rapidly at the expense of Burmese and Khmer empires.

1605–10
King Ekatotsarot develops significant economic ties with Europeans.

1610–28
Reign of King Songtham. British arrive and obtain land for a trading factory.

1628–55
Reign of Prasat Thong. Trading concessions expand and regular trade with China and Europe is established.

1656–88
Reign of King Narai. British influence expands. The reputation of Ayutthaya as a magnificent city and a remarkable royal court spreads in Europe.

1678
Constantine Phaulkon arrives at Narai's court and gains great influence; French presence expands.

1688
Narai dies and Phaulkon is executed.

1733–58
Reign of King Boromakot. Ayutthaya enters a period

of peace; the arts and literature flourish.

1767
Burmese King Alaungpaya captures and sacks Ayutthaya, destroying four centuries of Thai civilisation. Seven months later General Phya Taksin returns, expels the Burmese and moves the capital from Ayutthaya to Thonburi, near Bangkok.

Beginning of Chakri Dynasty
1767
Phya Taksin crowned as King Taksin.

1779
Generals Chao Phya Chakri and Chao Phya Surasi conquer Chiang Mai, expel the Burmese from what is now Thailand and take

control of most of the Khmer and Lao kingdoms. The statue of the Emerald Buddha is brought from Vientiane in Laos, to Thonburi.

1782
Taksin is deposed, and Chao Phya Chakri is offered the throne, founding the Chakri dynasty and assuming the name Ramathibodi (later Rama I). Capital is moved across the river to Bangkok. Under Rama I, Siam consolidates and expands its strength. Rama I revives Thai art, religion and culture. Work begins on the Grand Palace and Wat Phra Kaew in Bangkok.

1809–24
Reign of Rama II, known as the poet king. His famous Boat Songs were often

17th-century lacquer painting depicting delegates of Louis XIV in the Kingdom of Siam.

odes to his favourite foods. The king reopens relations with the West, which had been suspended since the time of King Narai.

1824–51
Reign of Rama III, who continues open-door policy with foreigners. Encourages American missionaries to introduce Western medicine to Siam.

1851
King Mongkut (Rama IV) ascends the throne. He is the first Thai king to understand Western culture and technology.

1868
Chulalongkorn (Rama V) ascends the throne, reigning for the next four decades. Schools, infrastructure, military and government modernised. Slavery is abolished.

Chulalongkorn (Rama V) and his wife.

1910–25
Reign of Vajiravudh (Rama VI), an Oxford-educated and Westernised ruler, who made Thai people adopt surnames.

1925–35
Reign of Prajadhipok (Rama VII). Economic pressures from the Great Depression rouse discontent among Thais.

Modern Thailand

1932
A coup ends the absolute monarchy and ushers in a constitutional monarchy.

1939
Siam's name is officially changed to Thailand, "Land of the Free".

1941
Japan invades Thailand with the acquiescence of the military government.

1946
King Ananda (Rama VIII) is killed by gunman; Bhumibol Adulyadej (Rama IX) ascends the throne.

1973–91
Bloody clashes between the army and students bring down the military government; political and economic blunders bring down the subsequent civilian government three years later. Various military-backed and civilian governments come and go for the next 20 years.

1992
Another clash between military forces and civilian demonstrators results in the military leaving government to civilian politicians. Thailand begins five years of unprecedented economic growth.

1996
King Bhumibol celebrates his golden jubilee of 50 years on the throne.

1997
Thailand's economy crashes. Start of the Asian economic crisis.

2001
Populist leader Thaksin Shinawatra is elected prime minister.

2004
Tsunami hits southern Thailand and causes widespread devastation.

2005
Thaksin is elected for a

second term as prime minister in February.

2006

Mass Bangkok demonstrations after Thaksin sells a company and pays no tax. The protestors unite under the People's Alliance for Democracy (PAD) banner. In September, a bloodless coup removes Thaksin, who remains in exile. Retired general Surayud Chulanont appointed interim premier.

Anti-government Red Shirt protester.

2007

Thaksin is banned from politics. His followers, the United Front for Democracy Against Dictatorship (UDD), launch protests. A Thaksin proxy, the People Power Party (PPP), wins the December election.

2008

The PAD occupies Government House and seizes the airport. In December, the courts disband the ruling party. The Democrat Party leader Abhisit Vejjajiva becomes prime minister.

2009

In April, UDD protests disrupt the ASEAN Summit in Pattaya, causing several heads of state to be airlifted to safety; Songkran riots erupt in Bangkok; PAD leader Sondhi Limthongkul is shot, but survives.

2010

In February the courts find Thaksin guilty of abuse of power and confiscate assets of B46 billion. April and May see thousands of Red Shirt demonstrators occupy various parts of the city, closing parliament for days and Pathumwan shopping malls for several weeks. Eighty-five people are killed and nearly 1,500 injured in clashes with the army on 10 April and 19 May, while banks, department stores and other major buildings are torched in the battles. Thaksin, still abroad, is charged with terrorism.

2014

The Puea Thai Party, led by Thakin's sister Yingluk, and its Yellow Shirts (plus affiliated groups) stage mass demonstrations, paving the way for the army to stage another coup. General Prayut Chanocah becomes the head of a military government and makes amends to the constitution. Decline in foreign investment and start of an economic downturn.

2016

King Bhumibol Adulyadej passes away on 13 October after a long illness. His son, Crown Prince Vajiralongkorn, becomes the new monarch.

2017

Elections are scheduled.

PAD protesters at the airport in 2008 celebrate the news that the ruling party has been disbanded.

Mural of the Grand Palace in Bangkok.

A CITY OF ANGELS

Whatever you call it – Bangkok, The Big Mango, Krung Thep or the City of Angels – this thriving metropolis dominates Thailand. It has been transformed from a sleepy riverside village where wild plum trees grew to a cosmopolitan community more than 30 times larger than any other city in the kingdom.

Bangkok's history as a town began in the 16th century when a short canal was dug across a loop of the Chao Phraya river to cut the distance between the sea and the Siamese capital at Ayutthaya. Over the years, monsoon floods scoured the banks of the canal until it widened to become the main course of the river. On its banks rose two towns – originally trading posts along the river route to Ayutthaya, 85km (55 miles) north – Thonburi on the west and, on the east, Bangkok. At the time, Bangkok was little more than a village (*bang*) in an orchard of wild plum trees (*kok*). Hence, the town's name, Bangkok, which translates as "village of the wild plum".

Ayutthaya prospered as the capital of Siam (the name of old Thailand) for more than four centuries, but in 1767 it was captured by the Burmese after a 14-month siege. The Burmese killed, looted and set fire to the whole city, plundering Ayutthaya's many rich temples and melting down all the gold from images of the Buddha. Members of the royal family, along with some 90,000 captives and the accumulated booty, were removed to Burma.

Despite their overwhelming victory, the Burmese didn't retain control of Siam for long. A young general named Phya Taksin gathered a small band of followers during the final Burmese siege of the Thai capital. He and his comrades broke through the Burmese encirclement and escaped to the southeast coast. There, Taksin assembled an army and a navy. Only seven months after the fall of Ayutthaya, Taksin's forces returned to the capital and expelled the Burmese occupiers.

European impression of 17th-century Ayutthaya.

THE LONGEST PLACE NAME EVER

In 1782, King Rama I decided the name Bangkok was insufficiently noble for a royal city so he renamed it *Krungthep mahanakhon amonrattanakosin mahintra ayutthaya mahadilok popnopparat ratchathani burirom udomratchaniwet mahasathan amonpiman avatansathit sakkathattiya visnukamprasit*. In English this means: "Great City of Angels, City of Immortals, Magnificent Jewelled City of the God Indra, Seat of the King of Ayutthaya, City of Gleaming Temples, City of the King's Most Excellent Palace and Dominions, Home of Vishnu and All the Gods". Most Thais, however, refer to Bangkok by just two syllables, Krung Thep, or "City of Angels", in everyday speech.

Bangkok canal in the late 19th century.

Move to Thonburi

Taksin had barely spent a night at Ayutthaya when he decided to transfer the site of his capital to Thonburi. Here he ruled until 1782. In the last years of his reign, he relied heavily on two trusted generals, the brothers Chao Phya Chakri and Chao Phya Surasi, who were given absolute command in their military campaigns. Meanwhile at Thonburi, Taksin's personality underwent a slow metamorphosis, from strong and just to cruel and unpredictable. When a revolt broke out in 1782, Taksin abdicated and entered a monastery, but was executed shortly thereafter.

Start of the Chakri dynasty

The official who engineered the revolt offered the throne to Chao Phya Chakri on his return from Cambodia. General Chakri assumed the kingship on 6 April – a date still commemorated as Chakri Day – thereby establishing the still reigning Chakri dynasty. On assuming the throne, Chakri took the name of Ramathibodi. Later known as Rama I, he ruled from 1782 until 1809. His first action as king was to transfer his capital from Thonburi to Bangkok.

Rama I was an ambitious man eager to re-establish the Thai kingdom as a dominant civilisation. He ordered the digging of a canal across a neck of land on the Bangkok side, creating an island and an inner city. Rama I envisioned this artificial island as the core of his new capital. Within its rim, he would concentrate the principal components of the Thai nation: religion, monarchy and administration.

French Jesuit ambassadors arriving in the Kingdom of Siam in the 17th century.

Artist's impression of King Mongkut (Rama IV).

To underscore his recognition of the power of the country's principal Buddha image, he called this island Rattanakosin) or the "Resting Place of the Emerald Buddha".

> After his abdication Taksin was executed in the traditional royal manner – with a blow to the neck by a sandalwood club concealed within a velvet bag.

To dedicate the area solely to statecraft and religion, he formally requested that the Chinese living there move to an area to the southeast. This new district, Sampeng, soon sprouted thriving shops and busy streets, becoming the commercial heart of the city in what is now known as Chinatown.

Rama I then turned his attention to constructing the royal island's principal buildings. First was a home for the Emerald Buddha, the most sacred image in the realm, which, until then, had been resting in a temple in Thonburi. Two years later, in 1784, Wat Phra Kaew was completed. A palace was next on his agenda; the Grand Palace was more than a home, it contained buildings for receiving royal visitors and debating matters of state. The last building to be constructed, the Chakri Maha Prasat, was not erected until late in the 19th century. Until 1946, the Grand Palace was home to Thailand's kings. The palace grounds also contain Wat Pho,

the National Museum, prestigious Thammasat University, the National Theatre, and various government offices.

Rama II and Rama III

Rama I's successors, Rama II and Rama III, completed both the consolidation of the Siamese kingdom and the revival of Ayutthaya's arts and culture. If Rama I laid the foundations of Bangkok, it was Rama II who instilled it with the spirit of the past. Best remembered as an artist, Rama II (ruled 1809–24), the second ruler of the Chakri dynasty, was responsible for building numerous Bangkok temples and repairing others, most famously Wat Arun, the Temple of Dawn, which was later enlarged to its present height by Rama IV. He is also said to have carved the great doors of Wat Suthat, throwing away the chisels so his work could never be replicated.

Rama II reopened relations with the West, which had been suspended since the time of former King Narai, and allowed the Portuguese to open the first Western embassy in Bangkok.

Rama III (ruled 1824–51) continued to open Siam's doors to foreigners. A pious Buddhist, Rama III was considered to be "austere and

King Mongkut (Rama IV) and his wife.

Chulalongkorn (Rama V) poses with the Crown Prince and other young students.

reactionary" by some Europeans. But he encouraged American missionaries to introduce Western medicine, such as smallpox vaccinations, to Siam.

Mongkut (Rama IV)

With the help of Hollywood, Rama IV (ruled 1851–68) became the most famous king of Siam. More commonly known as King Mongkut, he was portrayed by Yul Brynner in *The King and I* as a frivolous, bald-headed despot – but nothing could have been further from the truth. He was the first Thai king to understand Western culture and technology, and his reign has been described as the bridge spanning the new and the old.

The younger brother of Rama III, King Mongkut spent 27 years as a Buddhist monk prior to his accession to the throne. This gave him a unique opportunity to roam as a commoner among the populace. He learned to read Buddhist scriptures in the Pali language; missionaries taught him Latin and English. As a monk, Mongkut delved into many subjects: history, geography and the sciences, but he had a particular passion for astronomy. Mongkut instituted a policy of modernisation, and England was the first European country to benefit from this, when an 1855 treaty granted extraterritorial privileges, a duty of only 3 percent on imports, and permission to import Indian opium duty-free. Other Western nations followed suit with similar treaties. When Mongkut lifted the state monopoly on rice, it rapidly became Siam's leading export.

In 1863, Mongkut built Bangkok's first paved road – Thanon Charoen Krung (Prosperous City) or, as it was known to foreigners, New Road. This 6km (4-mile) -long street, running from the Grand Palace southeast along the river, was lined with shops and houses. He also introduced new technology to encourage commerce. The foreign community moved into the areas opened by the construction of New Road. They built their homes in the area where the Mandarin Oriental Hotel now stands, and along Thanon Silom and Thanon Sathorn, both rural retreats at the time.

Chulalongkorn with his son Vajiravudh

BANGKOK'S PIG SHRINE

Close by Wat Ratchabophit in downtown Bangkok is an unusual shrine in the likeness of a golden pig. It is dedicated to the chief consort of King Chulalongkorn, Queen Saowapha (1864–1919), who was born in the Chinese zodiacal Year of the Pig. The "pig shrine" is also an early monument to the women's movement in Thailand. In 1897, Queen Saowapha founded a college of midwifery in Bangkok. She also founded the Thai Red Cross Society, and built schools for girls in Bangkok and in the provinces. Her court was recognised as a centre for fine arts; young girls attached to the Siamese court attained the equivalent of a university education.

Procession of royal barges along the Chao Phraya River at Prajadhipok's (Rama VII) 1925 coronation.

King Chulalongkorn, who was just 15 when he ascended the throne, went on to abolish slavery and completely modernise Thailand's institutions, improving both education and health care.

Chulalongkorn (Rama V)

Mongkut's son, Chulalongkorn (Rama V), was only 15 when he ascended the throne in 1868. The farsighted king immediately revolutionised his court by ending the ancient custom of prostration, and by allowing officials to sit on chairs during royal audiences. Chulalongkorn's reign was truly revolutionary. When he assumed power, Siam had an under-equipped military force, few roads, and no schools, railways or hospitals. He brought in foreign advisors and sent his sons and other young men to be educated abroad. He also founded a palace school for children of the aristocracy, following this with other schools and vocational centres. During his reign, Chulalongkorn abolished the last vestiges of slavery and, in 1884, introduced electric lighting. He hired Danish engineers to build an electric tram system 10 years before the one in Copenhagen was completed, and encouraged the import of automobiles about the same time they began appearing on American streets.

Chulalongkorn changed the face of Bangkok. By 1900, the city was growing rapidly eastward. In the Dusit area, he built a palace, the Vimanmek Mansion and constructed roads to link it with the Grand Palace. Other noble families followed, building elegant mansions. In the same area, he constructed Wat Benjamabophit, the last major Buddhist temple built in Bangkok.

In the area of foreign relations, however, Chulalongkorn had to compromise and give up parts of his kingdom in order to protect Siam from foreign colonisation. When France conquered Annam in 1883 and Britain annexed Upper Burma in 1886, Siam found itself sandwiched between two rival expansionist powers. Siam was forced to surrender to France its claims to Laos and western Cambodia. Similarly, certain Malay Peninsula territories were ceded to Britain in exchange for renunciation of British extraterritorial rights in Siam. By the end of Chulalongkorn's reign, Siam had given up sizeable tracts of fringe territory. But that was a small price for maintaining the country's peace and independence. Unlike its neighbours, Siam has never been under colonial rule.

1947 coronation of King Bhumibol Adulyadej.

Vajiravudh (Rama VI)

King Chulalongkorn's successor, his son Vajiravudh, started his reign (1910–25) with a lavish coronation. He was educated at Oxford and was thoroughly anglicised, and his Western-inspired reforms aimed at modernising Siam had a profound effect on modern Thai society.

One of the first changes that Vajiravudh instituted was a 1913 edict which demanded that his subjects adopt surnames. In the absence of a clan or caste system, genealogy was virtually unheard of in Siam at that time. Previously, Thais had used first names, a practice that the king considered uncivilised. The law generated much initial bewilderment, especially in rural areas, and Vajiravudh personally coined patronymics for hundreds of families. To simplify his forebears' lengthy titles, he invented the Chakri dynastic name, Rama, to be followed by the proper reign number. He started with himself, as Rama VI.

To bring Thai ideals of femininity into line with Western fashions, women were encouraged to grow their hair long instead of having it close-cropped, and to replace their *dhoti*, or wide-legged Thai trousers, with the *panung*, a Thai-style sarong. Primary education was made compulsory throughout the kingdom; Chulalongkorn University, the first in Siam, was founded, and schools for both sexes flourished during Vajiravudh's reign.

Vajiravudh preferred individual ministerial consultations to summoning his appointed cabinet. His regime was therefore criticised as autocratic and lacking in coordination. His extravagance soon emptied the funds built up by Chulalongkorn; near the end of Vajiravudh's

FROM SIAM TO THAILAND

The man partly responsible for the end of Thailand's centuries-old absolute monarchy, Luang Phibulsongkh-ram, or Pibul, tried to instil a sense of mass nationalism in the Thais when he was elected PM in 1938. With tight control over the media and a creative propaganda department, Pibul whipped up sentiment against the Chinese. Chinese immigration was restricted, Chinese workers were barred from certain jobs, and state enterprises were set up to compete in Chinese-dominated industries. By changing the country's name from Siam to Thailand in 1939, Pibul intended to emphasise that it belonged to Thai ethnic groups and not to the Chinese.

Vajiravudh (Rama VI).

reign, the national treasury had to meet the deficits caused by his personal expenses.

The king married late. His only daughter was born one day before he died in 1925. He was succeeded by his youngest brother, Prajadhipok, who inherited the problems created by the brilliant but controversial former ruler.

Prajadhipok (Rama VII)

Prajadhipok's prudent economic policies, combined with the increased revenue from foreign trade, amply paid off for the kingdom. In the early years of his reign, communications were improved by the advent of a wireless service, and Don Muang Airport began to operate as an international air centre. It was also during the course of his reign that Siam saw the establishment of the Fine Arts Department, the National Library and the National Museum, institutions that continue today as important preservers of Thai culture.

The worldwide economic crisis of 1931 affected Siam's rice export and the government was forced to cut the salaries of junior personnel, and retrench officers in the armed services. Discontent brewed among army officials and bureaucrats. In 1932, a coup d'état ended absolute rule by Thai monarchs. The coup was staged by the People's Party, a military and civilian group masterminded by foreign-educated Thais. The chief ideologist was Pridi Banomyong, a young lawyer trained in France, who is now often cited as "The Father of Thai Democracy". On the military side, Capt. Luang

Phibulsongkhram (Pibul) was responsible for gaining the support of important army colonels.

With only a few tanks, the 70 conspirators sparked off the "revolution" by occupying strategic areas and holding the senior princes hostage. Other army officers stood by as the public watched. At the time, Prajadhipok was in Hua Hin, a royal retreat to the south. Perceiving he had little choice and to avoid bloodshed, he agreed to accept a provisional constitution by which he continued to reign.

The power of Pibul and the army was further strengthened in October 1933 by the decisive defeat of a rebellion led by Prince Boworadet, who had been the war minister under King Prajadhipok. The king had no part in the rebellion, but had become increasingly dismayed by quarrels within the new government. He moved to England in 1934 and abdicated in 1935. Ananda Mahidol (Rama VIII), a 10-year-old half-nephew, agreed to take the throne, but remained in Switzerland to complete his schooling.

After a series of crises and an election in 1938, Pibul became prime minister. His rule, however, grew more authoritarian. While some Thai officers favoured the model of the Japanese military regime, Pibul admired – and sought to emulate – Hitler and Mussolini.

Thai school children in the late 1940s.

Borrowing many ideas from European fascism, he attempted to instil a sense of mass nationalism in the Thais (see box).

Post World War II

On 7 December 1941, the Japanese bombed Pearl Harbor and launched invasions throughout Southeast Asia. Thailand was invaded at nine points. Despite a decade of military build-up, resistance lasted less than a day. Pibul acceded to Japan's request for "passage rights", signed a treaty with Japan and declared war on the Allies. Thailand's ambassador in the US, MR Seni Pramoj, famously collaborated with the Americans, who refused to accept the declaration of war. Seni formed a Free Thai movement. In Bangkok, Pridi Banomyong, who had been marginalised by Pibul due to his attempted reforms, which were perceived as Communist, established a local resistance movement, the Seri Thai.

By 1944, Thailand's initial enthusiasm for its Japanese partners had evaporated. The country faced runaway inflation, food shortages, rationing and black markets. The assembly forced Pibul out of office.

Pridi Banomyong's struggle for power with Pibul and later Seni Pramoj lasted several years, and he became prime minister in 1946. In the

King Prajadhipok in 1926.

same year, while on a visit to Thailand from school in Europe, the now adult King Ananda was found shot dead in his palace bedroom. Of the many rumours and conspiracy theories surrounding this incident, one of the most significant claimed that Pridi was involved.

Prajadhipok visits Berlin in 1934.

When Thailand, then an ally of Japan, declared war on the US in 1942, the Americans refused to accept it, and a Thai resistance movement, the Seri Thai, was formed.

He resigned and the following year fled to Singapore after his house was attacked during a military coup. After a failed armed rebellion against the Pibul government in 1949, Pridi left for China, and never returned. The protracted murder trial of King Ananda's alleged killers finally convicted and sentenced to death three palace aides for conspiracy, although a gunman was never formally identified. The circumstances of the king's death have still not been satisfactorily explained; the incident is still discussed and most people have their own theories.

King Ananda was succeeded by his younger brother, Bhumibol Adulyadej (Rama IX), (see page 47), who returned to Switzerland to complete law studies. He did not, however, take up active duties until the 1950s. By then, Thailand had been without a resident king for 20 years.

In 1957, a clique of his one-time protégés overthrew Pibul. Their leader, General Sarit Thanarat, and two cohort generals, Thanom Kittikachorn and Prapas Charusathien, ran the government until 1973, employing martial law. The military, which had steadily been gaining power, reached its peak of influence during these years. The generals' ascendancy coincided with America's involvement in the Vietnam War. Large infusions of money flowed from the US to Thailand, America's staunchest ally, resulting in a burgeoning economy. Health standards improved; the business sector expanded; construction boomed; the population swelled in response to new jobs; and a middle class began to emerge. And the generals, now called "The Three Tyrants", used their power to amass huge personal fortunes. But the socio-economic changes also brought new aspirations to the population.

The October 1973 uprising

Following the arrest of student leaders for distributing anti-government leaflets, protests broke out around the country, including 400,000 people at Bangkok's Democracy Monument. Clashes on 14 October 1973 between troops and students left many students dead

Billboard, c.1950.

(the official figure was 77, press estimated 400). Under pressure from several influential factions, The Three Tyrants fled to the US.

Two subsequent elections produced civilian governments, but the fledgling democracy was hampered by the diverse interests of new political parties, labour unions and farming organisations. The middle class, originally strongly supportive of the student revolution, along with

TRAFFIC WOES

The 1980s and '90s saw the vertical growth of Bangkok. Its skyline changed dramatically but along with it came congested roads and notorious traffic jams. In the early 1980s, various government officials suggested solutions to ease Bangkok's traffic problem. Eventually the ideas evaporated, mired in corruption or woefully poor cooperation between competing agencies – only to be recycled a year or two later. Thankfully, the situation has improved vastly with the construction of a complex network of elevated expressways. To ease traffic further, in 1999, Bangkok's first mass transit system, the Skytrain, started operations, and in 2004 a metro line opened.

Field Marshal Thanom Kittikachorn at a news conference in 1971.

some of the upper class, came to fear that total chaos or a Communist takeover would emerge.

The 1976 return of General Thanom, ostensibly to become a monk, sparked more student protests. After two were garrotted, allegedly

Soldier occupying Thammasat University during the 1976 student protests.

by police, students occupied Thammasat University. On 6 October, police, troops and paramilitary organisations stormed the grounds, raping and killing many people. Within hours the army had seized power in a coup. Self-government had lasted but three years. Ironically, the civilian judge appointed to be prime minister, Thanin Kraivichien, turned out to be more brutal than any of his uniformed predecessors. Yet another military coup ousted Thanin in October 1977. For the next decade there was relatively moderate military rule, and under General Prem Tinsulanond the foundations were laid for new elections, which ushered in a civilian government.

Another military coup

After a bloodless military coup in 1991, spearheaded by General Suchinda Kraprayoon, the junta installed a businessman and ex-diplomat, Anand Panyacharun, as a caretaker premier until elections planned the following year. Anand earned plaudits for running the cleanest government in memory and is still a highly respected figure in Thai politics.

A political party newly formed by the junta won the most seats at the election, but General

Suchinda unseated the intended prime minister and installed himself as leader. The middle classes protested, gathering at rallies, inspired by former Bangkok Governor Chamlong Srimuang, a figure who would have great impact on Thai politics into the new millennium. More than 70,000 people alone met at Sanam Luang on 17 May 1992. Late in the evening, soldiers fired on unarmed demonstrators. Killings, beatings, riots and arson attacks continued sporadically for the next three days. The Thai broadcast media, controlled by the government, were obliged to impose a news blackout, but owners of satellite dishes, along with viewers around the world, watched the coverage of "Bloody May". The crisis ended when King Bhumibol intervened. A little later, the unrepentant Suchinda bowed out and left the country. The Democrat Party and other prominent Suchinda critics prevailed in the September 1992 re-elections.

Democracy prevails

Prime Minister Chuan Leekpai, considered honest but ineffectual, persisted for almost three years from 1992 to 1995, a record for a civilian government. Setting another record, he was not toppled by a coup. But by the end, Chuan had lost much of the goodwill of the pro-democracy groups that had lifted him to power.

Chuan battled constantly to keep his coalition working together. It finally disintegrated when some members of Chuan's own party were implicated in a land-reform scandal. Elections in July 1995 brought an old-style politician, Banharn Silpa-archa, to the premiership. As the Thai press phrased it at the time, both Banharn and his party, Chart Thai, had a strong "reputation" for corruption.

Economic crisis

The Thai economy, which registered phenomenal annual growth rates for over a decade to emerge as one of the famous "Tiger" economies of Southeast Asia, suddenly saw the good times come to an end. By late 1996, inflationary pressures, a widening current account deficit and slower economic growth led to a censure motion against the 14-month-old government led by Banharn Silpa-archa. Elections held in November 1996 saw a coalition headed by the New Aspiration Party come to power. NAP leader Chavalit Yongchaiyudh became

Thailand's 22nd prime minister, but many of his partners in government were the same as in the previous administration and little was done to stem the economic rot that had set in.

By February 1997, ratings agency Moody's had downgraded Thailand's credit rating. A few months later, the government ordered the closure of 16 finance companies that were in the red. The final straw came shortly afterwards, on 2 July, when the Chavalit administration decided to drop the traditional currency peg in favour of a "managed float". This had the disastrous double effect of sending the currency down in a devaluation spiral and making the foreign debts of local corporations skyrocket.

The pressure to float the baht was partly caused by aggressive attacks by foreign hedge funds; enormous sums from the country's foreign exchange reserves were spent in its defence. In the end, the government was forced to ask

Protesters are forced to the ground when government troops open fire during the "Bloody May" crisis of 1992.

Leader of the New Aspiration Party, Chavalit Yongchaiyudh, who became Prime Minister in 1996.

the IMF for US$17 billion to help keep the country afloat. The crisis saw businesses go bankrupt and many thousands lose their jobs, due to closures or downsizing.

Amid all this, changes to Thailand's constitution were promulgated on 11 October 1997 by the Chavalit government. It set up positive new measures for Thai democracy, including a bicameral legislature and independent bodies to monitor the government. The new document, however, was not enough to save the government, and Chavalit stepped down under intense public pressure in September 1998 as the country's economic gloom deepened.

This brought in a Democrat government headed by Prime Minister Chuan Leekpai. After over a year of hard work, the economy, which had bottomed out, began showing gradual signs of recovery. The process was helped along by a banking reform package in August 1998 that helped boost confidence in the country among foreign investors. The government also pushed forward business laws to help speed up corporate debt restructuring.

The Thaksin administration

In 2001, general elections installed the populist billionaire entrepreneur Thaksin Shinawatra and his newly formed Thai Rak Thai (Thai Love Thai) party.

Thaksin's governance proved almost immediately controversial. He faced, and successfully defended, charges of corruption; he was widely condemned after hundreds were killed in his "War on Drugs"; and he was slammed for suppressing the media. But his leadership was a breath of air to many. His "populist" approach saw loans and cheap health care for the poor, and he brought a swagger and confidence to Thailand's self-perception on the world stage, famously dismissing international criticism on one occasion by declaring: "The UN is not my father". However, as he became wildly popular in poorer rural areas, particularly in the north and northeast, his "CEO style" of government was increasingly annoying traditional powers in the country, centred in Bangkok.

In 2005, an alliance of opposition interests formed, led by Chamlong Srimuang and former Thaksin supporter Sondhi Limthongkul. They united under the name the People's Alliance for Democracy (PAD), and began anti-Thaksin street demonstrations. They adopted the colour yellow to show allegiance to the monarchy. The movement intensified after Thaksin, already the richest man in Thailand, sold his telecommunications company to an arm of the Singapore government for US$1.9 billion and paid no tax.

Yet another coup

In response, Thaksin announced a snap election in April 2006. Opposition parties boycotted the

Prime Minister Chuan Leekpai casts his vote in the 1995 elections.

Street celebrations in honour of King Bhumibol's 80th birthday in 2008.

process, and although Thaksin won again, he resigned as prime minister in the face of mass protests, appointing his deputy, Chidchai Wannasathit, as the new caretaker premier. Thaksin was plagued by claims of rigged bids for the new Suvarnabhumi Airport, *lèse majesté* against the beloved King Bhumibol, alleged vote-buying and a worsening Muslim insurgency in the south, which by then had claimed over 2,000 lives.

Following months of protests, the army staged a bloodless coup on 19 September 2006, when Thaksin was in New York attending a United Nations summit. Following up on charges of election irregularities, the new authorities banned 111 Thai Rak Thai officials from politics, including Thaksin, and froze his bank accounts in the country. As Thaksin lived in exile in London, his followers, calling themselves the United Front for Democracy Against Dictatorship (UDD), and wearing red shirts, launched protests against the military government. A Thaksin proxy, the People Power Party (PPP), won the next general election in December 2007, and Thaksin returned the following year, only to later skip bail on corruption charges and flee once again to London.

Red Shirt, Yellow Shirt

Meanwhile, the yellow shirt PAD demonstrations resumed. During late 2008, they occupied Government House, sometimes clashing violently with Thaksin supporters, and finally seized the airport, bringing the country to a standstill. In December that year, the courts disbanded the ruling party, and, in a deal largely seen as being brokered by the army, some key Thaksin allies jumped ship. The Democrat Party took office with Abhisit Vejjajiva as prime minister.

As befits a telecoms tycoon, Thaksin mobilised his followers with a series of satellite phone-ins and video links, launched internet sites, and began twittering on a daily basis. In April 2009, Red Shirt protests intensified. They disrupted the ASEAN Summit in Pattaya, causing several heads of state to be airlifted to safety, and Songkran riots erupted in Bangkok. In the same month, PAD leader Sondhi Limthongkul was shot, but survived the assassination attempt.

In a provocative twist, and revealing his links with regional powers were still significant, Thaksin was appointed as financial advisor to the Cambodian government late in the year. Tensions between Thailand and Cambodia were

Anti-government "red shirt" protesters in Bangkok's main shopping district, April 2010.

already high over the disputed lands around the Preah Vihear Temple on the Cambodian border. Troop numbers were increased and ambassadors recalled by both countries.

As the New Year approached, commentators were increasingly debating the possibility of civil war breaking out at some level, particularly as factions either within the army, or with strong army connections, began to reveal themselves as Thaksin supporters.

In February 2010, outstanding corruption charges against Thaksin were finally heard. The courts found him guilty of abuse of power and confiscated assets of B46 billion. Still immensely rich, Thaksin vowed to fight on.

Post-Thaksin life

In 2014, after successive Thaksin-backed governments win elections, under the new banner of the Puea Thai Party, led by his sister Yingluk, the opposition Yellow Shirts (and affiliated groups) stage mass demonstrations. Thaksin's influence in politics wanes. Led by Suthep Thaugsuban, the opposition is successful in bringing enough chaos to the streets to allow for the army to

stage another coup, ostensibly to bring calm to a precarious social and economic situation that has been volatile since 2006. General Prayut Chanocah is sworn in as the new leader of a military government with promises for elections within two years. Machinations and problems in the constitution writing process delay the initial timetable and elections are delayed until 2017. The new constitution is eventually passed via a nationwide referendum which leaves the possibility of an unelected prime minister being appointed after fresh elections.

As a result of this period of political instability, Thailand sees a decline in foreign investment and enters a period of economic downturn.

King Bhumibol's passing

After a long illness, King Bhumibol passes away on 13th October 2016. The country starts a year-long period of mourning. The authorities ask for entertainment venues to tone down as a mark of respect and people are encouraged to wear black or dark clothing. Bhumibol's son, Maha Vajiralongkorn, is crowned king 50 days after his father's death.

The Monarchy

Thailand is officially a constitutional monarchy, but the king's importance in the nation's life is apparent everywhere, from official buildings to people's homes.

Although an army-led bloodless coup in 1932 removed the absolute powers of Thailand's King Prajadhipok (Rama VII), the monarchy remains one of the most influential institutions in the land, and is omnipresent.

The monarchy is represented by the blue bar of the Thai tricolour (red stands for the nation, white is religion), while photographs of the late King Bhumibol Adulyadej adorn government buildings and public spaces, and legal regard is enshrined in *lèse majesté* laws, which carry a maximum penalty of seven years imprisonment for anyone convicted of insulting the royal family.

King Bhumibol ascended the throne in 1946, following the death, in mysterious circumstances, of his brother King Ananda Mahidol (Rama VIII), and was, until his death in 2016, the world's longest-reigning monarch. Respect for King Bhumibol was enhanced by a sense of his morality and representation of traditional Thai values in the face of corrupt governments. He was seen as the ameliorating figure in the turbulent conflicts of 1973, 1976 and 1992, when the army and police killed many civilians. He endured pockets of unprecedented criticism from some supporters of Thaksin Shinawatra, who believe the king and other elements of the traditional elite were involved in the overthrow of the fugitive ex-prime minister. The *lèse majesté* laws have been used more widely than usual during recent years.

Books and films about King Mongkut based on the memoirs of Anna Leonowens, titled *The English Governess at the Siamese Court*, are all banned in Thailand. These include the Hollywood favourite *The King and I*, starring Yul Brynner. Leonowens was a tutor of the royal children, but is regarded as having misrepresented both her role and life in the palace.

Radio and TV stations play the national, or King's anthem, regularly, as do cinemas and railway and bus stations, when people will stand respectfully for the duration. Indeed, his subjects had a famed love of the king and would generally take offence at anyone speaking ill of the monarchy. Photographs of the late King Bhumibol are widespread in shops and homes, along with those of his predecessors, particularly King Mongkut and King Chulalongkorn, who were the modernisers of Thailand in the late 19th and early 20th centuries.

Thailand's new king, Maha Vajiralongkorn (Rama X).

King Bhumibol was seen as a man of the people, particularly through his work in the King's Project, which is concerned with the development of small agricultural communities. His subjects were also genuinely proud of his achievements in the field of jazz (see page 86); the king penned many tunes, including the humorously named "HM Blues". The nation's monarchist fervour saw crowds turn out in huge numbers for the king's birthday celebrations in Sanam Luang in December.

On 13th October 2016 the king passed away after a long illness. His heir apparent, the Crown Prince Maha Vajiralongkorn, succeeded him on the throne on 1st December 2016.

The colourful rooftops of Wat Traimit.

RELIGION

Buddhism is central to the lives of most Thais, as shown by the many rituals and practices that are part of daily routine. Yet a strong thread of animism persists: people wear amulets to ward off bad luck, while buildings have tiny "spirit houses" to appease previous occupants.

Though it is predominantly Buddhist, Thailand has historically been tolerant of other religions. According to the government census, 94 percent of the population are Theravada Buddhists, 3.9 percent are Muslims, 1.7 percent Confucians and 0.6 percent Christians (mostly hill-tribe people living in the north). Buddhism – a philosophy, rather than a religion – has played a profound role in shaping the Thai character, particularly in the way in which people react to events. The Buddhist concept of the impermanence of life and possessions, and of the necessity to avoid extremes of emotion or behaviour, has done much to create the relaxed, carefree charm that is one of the most appealing characteristics of the Thai people.

Theravada Buddhism

Most of the Thai population subscribe to Theravada Buddhism, which is also the main Buddhist form practised in neighbouring countries like Laos, Cambodia and Burma (Myanmar), as well as Sri Lanka. Nevertheless, even a casual visitor to temples in these countries will quickly see differences between them. As they have done with most outside influences – Khmer temple decorations and Chinese food, for instance – the Thais have evolved a Buddhism of their own cast over the centuries.

Theravada Buddhism is a mixture of Buddhist, Hindu and animistic beliefs, and, as the oldest of all Buddhist faiths, it is the only one to trace its origins directly back to the 6th century BC teachings of Siddhartha Gautama, the Indian prince who gave up his royal privileges

Monks at prayer in Wat Suthat.

to follow an ascetic life, and became the Buddha. The central doctrines are based on *dukkha* (stress, misery), *anicca* (impermanence) and *anatta* (the absence of self).

The Buddha taught that the craving for self-worth and possessions creates misery, and that because everything is impermanent and cannot be possessed, the exercise is in any case senseless. If we suppress desire and practise detachment we will no longer be unhappy.

To reach this state, Gautama advocated a method of living he called the Middle Way (or Eightfold Path), which leads to enlightenment. At the time of enlightenment, Gautama became the Buddha and ascended into Nirvana, an event now represented by reclining Buddha statues and celebrated on Visakha Puja Day, each May.

Adherents believe the Buddha lived 500 lives, and that they themselves will be reincarnated (an idea adopted from Hinduism) and finally, if they live a good cycle of lives, will reach Nirvana. Living a good cycle requires rightful and mindful actions and thoughts, and is significantly aided by *tham boon* (merit making). People can make merit in many ways. A man who spends some part of his life as a monk will earn merit by living in accordance with the strict rules governing monastic life. So, too, a person who supports the monks on a daily basis by donating food, or who visits a temple to pray for a sick person. People can also make merit by releasing birds or fish, which market stalls sell for the purpose. And a donation to a worthy cause is always helpful.

The Buddha image in front of which prayers are offered provides only a formal background for these activities. The image and the Buddha himself are there as inspiration rather than objects to be worshipped.

Mahayana Buddhism

In addition to Theravada Buddhism, there is Mahayana Buddhism that is practised by those of Chinese descent. Visitors are likely to spot Mahayana temples in Bangkok's Chinatown. Mahayana literally means "Greater Vehicle"; the defining belief, according to this doctrine, is that those who have attained Nirvana return to help others reach the same state. The various Buddhist sects and practices that predominate in China, Tibet, Taiwan, Japan, Korea and Vietnam are classified as Mahayana.

Chinese Buddhism, at least that practised in Thailand, primarily consists of incense, lucky charms, and heaps of other folk practices. The visitor entering a *sanjao*, or inner shrine, of such a temple will have a chance to shake sticks out of a canister, from which a fortune can be told. At funerals, paper money and doll-size cardboard houses (complete with paper Mercedes Benz cars) are burned to assist the deceased in his or her next life.

Making a request at Erawan Shrine.

Offerings of food at a Buddhist temple.

Admiring the Phra Sri Sakyamuni Buddha in Wat Suthat.

A little over 90 percent of the Thai people are Buddhist, but religious tolerance is extended to other religions. Around 3.9 percent of Thais are Muslim, with the remainder Christian, Hindu and Sikh.

Temple life

Most of Thailand's 300,000 or so monks live in *wat* (temples), practising and teaching the rules of human conduct laid down by the Buddha. There are literally hundreds of Buddhist temples in the city and suburbs, usually sited in serene pockets of densely packed neighbourhoods and serving as hubs for the spiritual and social life of the community.

The term *wat* defines a large, walled compound made up of several buildings, including a *bot* or hall where new monks are ordained, and one or more *viharn* where sermons are delivered. It may also contain a belltower, a *ho trai* (library) and *guti*, or monk meditation cells, as well as a domed edifice, called *chedi* in Thailand, or *prang*

in Cambodia, and *stupa* or *pagoda* in other countries. *Chedi* contain the ashes or relics of wealthy donors, emulating the Buddha, whose ashes and relics were placed according to his instruction in a mound of earth.

Tradition requires that every Buddhist male enter the monkhood for a brief period before marriage, and companies customarily grant

BRAHMAN BELIEFS

Many of the Thais' non-Buddhist beliefs are Brahman in origin, and even today Brahman priests officiate at major ceremonies. The Thai wedding ceremony is almost entirely Brahman, as are many funeral rites. The rites of statecraft pertaining to the royal family are presided over by Brahman priests. One of the most popular of these, the Ploughing Ceremony (Raek Na), takes place each May in Bangkok. To signal the start of the rice-planting season, sacred oxen are offered a selection of grains. Astrologers watch the events carefully, as the grains the oxen choose will determine the amount of rainfall to come and the success or failure of the crops in the year ahead.

paid leave for male employees wishing to do so. The entry of a young man into monkhood is seen as repayment to parents for his upbringing, and as bestowing special merit on them, particularly his mother. Unlike other Buddhist countries, women cannot be ordained in Thailand. It is thus popularly believed that a son, as a monk, can earn merit for his mother and other female relatives.

For all its spartan life, however, a Buddhist *wat* in Thailand is by no means isolated from the real world. In addition to the schools that are attached to most *wat* (for centuries, the only schools were those run by monks), the *wat* has traditionally been the centre of social and communal life in the villages. Monks serve as herbal doctors, psychological counsellors and arbitrators of disputes. They also play an important part in daily life, such as blessing a new building, or at birthdays and funerals.

Spirits and amulets

When Buddhism started in what is now Thailand in the early years, it promised a better life for farmers. But as it provided little assistance with the unfathomable tragedies of daily

Miniature Buddha statue.

life, and certainly no answer to the questions of the supernatural, the people continued to worship their old deities and spirits to fill in what they saw as gaps in Buddhism.

The variety of *phi* (spirits) in Thailand is legendary. A seductive female *phi*, believed to reside in a banana plant, is said to torment young men who come near it. Another bothersome one takes possession of her victims and forces them to remove their clothes in public. (For some reason, the most destructive spirits seem to be female.)

To counteract the spirits and potential dangers in life, protective spells are cast and kept in small amulets mostly worn around the neck. Curiously, the amulets are not bought, but rather rented on an indefinite lease from "landlords", often monks considered to possess magic powers. There are amulets that offer protection against accidents

> *Some idols blessed by monks are believed to be so powerful that cult followings develop around them. Fortunes can be won and lost depending on the state of the market in these talismans.*

while travelling or against bullet and knife wounds; some even boost sexual attraction.

All this has no more to do with Buddhism than the protective blue-patterned tattoos sported by some Thais to ward off evil. But some monasteries have been turned into highly profitable factories for the production of amulets. In 2007 a great cult following grew around idols called Jatukam Ramathep, which were believed to be particularly powerful. Thousands all over the country exchanged hands for ever-increasing prices, and many people saw an opportunity to make a fast profit. But the bubble burst and some temples were left in financial difficulties because they had over-stocked.

Spirit houses

No building in Thailand, not even the humblest wooden hut, will be seen today without a "spirit house", or at least a house altar. In ordinary residences, the small doll-like house may resemble a Thai dwelling; in hotels and offices, it is usually an elaborately decorated mini-temple. In either case, these spirit houses serve as the abodes of the resident spirits. As it

A spirit house.

Phalluses at the Chao Mae Tuptim shrine in the grounds of the Lai Nert Park Hotel.

is within their power either to favour or plague the human inhabitants of the actual house or building, the spirit house is regularly adorned with placatory offerings of food, fresh flowers and incense sticks. If any calamity or ill luck befalls the members of the compound, it may be necessary to call in an expert to consult the spirit to determine what is wrong.

One of the most famous spirit houses in Bangkok is the Erawan Shrine, at the intersection of Ratchadamri and Ploenchit roads. This shrine, honouring the Hindu god Brahma, was erected by the owners during the construction of the original Erawan Hotel in the 1950s, after several workers were injured in mysterious accidents. The shrine soon acquired a widespread reputation for bringing good fortune to outsiders as well.

A less well-known shrine sits in the compound of Bangkok's Lai Nert Park Hotel, known as the Chao Mae Tuptim shrine. Its offerings consist entirely of phalluses, ranging from small to gargantuan, sculpted from wood, wax, stone or cement, and with fidelity to real life. They are left by women hoping to conceive a child.

TEMPLE ART AND ARCHITECTURE

The temple *(wat)* plays a vital role in every community, large or small; for many visitors Thailand's temples are the country's most enduring sights.

A typical Thai *wat* (temple) has two enclosing walls that divide it from the secular world. The monks' quarters are situated between the outer and inner walls. In larger temples the inner walls may be lined with Buddha images and serve as cloisters for meditation. This part of the temple is called *buddhavasa* or *phutthawat*. Inside the inner walls is the *bot* or *ubosot* (ordination hall), surrounded by eight stone tablets and set on consecrated ground. This is the most sacred part of the temple and only monks can enter it. The *bot* contains a Buddha image, but it is the *viharn* (sermon hall) that contains the principal Buddha images. Also in the inner courtyard are the bell-shaped *chedi* (relic chambers), as well as towering Khmer-style spires called *prang*, which are a variation of *chedi* and similarly contain the relics of either the Buddha or pious or distinguished people. *Salas* (pavilions) can be found all around the temple; the largest of these areas is the *sala kan prian* (study hall), used for saying afternoon prayers. Apart from Buddha images, various mythological creatures (see page 110) are found within the temple compound.

The cloisters at Wat Suthat are lined with Buddha statues, these portrayed in the "Subduing Mara" position, denoting a renunciation of worldly desire.

Gilded chofa (bird-like decorations), intricately carved gables, and green and ochre coloured tiles are common features of Thai temple roofs.

Temple exteriors are often very ornate, such as that of the bot of the Emerald Buddha at Wat Phra Kaew. Gold tiles, glass mosaic, lacquer and mother-of-pearl are some of the materials used.

Thai temple murals are created on a background that has been prepared and dried before the artist paints on it using coloured pigments mixed with glue. Often featured on the interior of temple walls, such murals depict the classic subjects of Thai painting, including tales from the Jataka (Buddha's birth and previous lives) and other Buddhist themes, and also vignettes of local life. During the reign of Rama III (1824–51), mural painting reached its peak, with artists not only following the principles of traditional Thai art but also introducing new elements, like Western perspective. The mural below, from Wat Suthat in Bangkok, is an example of the late 18th-century art style (better known as the Rattanakosin Period).

The gleaming Phra Si Rattana chedi at Wat Phra Kaew is bell-shaped with a ringed spire and a three-tiered base – a feature of Sri Lankan reliquary towers. Close-up inspection will reveal a surface made up of thousands of tiny gold mosaic pieces.

These towering chedi at Wat Pho sit on square bases and have graceful and elegant proportions, reminiscent of the Lanna-style architecture of north Thailand. Decorated with coloured tiles, the chedi are memorials to the first four Chakri kings.

Wat Arun features five rounded prang – reflecting Cambodian-Khmer influence – encrusted with thousands of broken porcelain pieces. These porcelain shards were leftover ballast from Chinese ships which visited Bangkok in its early days.

Lakhon dancers wear elaborate costumes.

THE CREATIVE ARTS

While Thailand's traditional dance-dramas are an enticing part of the Thai experience for visitors, its young indie movie industry, cutting-edge contemporary theatre and dance, and modern artists and sculptors are fast gaining international attention.

Like most of Southeast Asia, Thailand's traditional cultural symbols and aesthetics are often most keenly appreciated by people outside the country. Abroad, for instance, Thai dance-drama is recognised as among the world's most dazzling and stylistically challenging; in Thailand performances are relatively rare outside tourist centres.

While the various forms of traditional artistry are delightful to watch, and enforce perceptions of exotic Thailand, it is also worth trying to catch some of Thailand's contemporary art scene, which is fast gaining recognition in international circles. The capital's modern art galleries, cutting-edge theatre and indie movies directed by a new breed of imaginative young directors are all part of the historical creative process that appears in traditional dance-drama and the faded beauty of temple murals.

Thai dance-drama

The origins of traditional Thai theatrical arts are entwined with court ceremony and religious ritual, some of which can still be seen today in Bangkok's Erawan Shrine or at the Lak Muang, where performers are hired to dance as a means of thanksgiving to the spirit gods. Drama and dance are inseparable as the dancer's hands and body express the emotions that the silent lips do not, with the storyline and lyrics provided by a singer and chorus on the side of the stage. A *phipat* orchestra (see box) creates not only the atmosphere, but also an emotive force.

It is thought that the movements of dance-drama originated in *nang yai* (shadow puppet) performances of the 16th and 17th centuries.

Lakhon dancers perform scenes from the epic Ramakien.

Huge buffalo hides were cut into the shapes of characters from the *Ramakien*. Against a torch-lit translucent screen, handlers manipulated puppets, using their silhouettes to tell complex tales of good and evil. As they moved the figures across the screen, the puppeteers danced the emotions they wanted the stiff figures to convey. These movements gradually evolved into an independent theatrical art.

The most identifiable form of dance-drama is *khon*, historically performed by a large troupe of male dancers wearing beautifully crafted masks. The performances were originally staged for the royal court. These days a condensed version of several episodes from the *Ramakien* – based on the Hindu epic *Ramayana* – is adapted into a short medley of palatable scenes for tourist dinner shows; the entire *Ramakien* would take 720 hours to perform. The colourful masks depict beasts and demons from the epic tale, with each performer trained to portray the particular character of each creature through gestures and actions.

The most graceful dance is the *lakhon*. There are two forms: the *lakhon nai* ("inside" *lakhon*), once performed only inside the palace walls by women, and the *lakhon nawk* ("outside" *lakhon*), performed beyond the palace by both sexes. Garbed in costumes as elaborate as their movements, the performers glide slowly about the stage, their stylised choreography conveying the plot. *Lakhon*'s rich repertoire includes scenes from the *Ramakien*, and tales like *Inao*, with its romantic storylines.

There have always been two cultures in Thailand: palace and village. The village arts are often parodies of the palace arts, but more

Saw-duang player.

burlesque, with pratfalls and bawdy humour. *Likay* is the village form of *lakhon*, played out against gaudy backdrops to an audience that walks in and out of the performance at will, eating and talking, regardless of what happens to the performers on stage.

Hanuman is a key character in the Ramakien.

THAI CLASSICAL MUSIC

To the uninitiated, classical Thai music sounds like a jarring and ear-piercing mishmash of contrasting tones without any pattern. The key is to listen to it as one would jazz, picking out one instrument and following it, switching to another as the mood moves one. Thai music is set to a scale of seven full steps, with a lilting and steady rhythm. Each instrument plays the same melody, but in its own way and seemingly without regard to how others are playing it. Seldom does an instrument rise in solo; it is always being challenged and cajoled by the other instruments of the orchestra.

A classical *phipat* orchestra is made up of a single reed instrument, the oboe-like *phinai*, and a variety of percussion instruments. The pitch favours the treble, with the pace set by the *ching*, a tiny cymbal, aided by the drums beaten with the fingers. The melody is played by two types of *ranad*, a bamboo-bar xylophone, and two sets of *gong wong*, tuned gongs arranged in a semi-circle around the player.

Another type of orchestra employs two violin-like instruments, the *saw-oo* and the *saw-duang*, and is usually heard accompanying a Thai dance-drama. A variation of the *phiphat* orchestra can be found performing at Thai boxing *(muay thai)* matches to spur the sinewy combatants to action.

The Joe Louis puppet troop performing the khon classical dance.

Puppet theatre

Traditional puppet theatre, like dance-drama, has also lost most of its Bangkok audiences to television. One troupe struggling to survive is the Joe Louis Theatre at Asiatique, a new waterfront dining, shopping and entertainment complex on Charoen Krung Road. . The company, which won the Best Performance Award at the World Festival of Puppet Arts in 2008, stages a *hun lakhon lek* puppet show nightly. Visually mesmerising and based on *khon* masked dance-drama, the performance requires three puppeteers who manipulate sticks attached to the marionettes to bring them to life. This endangered art form was revived by the late Sakorn Yangkeawsot, who went by the moniker Joe Louis.

He succeeded in updating *hun lakhon lek*, without diluting its origins, by allowing freer movement and more detailed costuming, and by incorporating contemporary themes based on social issues and modern speech.

Modern theatre and dance

Sadly, this is one area where modern innovation has been stifled, compounded by language barriers (for international appreciation) and budget limitations.

The last venue that regularly staged and produced quality modern productions was

> In traditional puppetry, the handlers also danced as they moved their puppets. Their complex choreography developed into the separate art form of Thai classical dance.

Patravadi Theatre, in Thonburi, but it closed down after the 2011 floods and the theatre moved its performances to Hua Hin. There are plans to bring modern dance back to Bangkok, but these have not come to fruition as yet. The open-air venue formerly run by Patravadi Mechudhon is now a café. The theatre in Hua Hin shows adaptations of classic Thai tales mixed with traditional local dance and theatre with modern Western styling. Some of its works fuse elements of Asian dance forms like Japanese *butoh* and Indonesian *wayang kulit*. Patravadi Theatre stages its acclaimed shows in its new location in Hua Hin (62–70 Petchkasem Road) on Saturday and Sunday nights.

Some productions tour overseas – notably the landmark *Sahatsadecha*, a mix of *khon* and *nang yai*, which played at the Biennale de la Danse, in Lyon, France. Past works have included *Monster*, a contemporary Japanese piece inspired by the artworks of Francis Bacon, and *The Ministry of Truth*, a performance

A Thai woodcarver.

when the Burmese sacked Ayutthaya in 1767. At the heart of Thai literature is the *Ramakien*, the Thai version of the Indian *Ramayana*. The enduring story has found a home in the literature, dance and drama of many Asian countries. Familiarity with the *Ramakien* enables one to comprehend a variety of dramatic forms, its significance for the Thai monarchy and its role as a model for exemplary behaviour.

The *Jataka* tales are also of Indian origin, telling of Buddha's reincarnations prior to enlightenment, though some are probably based on tales that existed before the Buddha lived. The first tales were translated from Pali script to Thai in the late 15th century. They have generated many other popular and classic stories, such as *Phra Aphaimani*, written by Sunthorn Phu, the 18th-century poet laureate.

Modern literature

It wasn't until the 1920s that Thai novels were published, with themes mainly touching on social or political issues. In the 1950s, however, censorship became so heavy and writers so harshly persecuted that quality fiction practically disappeared for 20 years. Thai writers since the 1980s have enjoyed a measure of political freedom. While they remain social critics, there are efforts to write fiction of literary merit. Many landmark Thai books were translated into English in the early 1990s. The late prime minister and cultural advocate Kukrit Pramoj's *Many Lives*, for instance, gives a good introduction to the Buddhist way of thinking. His *Four Reigns* is a fictional yet accurate account of court life in the 19th and 20th centuries. Also

described as discomfiting, in which German dancers and Thai ladyboys explored the human need to control and be controlled. Patravadi Theatre also hosts the annual Fringe Festival of dance, drama and music in Hua Hin.

Classical literature

Thais have always placed a heavy emphasis on oral tradition. Unfortunately, most of the country's classical written literature was destroyed

---

BUDDHA IMAGES

The focal point of the *bot* and *viharn* (ordination and sermon halls) of a Thai temple is the Buddha image. The image is not considered a representation of the Buddha, but is meant to serve as a reminder of his teachings. Buddha images cast in bronze, or carved in wood or stone, constitute the bulk of classic Thai sculpture. They epitomise the zenith of sculpting and employ some of the finest artistry (and some of the highest prices) of any arts. Superb examples of bas-relief sandstone carving can be seen around the base of the *bot* of Bangkok's Wat Pho. Delicately executed, the dozens of panels depict scenes from the *Ramakien*.

Buddha images conform to aesthetic rules, including being placed in one of four positions – sitting, standing, walking or reclining – and possessing distinguishing features *(laksanas)*, such as slender fingers and long eyelashes. The hand positions *(mudras)* are also significant, and are sometimes adopted by Buddhists to help focus during meditation. For instance, the hands in the lap, pointing up, indicate a disciplined mind. The *mudras* relate to events in the Buddha's life. The thumb and forefinger joined to make a circle represents the Buddha's first sermon after enlightenment. It signifies the Wheel of Dharma (Buddhist teachings).

Ramakien murals in the walls surrounding Wat Phra Kaew.

of note are Kampoon Boontawee's *Children of Isaan* and Botan's *Letters from Thailand*.

The highlight of the literary calendar is the SEA Write awards, held every August/September. Past Thai winners have included Uthis Haemamool for the novel *Laplae, Kaeng Khoi*, and Prabda Yoon, who stirred things up with the old establishment by penning works that connect to Thai youth.

Expatriate writers like Jake Needham and Christopher Moore bring a Western perspective to life in the kingdom, mainly using the hard-boiled detective genre to focus on the seedier aspects of the capital's nightlife. The most widely acclaimed has been John Burdett with *Bangkok 8*.

Traditional art

The inner walls of the *bot* (ordination hall) and *viharn* (sermon hall) in Thai temples are traditionally covered with murals (see page 57). In the days before public education, the temple was the principal repository of knowledge for the common person. Monks were the teachers, and the interior walls of the temples were illustrated lectures. The principal themes are the life of Buddha, with the back wall generally depicting

the *Maravijaya*, in which all earthly temptations are united to break the meditating Buddha's will and prevent his achieving Nirvana.

The murals at Buddhaisawan Chapel in Bangkok's National Museum are among the finest examples of Thai painting. Others include the

Mother-of-pearl inlay on door at Wat Ratchabophit.

Contemporary Thai art.

murals at Wat Suthat and the 19th-century paintings at Wat Bowonniwet. Although restored several times with less than perfect accuracy, the *Ramakien* murals on the walls surrounding Wat Phra Kaew include wonderful scenes of village and palace life.

Traditional art is also executed in the form of lacquer and gold paintings found on the shutters of most Thai temples. The best examples of lacquer painting can be found on the walls of the Lacquer Pavilion at Suan Pakkad Palace. Equally stunning is the intricate mother-of-pearl work by Thai artisans.

Contemporary art

At the turn of the 20th century, King Chulalongkorn commissioned several European artists to embark on projects in Bangkok, a trend the government continued in 1923 when they invited Italian sculptor Corrado Feroci to teach sculpture at the Fine Arts Department of the Ministry of Palace Affairs. The Florentine artist proved catalytic in the development of modern Thai art right through the 1960s; locals even gave him the adopted name of Silpa Bhirasri. He is regarded as the forefather of modern art in Thailand, and established the country's first school of fine arts, which later became Silpakorn University.

Spirituality and Buddhism have been, and still are, major precepts in contemporary art – whether created by neo-traditionalist painters like Thawan Duchanee and Chalermchai Kositpipat, whose late 20th-century paintings reinvigorate traditional perceptions of Thai identity, or the meditative installations in the 1990s by the late Montien Boonma. Internationally acclaimed Sakarin Krue-on uses spiritual metaphors as his basis, appropriating traditional imagery to question the blind adoption of Western trends.

Aside from the spiritual, since the 1997 economic collapse, many local artists have begun to question the effects of globalisation on the Thai populace. Rebellious artist Vasan Sitthiket blurs his art with faux political campaigning to highlight his contempt for national policies, while conceptual photographer Manit Sriwanichpoom ridicules the Thai urbanite's consumerist compulsions with his satirical *Pink Man* series.

The 11-storey Bangkok Arts and Culture Centre, despite political infighting and being a less than perfect space, is the most significant exhibition centre in the city, running shows with both local and international artists.

Cinema

Like most places in the world, Hollywood blockbusters dominate the cinemas. Of late however, a few talented Thai directors have been receiving

Modern pieces often have a political message.

Scene from the award-winning film, 'Last Life in the Universe'.

acclaim for their works on the international film circuit. Leading the charge is the new wave director Apichatpong Weerasethakul, whose 2002 film *Blissfully Yours* was awarded the *Prix un certain regard* at the Cannes Film Festival, followed by his atmospheric 2004 film *Tropical Malady* (*Sud Pralad*), which also picked up a special prize at Cannes. Apichatpong's 2004 collaboration with Thai–American artist Michael Shaowansai on the hilariously campy *The Adventures of Iron Pussy* – about a cross-dressing superhero – is proof that Thai cinema is engaging and provocative to both domestic and international audiences. Another Thai filmmaker to watch is Pen-Ek Ratanaruang who has produced two successful films, *Last Life in the Universe* (2004) and *Invisible Waves* (2006), starring the Japanese superstar actor Tadanobu Asano. He also wrote and directed *Ploy*, which premiered at Cannes in 2007, about a couple questioning their relationship upon returning to Thailand from living in America. Another Cannes favourite is Apichatpong Weerasethakul, who won the prestigious *Palme d'Or* in 2010 for his *Uncle Boonmee who can Recall his Past Lives*, a movie about the history and struggles of the Isaan region of Thailand.

However, many such films don't get the airing they deserve in Bangkok – the only real indie cinema is House on RCA, with occasional screenings at Lido in Siam Square. Additionally, there are film festivals, including the World Film Festival, EU Film Festival, and the big one, the Bangkok International Film Festival.

Michael Shaowanasai, the star of the musical comedy, 'The Adventures of Iron Pussy'.

Eating out in Bangkok: the busiest places are usually the best.

CUISINE

Thai cuisine is not just about tongue-numbing spices. Distinct regional, ethnic–migrant and Thai-fusion styles create a fabulous variety of complex flavours that appeal to the serious gourmand. And if you want a change from Thai, the city abounds with international restaurants.

Thai food is expanding faster globally than any other cuisine, and it's easy to see why. Less a dining experience than a sensory attack, it's one of the few cuisines in the world capable of drawing people to a country purely on its own merits.

It's the explosive spiciness of Thai food that initially overwhelms, but what's most impressive is the extraordinary complex balance of flavours that lie underneath. And contrary to what most people think, it's not all blatantly spicy: most Thai meals will include a sampling of less aggressive dishes, some subtly flavoured with only garlic and herbs.

The variation of foods and cooking styles is immense, as each of Thailand's four regions has a distinct cuisine of its own. The northeast is influenced by Laos, the south by Malaysia and Indonesia, the central area by the cuisine of the Royal Thai kitchens of the capital (the one people are most familiar with) and the north

Massaman curry, a creamy dish of Persian origin.

Thai chefs are adept at adapting foreign influences for local cooking styles. China, Malaysia, Laos, and even Portugal, have left their tastes on the Thai dinner table.

by Burma and Yunnan. All types are available in Bangkok, and often at street stalls and markets serving the city's migrant communities. As usual, the busiest spots have the best food.

But Bangkok offers far more than Thai food. It's fast emerging as an international culinary hot-spot, with options that include Mexican, Italian, Lebanese, Spanish and even the franchise of a hip Michelin-starred French restaurant. Adding excitement is a clutch of new-wave fusion restaurants that are boldly experimenting with Thai and Western ingredients and methods of preparation.

How to eat Thai food

Most Thai meals have dishes placed in the middle of the table to be shared by all; the larger the group the more dishes you can try. Heap a little rice onto your plate, together with small

ORIGINS OF ROYAL THAI CUISINE

Royal Thai cuisine has hugely influenced the food of the Central Plains, with dishes such as green curry and the hot and sour shrimp soup *tom yum goong*. The great-grandson of King Rama IV, MR Sorut Visuddhi, co-owner of Bangkok's Thanying (www.thanying.com), a royal Thai restaurant that serves the recipes of his mother, Princess Sulap-Walleng Visuddhi, explains: "In the palace it was considered bad manners to perspire at the table or to eat foods that had strong smells. So we would use coconut milk to cut down on these tastes. This had a big influence on Central cooking."

The Grand Palace had many residences where each princess cooked what was called *ahaan chawang* (food

for the palace people). These recipes spread through the wealthy classes via palace finishing schools and publications such as *Mae Krua Hua Baak*, the country's first cookbook, written by Thanpuying Pliang Pasonakorn, a descendant of King Rama II.

Later, when the royal families moved out of the palaces, the kitchen hands they hired learnt the recipes and started cooking them at home. A number of royally connected Thai restaurants began to open from the 1980s, but few authentic ones remain today. The intricate fruit and vegetable carving seen at fine Thai restaurants – like the Sala Rim Naam at the Oriental hotel – is also a legacy of Royal Thai cuisine.

portions of various dishes at the side (it's polite to take only a little at a time). Eat with a fork and spoon, using the fork to push food onto the spoon. Chopsticks are only for Chinese and noodle dishes.

Rice is the staple; in the past it sustained workers throughout the day, with just small portions of chilli, curry or sauce added for flavour. Even

now, rural Thais eat large helpings of rice with just morsels of dried or salted fish. Thankfully, jasmine-scented Thai rice is one of the most delicious in Asia, regarded as being so valuable that the government has patented its genetic code.

Condiments on the table usually include dried, ground red chilli, sliced chilli with vinegar, sliced chilli with *nam pla* (fish sauce),

Noodle stand in Talad Kao Market.

Hot green chillis, a key ingredient of many dishes.

Exquisitely presented dishes at the Sala Rim Naam restaurant, at the Mandarin Oriental Hotel.

> *Thai cooks use several types of chilli (prik), both red and green, some relatively mild, and some very fiery. When sliced and served in fish sauce (nam pla) as a condiment, it's called prik nam pla.*

and white sugar. These are mainly used to add extra flavour to noodle dishes. Many visitors are surprised to find that the peanut sauce condiment used in many Thai restaurants in Western countries is of Malaysian or Indonesian origin; in Thailand it's only used as a dip for satay.

Northern cuisine

This is the mildest of Thai foods. Northerners generally eat *khao nio* (sticky rice), kneading it into a ball to dip into sauces and curries such as the Burmese *kaeng hanglay*, a sweet and tamarind-sour pork dish. *Khao soi* is also found in Burma, but is possibly of Chinese origin. Usually made with chicken, it has fresh egg noodles swimming in a mild coconut curry, with crispy noodles sprinkled on top.

Other northern Thai specialities include sausages, such as the spicy pork *sai oua* (roasted over a coconut husk fire to impart aroma and flavour) and *naem* (fermented raw pork and pork skin seasoned with garlic and chilli). *Laab* is a salad dish of minced pork, chicken, beef or fish, served with mint leaves and raw vegetables to cool the spices. It's also common in the northeast.

Dipping sauces include *nam prik ong* (minced pork, mild chillies, tomatoes, garlic and shrimp paste) and the potent northern classic, *nam prik noom* (grilled chillies, onions and garlic). Both are eaten with the popular snack called *khaep moo* (crispy pork rind).

Northeastern cuisine

Northeastern (Isaan) food is simple, generally spicy, and eaten with mounds of sticky rice kept in bamboo baskets. Hot dishes include the legendary *som tam* (shredded green papaya, garlic, chillies, lime juice, and variations of tomatoes, dried shrimp, preserved crab and fermented fish) and a version of *laab*, which is spicier and sourer than its northern sister.

An array of curries at a food market.

But perhaps the most popular Isaan food is not hot at all. *Gai yang* is chicken grilled in a marinade of peppercorns, garlic, fish sauce, coriander and palm sugar, and served with both hot and sweet dipping sauces.

Southern cuisine

The south – notable for Thailand's hottest dishes – also has gentler specialties such as *khao yam*,

an innocuous salad of rice, vegetables, pounded dried fish and a southern fish sauce called *budu*. Slightly spicier are *phad sataw*, a stir-fry usually with pork or shrimp, and *sataw*, a large lima bean look-alike with a strong flavour and aroma. *Khao moke gai* is roasted chicken with turmeric-seasoned yellow rice – like an Indian *biryani*, often sprinkled with crispy fried onions.

Hot dishes include *kaeng tai plaa*. Fishermen who needed food that would last for days at sea are said to have created it by blending the fermented stomachs of fish with chillies, bamboo shoots and vegetables together with an intensely hot sauce. Even hotter is *kaeng leuang* (yellow curry), a variant of the central Thai *kaeng som*, with fish, green papaya and bamboo shoots or palm hearts in an explosive sauce.

Central cuisine

Central cuisine, which has been influenced by the royal palaces (see page 68), includes many of the dishes made internationally famous at Thai restaurants abroad. It's notable for the use of coconut milk and even modern garnishes such as grapes, which mellow the chilli heat and

---

THAI CHINESE CUISINE

Many ethnic Chinese in Thailand still speak the Teochew dialect of their southern Chinese ancestry, and most Chinese restaurants serve Teochew or Cantonese food. Especially famous are goose feet cooked in soy sauce, Peking duck, a wide variety of steamed and fried fish dishes, and the bite-sized lunchtime snacks called *dim sum*. Poultry, pork, seafood and mushrooms are ubiquitous items along with noodles or rice, while piping-hot Chinese tea is an integral part of every meal. Chinatown is awash with dining options although it has surprisingly few actual restaurants. Most people choose to eat at street stalls or in tiny shophouse cafés.

Street-side noodle stalls are ubiquitous in some areas of the city.

kratiam prik Thai) or the sweet and sour *muu pad prio waan*, probably of Portuguese origin, brought to Thailand by Chinese immigrants. *Neua pad nam man hoi* is a mild, delicate dish of beef fried with oyster sauce, spring onions and mushrooms. The popular and very spicy *pat pet pat bai kaprao* dishes include meat stir-fried with chillies, garlic, onions and holy basil (*bai kaprao*). Main ingredients to note are: chicken (*gai*), pork (*muu*), beef (*neua*), duck (*ped*), seafood (*talay*) and shrimp (*goong*).

Noodles and rice

Noodles – a Chinese import – have a place in Thai restaurants. The ubiquitous street-side noodle shop sells two types: *kuay tiaw*, made from rice flour, and *ba mee*, from wheat flour. Both can be ordered broad (*sen yai*), narrow (*sen lek*) or very narrow (*sen mee*), and with broth (*sai naam*) or without (*haeng*).

add a little sweetness. It's still fiery, though, so take care. Trademark dishes include *tom kha gai*, a soup of chicken, coconut milk and galangal, the celebrated hot and sour shrimp soup *tom yum goong*, and *kaeng khio waan* (green curry), with chicken or beef, basil leaves and pea-sized green aubergines. Stir-fries and noodle dishes are everywhere, due to the large Chinese presence in the central region.

Common dishes to try

Kaeng is usually translated as curry, but it covers a broad range, from thin soups to near-dry dishes like the northern *kaeng ho*. Many *kaeng* are made with coconut cream, like the spicy red curry (*kaeng pet*) and *kaeng mussaman*, a rich, sweetish dish of Persian origin with meat, potatoes and onions. *Kaeng* without coconut milk include "jungle curries", which are very spicy.

Fish and seafood have featured largely in Thai cooking since ancient times. *Haw mok talay* is mixed seafood in a curried coconut custard and steamed in a banana-leaf cup or coconut shell. Other delicious choices to try are *poo pat pong karee* (steamed chunks of crab in an egg-thickened curry sauce with crunchy spring onion) and *hoi malaeng poo op maw din* (mussels in their shells, steamed in a clay pot with lime juice and aromatic herbs).

Meat – usually chicken, pork or beef – is cooked in all manner of styles, such as pork fried with garlic and black pepper (*muu thawd*

Typical Isaan dishes from northeastern Thailand, including som tam and gai yang.

Common dishes are *kuay tiaw raad naa* (rice noodles flash-fried and topped with sliced meat and greens in a thick, mild sauce) and *paad thai* (narrow pan-fried rice noodles with egg, dried and fresh shrimp, spring onions, tofu, crushed peanuts and bean sprouts). In *mee krawp*, the rice noodles are fried crispy, tossed in sweet-and-sour sauce and topped with sliced chillies, pickled garlic and slivers of lime rind.

Many lunchtime rice dishes are of Chinese origin. They include *khao man gai* (chicken with rice cooked in chicken broth), *khao moo daeng* (with Chinese red pork) and *khao kaa moo* (with stewed pork leg and greens). At night and in the early morning, two soup-like rice dishes are favoured. *Khao tom* comes in the water it was boiled in (with additions such as garlic-fried pork, salted egg or pickled ginger) and the close relative *joke*, which is porridge-like rice seasoned with minced pork, coriander and slivers of fresh ginger. Crispy *pathongko* (fried dough) pieces float on top.

Thai desserts

In Bangkok, *khanom* (desserts) come in bewildering variety, from light concoctions with

Singha beer, popular with Thais and farang alike.

THE KING OF FRUIT

The notorious durian, often avoided by foreigners for a smell they liken to toilets, is so prized by Thais they call it the King of Fruit. The outer appearance is like a large, spiky green rugby ball, while inside it has a creamy flesh with a unique, slightly burning sweetness that tastes much better than it smells.

Of the many varieties, which are in season from May to August, Chanee and Monthong are said to be the best, and those grown in Nonthaburi the best of all. Some upmarket restaurants now include durian ice cream and durian cheesecake on their menus, which entice more foreigners to their charms.

crushed ice and syrup, to custards, ice creams and little cakes, and an entire category based on egg yolks cooked in flower-scented syrups.

The heavier Thai confections are rarely eaten after a big meal. After-meal desserts, served in small bowls, are generally light and elegant. *Kluay buat chee* has banana slices in sweetened and salted warm coconut cream. *Kluay kaek* uses bananas sliced lengthwise, dipped in coconut cream and rice flour, and deep-fried until crisp. Other favourites are *taap tim krawp* (water chestnut pieces covered in red-dyed tapioca flour and served in coconut cream and crushed ice) and *sangkhaya ma-praoawn*, a coconut cream custard steamed in a young coconut or a small pumpkin.

Mango with sticky rice and coconut cream, a truly sumptuous dessert.

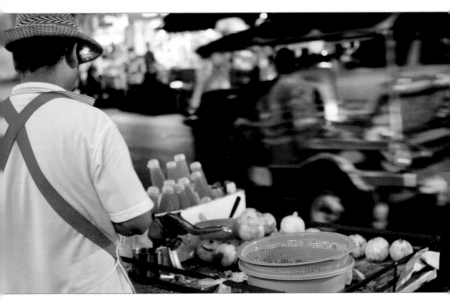

Fresh-juice stall.

Many desserts are startlingly inventive – you may finish a rich pudding before realising that its tantalising flavour comes from crisp fried onions. Look out for market vendors who sell "roof-tile cookies" (*khanom beuang*), crispy shells filled with strands of egg yolk cooked in syrup with shredded coconut, sweet and spicy dried shrimp, coriander and coconut cream. But, if you sample nothing else in Thailand, don't miss the heavenly *khao niao ma-muand* (mango with sticky rice and coconut cream).

Thai fusion cuisine

There have been foreign influences in Thai food for centuries (even chilli, which is another Portuguese import), but recent years have seen the growth of a dedicated style of Thai-fusion dishes. It often takes the form of Italian–Thai blends such as Thai-style spaghetti with anchovies and chilli, served at modern cafés like Greyhound (several branches in the city; www. greyhoundcafe.co.th).

Other modern Thai restaurants, like Mahanaga (www.mahanaga.com) for instance, use non-traditional ingredients such as lamb and salmon, and plate their essentially Thai dishes Western style. When international Thai restaurant chain The Blue Elephant opened its Bangkok branch (www.blueelephant.com/bangkok), it introduced several fusion items, including salmon *laab*. The hot shot is Long Table (www.longtablebangkok. com), where ex-Bed Supperclub chef Dan Ivarie designed a menu with interesting combinations like foie gras with dried shrimp and tamarind. And at Breeze they incorporate Thai flavours into their pan-Asian menu with delicious flare.

Refreshments

With meals Thais drink locally brewed beers such as Singha, Leo and the stronger Beer Chang. Foreign brands brewed on licence include Heineken. The middle-class obsession with French wines is waning, and there is now a decent selection available from the New World. Thailand itself is even producing its own wines (see page 224).

Among the working classes, the rice whisky brands Maekhong and Saeng Thip are popular, usually served as a "set" with ice, soda and lime. Note: fresh fruit and ice drinks will often get a splash of syrup (and salt) unless you request otherwise.

SHOPPING

Brush up your bargaining skills and fill your pockets with baht, because Bangkok is a retail heaven. Colourful markets sell everything from cheap clothes to snakes and violins, while gigantic high-gloss malls take care of the Gucci crowd.

Bangkok is one of the shopping capitals of the world. It's a city where you can sniff out an antique treasure under the sweltering awnings of an outdoor market or pick up a Hermès handbag from a luxury marble-clad mall. If you know where to look for it, just about anything is available – from Siamese pottery and hand-woven silks to cutting-edge home furnishings and funky street wear. The city caters to both spendthrifts and penny pinchers, with shops open seven days a week. Bangkok's Skytrain conveniently connects the best shopping areas and you can glide above the traffic in air-conditioned comfort from Emporium, a glitzy shopping mall offering brands like Prada, Versace and Chanel, to the rough and ready Chatuchak Weekend Market, where thousands of stalls sell everything from hill-tribe clothing to quirky home accessories.

The main shopping areas converge around Thanon Rama I and Thanon Ploenchit and are linked by the Skywalk – a covered walkway beneath the Skytrain tracks – which connects the Chidlom, Siam Square and National Stadium Skytrain stations. This means you can walk from mall to mall without ever touching terra firma. Just a stone's throw from Siam Square, a warren of market stalls and shops catering to a trendy teenage clientele, is the high-end Siam Discovery Centre, as well as Mahboonkrong (MBK), a multi-storey bargain-hunter's heaven. Nearby is the gargantuan Siam Paragon mall, are peppered with high-end boutiques, cafés, and even a giant aquarium and a Ferrari showroom. Further down the road is the even bigger Central World mall. At the other end of the Skywalk is luxury

Night markets are great places to pick up unusual and inexpensive souvenirs.

THE ART OF BARGAINING

First, don't start bargaining unless you really want to buy. Stage One involves asking the price. At Stage Two you say it is too much, and they will (99 percent of the time) lower the original price, signalling they are open to offers. Then you offer your first price, which is always too low, and from there the volley of bargaining begins until the final price is agreed. It's a good idea, if you can, to watch local shoppers to see what price they get. And walking away is a good tactic. You may be called back with a better price, and if not you've at least established some groundwork for trying at another stall (many stock the same items).

COUNTERFEIT CITY

Bangkok has long had an unwelcome reputation for its fakes, from Louis Vuitton handbags to pirated copies of the latest Hollywood movies. For a fraction of the price of the real thing you can buy reproductions of Rolex, Cartier or Tag Heuer watches. Bear in mind that some reproductions are better than others – a dud "Rolex" may stop running a few weeks after purchase. Clothes are a safer bet. Popular knock-offs include Nike, Hilfiger, Armani, DKNY and Ralph Lauren. The quality can vary tremendously, so inspect each garment carefully.

With increasing pressure from international companies, the Thai government musters half-hearted crackdowns on counterfeit goods from time to time, but the trade is fairly open. Sporadic government raids only mean that watches, DVDs or audio CDs are sometimes sold more surreptitiously. The covers of pirated DVDs, for instance, are displayed in albums at street-side stalls; once buyers have made their choices, vendors will disappear to a hidden stash nearby and minutes later return with the merchandise.

Fake goods can be found almost anywhere in Bangkok's markets and shopping malls, but they proliferate mainly around the Thanon Silom and Patpong night markets, MBK Centre and the stalls that spring up along Thanon Sukhumvit (Soi 5 to Soi 11) each evening.

shopping at Gaysorn Plaza and Erawan Bangkok, where you can find the latest bags from Burberry, Coach and Mulberry.

Other good areas for shopping are Chinatown, where the maze of crowded streets gives a taste of old Bangkok without the tacky tourist goods; Thanon Khao San, catering to its backpacker clientele, so shops there specialise in tattooing, hair-braiding, funky clothes, used books and silver jewellery; and Pratunam for its interesting market and also for Panthip Plaza, where various shops sell computers, software, games and DVDs.

The best times to shop

Shops in the main downtown and tourist areas open daily, usually from 10am to 10pm, but in the Old City and Chinatown they will normally close on Sundays. Bangkok hosts a number of seasonal sales that offer unique items, such as the twice-yearly prison sale of wooden furniture made by Thai prisoners. Check the local English-language newspaper listing sections for details. Also worth attending are the annual export sales events such as Made in Thailand, the Bangkok International Gift Fair (BIG) and

Lacquerware at Chatuchak market.

Elaborate wood carving of a fiery dragon.

A scene from the Ramakien carved into wood.

the Bangkok International Houseware Fair (BIH). Every June–July and December–January, major department stores and malls take part in the Thailand Grand Sales, though many also offer a 5 percent tourist discount year-round – simply show your passport at the point of purchase. Additionally, you can claim the 7 percent VAT refund at the airport (see page 243).

Traditional Thai products

Thailand is famous the world over for the fine quality of its traditional handicrafts, and there is an extraordinary variety on offer.

Northern silversmiths pound out bowls coated with an extract of tamarind to enhance their sheen. Teakwood is carved into practical items such as breadboards and salad bowls, as well as more decorative trivets and statues of mythical gods, angels and elephants. Bronze statues of classical drama figures like the recumbent deer from the *Ramakien* make elegant decorations. Brassware, like the large noodle cabinets which street vendors sling on bamboo poles, can double up as small side tables. Natural fibre woven into placemats, laundry baskets and handbags also make great buys.

Thai craftsmen excel at lacquerware, the art of overlaying wooden or bamboo items with glossy black lacquer, then painting scenes in gold leaf on this black "canvas". Bowls and trays are the main items sold. One of Thailand's lesser-known arts is nielloware, which involves applying an amalgam of black metal onto etched portions of silver or, to a lesser extent, gold. Thai craftsmen are also supremely skilled at setting oyster shells aglow in black lacquer backgrounds to create scenes of enchanting beauty.

Kitsch trinkets.

Ornate lacquer jewellery.

Thais have been crafting pots for over 5,000 years with great skill. While original antiques are rarities, most ceramics are still thrown in the same shapes and designs as their age-old counterparts. Among the best-known are Sangkhaloke ceramic plates from ancient Sukhothai, with their distinctive twin-fish design. Celadon is a beautiful stoneware with a light jade green or dark-brown glaze, and is used to make dinnerware, lamps and statuary. *Bencharong* originated in China and was later developed by Thai artists. Its name describes its look: *bencha* is Sanskrit for five, and *rong* means colour. The five colours of *bencharong* – red, blue, yellow, green and white – appear on delicate porcelain bowls, containers, ashtrays and decorative items. Popular blue-and-white porcelain, which also originated in China, has been produced extensively in Thailand for centuries.

Thai handicrafts are found in shops and markets all over the city, and some of the more specialist shops are worth seeking out. If pressed for time, head for Nayarana Phand in Thanon Ratchadamri, a one-stop shop for all things Thai.

Antiques

Thai and Burmese antiques are among the finest in Asia, although the real thing is hard to find these days. The tenacious and well-informed can still unearth treasures, but the rule of thumb is to take claims of antiquity with a pinch of salt unless you really know what you're doing; things are not always what they seem. The centre of the city's antiques trade is located on the upper floors of River City, an array of shops selling genuine antiques as well as lookalike *objets d'art*. Note: the Fine Arts Department maintains strict control over the export of religious antiques (see box); dealers are usually able to

EXPORT PERMITS

The Thai Department of Fine Arts prohibits the export of all Thai Buddha images, images of other deities and fragments (hands or heads) of images dating before the 18th century. All antiques must be registered with them. The shop will usually do this for you, or you can take the piece yourself to the office at Thanon Na Prathat (tel: 0-2226 1661) together with two postcard-sized photos of it. The export fee ranges from B50 to B200 depending on the antiquity of the piece. Fake antiques do not require export permits, but airport customs officials are not art experts and may mistake these for genuine pieces. If it looks authentic, clear it at the Department of Fine Arts to avoid problems later.

Despite recent campaigns to make tourists aware of the laws regarding the purchase and export of Buddha images, these campaigns remain reasonably ineffective, with many market stall vendors ignoring the Thai government wishes.

Toy cars made from recycled beer cans.

The place to go for a tailor-made silk suit.

Thailand has one of the world's leading markets in gemstones and jewellery products, with all aspects of the trade covered in the country, from mining to the finished product.

clear buyers' purchases by obtaining export permits and shipping them abroad.

Gems and jewellery

Thailand mines its own rubies and sapphires from the eastern coast city of Chantaburi, and also acts as a conduit for stones from Burma and Cambodia. Globally, Thailand is a major player in the international jewellery market, and Bangkok is home to the world's leading cutters of coloured gems. Rubies range from pale to deep red (including the famous "pigeon's blood" red); sapphires come in blue, green and yellow, as well as in the form most associated with Thailand – the star sapphire. Thai jewellers can turn gold, white-gold, silver and platinum into delicate jewellery settings and are able to produce both traditional and modern designs.

Be careful when shopping for gems and jewellery; on streets and in some small shops, the stones may not be of the quality and weight advertised. The Tourism Authority of Thailand has joined hands with gem-trading organisations to provide quality control through the Jewel Fest Club – look for the ruby-ring logo on shop fronts.

Textiles and tailoring

The potential glamour of Thai silk was recognised in the late 1940s by American entrepreneur Jim Thompson. He promoted it abroad where it quickly gained wide acceptance for its bumpy texture and shimmering iridescence. Today, silk has become a major Thai industry. While the Jim Thompson shop offers an excellent range of coloured silks and ready-made products, bargains can also be gleaned from the lesser-known Jim Thompson Factory Outlet.

Also worth buying is *mudmee*, a northeastern silk characterised by subtle zigzagging lines and in more sombre hues such as dark blue, maroon and deep yellow. Dazzling embroidery can be found in the modern-day versions of *teen chok* – a method with which women of the ancient Lanna kingdom in the north of Thailand symbolically wove their family histories into their sarongs. The country's northern hill-tribes each have their own distinctive patchwork and embroidery designs, mainly in bright blues,

Designer kitchen utensils.

Lane in Chinatown. Though some shops offer a 24-hour service, it's always best to return for at least one fitting to ensure the best results.

Cutting-edge Thai

Thai craftsmanship and creativity extends far beyond the realm of the traditional, and Bangkok is fast becoming a hub for cutting-edge design. Keep an eye out for some of Thailand's up-and-coming homegrown fashion labels such as the flamboyant offerings from Fly Now and Jaspal, or the more understated designs from Greyhound. Thai designers are also making waves in the area of home decor. Propaganda (at Siam Discovery Centre and Emporium) produces innovative accessories, while Ayodhya (at Gaysorn Plaza) offers a line of chi-chi throws and water hyacinth furniture. Thai cosmetics companies, such as Harnn, are also reinventing natural Thai beauty products like jasmine rice soap and tamarind facial scrubs, and packaging them in elegant rattan baskets.

magentas and yellows. At the Siam Centre's Mae Fah Luang shop – a royal initiative to promote the livelihood of Thai villagers through traditional means – you can purchase hand-woven silks and cottons in lengths, or ready-made into cushion covers and clothes.

Using local and imported fabrics, Bangkok's excellent tailors can whip up perfectly fitted three-piece suits for men as well as elegant dresses with appliqué and beadwork for women. Choose designs from catalogues, conjure up your own creations or have your old favourites copied. If using your own material, rummage at Bangkok's famous fabric market on Sampeng

Even the shopping experience is being repackaged; if you get bored with the city's seemingly limitless supply of department stores and malls, you can sample more eclectic boutique shops like It's Happened to Be a Closet (Emporium mall), where customers are encouraged to mix-and-match vintage dress designs with homeware products and accessories, before dining in their coffee shop or popping into their hair stylist.

Thai designer Chamnan Pakdeesuk shows off his creations at Bangkok International Fashion Week.

Bangkok Bazaar

Markets are an essential Bangkok experience. In fact, they're hard to avoid: shops spill onto every street, and vendors hawk goods off metal carts and tarpaulin sheets.

The colours, noise and pungent aromas of Bangkok's markets *(talad)* are a tantalising assault on the senses. And Bangkok has a market for just about every neighbourhood, and every hour of the day or night.

The ultimate bazaar is **Chatuchak Weekend Market** affectionately dubbed "JJ" due to the alternative Thai spelling, Jatujak. Some 15,000 stalls offer a mind-boggling variety of goods. From pedigree pooches to hill-tribe fabrics, old Thai movie posters and hand-made paper… you name it, it's here.

There are numerous markets tucked around the shopping malls and department stores of central Bangkok. **Pratunam Market** rivals Chatuchak for its selection of clothing. At midday the stalls at **Soi La Lai Sap** (literally "lane which melts your money away") sell shoes, handbags and myriad accessories. **Thanon Khao San** is lined with stalls offering backpacker requisites such as silver jewellery, hand-painted cards and second-hand books.

For a real flavour of **Chinatown** wander the length of **Soi Itsaranuphap**, passing spice shops, a fish market and stores selling religious paraphernalia. At its river end, **Talad Kao** sells fresh produce. Also in Chinatown, at the so-called "Thieves Market", where in the past residents would look for items burgled from their homes, you find musical instrument shops and antiques. Retaining more of its traditional atmosphere is **Faichai**, or Flashlight Market, held on Saturday evenings along the labyrinth of streets around Central Hospital near Chinatown. It sells a variety of goods and bric-a-brac. **Pahurat Market** has all things Indian, from saris to henna dyes, and don't miss the 24-hour **Flower Market**, which spills into the clothes and accessories stalls of **Saphan Phut Market** come nightfall.

For more night time shopping, head to **Ractchada Train Market behind Esplinade Mall on Ratchada Road.** With stalls selling handicrafts, clothes and furniture, it's a smaller version of Chatuchak without the midday heat and crowds. Other evening markets, like those along **Thanon Silom** and in **Patpong**, as well as the stalls along **Thanon Sukhumvit** (roughly Soi 5 to

Sukhumvit night market.

Soi 11), are a treasure-trove of counterfeit goods and souvenirs, and are open until midnight. **Damnoen Saduak**, the most famous floating market, selling vegetables and fruit on the outskirts of Bangkok, is now mainly a tourist attraction, but still worth a visit.

The night comes alive at infamous Patpong.

BANGKOK AFTER DARK

Bangkok struts to live jazz, rock and indie music with a thriving scene full of hip clubs and cool bars. You can sip champagne cocktails on a rooftop 63 storeys up, or down cheap beers in a bar with no walls. There really is something here for everyone.

Many visitors' expectations of Bangkok nightlife extend no further than the much-hyped Patpong go-go bar scene, but this cosmopolitan city has plenty of options for entertainment once the sun goes down. The Thai craving for *sanuk* (fun) has in recent years seen booms in everything from microbreweries and bars offering Cuban cigars and art on the walls to clubs specialising in music as diverse as jazz, Latin, hip hop, house and mind-numbing techno, often all on the same street. In addition, there is traditional dance, theatre, opera, classical music, indie films and evening sports aplenty. Bangkok really comes alive under the cover of darkness, and never before has it offered so much choice to the night-time reveller.

Nightlife zones

Officially, for the purposes of nightlife entertainment, Bangkok is divided into three zones: Thanon Silom, Thanon Ratchadaphisek and Royal City Avenue (RCA), where venues with valid dance licences can officially stay open until 2am. The rest should close by 1am. This system was introduced early this century, following a clampdown on drugs, underage drinking and inappropriate behaviour close to temples and schools. But habits die hard: Bangkok has long had a party atmosphere, and although the zones survive, the restrictions in other areas are intermittently less strictly enforced. If anything, the extra regulations merely provide extra opportunities for the local police to collect bribes. A venue may or may not close according to law, and there are generally places to carry on drinking if you follow

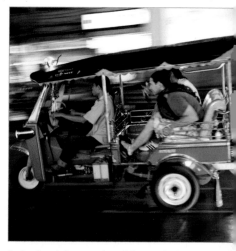

Racing through the streets of Bangkok on a tuk-tuk.

your nose. One lingering effect of the crackdown is that you have to be over 20 to enter clubs and almost all require you to show ID, whatever your age. There have been purges on patrons in late-night venues with arrests being made for positive drugs tests and not having official government identification (for foreigners this usually means a passport). If you do not want to carry your passport, do take a photocopy with you.

The Silom zone includes the famous Patpong red-light district as well as numerous pubs and restaurants, but little in the way of dance clubs outside Soi 2 and Soi 4. Thanon

THAI ROCK AND COUNTRY

Three types of music dominate Thai-style rock and country clubs. The rock-format *plaeng puer cheewit* (Songs For Life) is played in countless Bangkok clubs notable for their kitschy decor of cowboy hats, buffalo horns and Confederate flags from the US Civil War. The music has its roots in the record collections of American GIs stationed in Thailand during the Vietnam War, and the lyrics developed as protest songs during Thailand's student uprisings of the early 1970s. The most famous practitioner of this music form is Ad Carabao, who still plays gigs with his band Carabao.

Luk thung (Child of the Rice Fields), as the name suggests, is Thai country music and mainly appeals to the working class. Its lyrics recount "real life" issues, ranging from unrequited love to poverty and despair. The genre of music is so popular it has spawned several magazines and TV programmes, and even a few films.

Morlam (Master Rap) is an upcountry form sung in the Lao dialect by singers sometimes dressed in ornate costumes inspired by the royal courts. The lyrics are usually improvised and are usually highly sexual or political. You'll hear *luk thung* and *morlam* played on taxi drivers' radios and in clubs primarily located on the outskirts of town where Isaan migrant communities congregate. Spicy food and copious amounts of local rice-based whiskies are the fuel for any of these gigs.

Ratchadaphisek has been the traditional stomping ground for huge gentlemen's clubs and even larger massage parlours, visited mainly by Thais and Asian tourists, but there's also a clutch of smaller bars and live music venues that attract young Thais. You'll occasionally find imported bands here as diverse as heavy metal to indie folk. Hip hop has taken root in the urban young and there has been an influx of foreign artists in recent years.

Of the three zones, it is RCA that has developed into the most focused club scene in town, with a stretch of hip bars and clubs that people flit in and out of. Dedicated restaurants are scarce in the area, but most bars and clubs in Bangkok have some provision for food, and there are reasonable Thai menus at most places on the strip. Current hot spots with dance floors include Route 66 and 808, the latter of which has a regular influx of international DJs.

Bangkok has no shortage of cocktail bars.

The club scene is alive and kicking.

The club scene

Bangkok's club scene is constantly expanding. Dance music has evolved from ear-bashing techno to include hip hop, deep house, jungle, Indian vibes, and countless variations led by cutting-edge dance clubs like LEVELS (Sukhumvit Soi 11), Club Culture (Thanon Sri Ayutthaya) and Glow (Sukhumvit 23), all of which draw multinational crowds. All these spots regularly import international DJs in addition to hosting an increasingly confident posse of local DJs who go by names like Nakadia, Dragon, Seed and Funky Gangster.

The lanes off Soi Thonglor have popular bars and clubs such as Demo that draw Thais and expats from around town. A Thai scene also flourishes in the backpacker quarter near Thanon Khao San, with hot venues like The Club and the Brick Bar.

Even some of the city's hotels are getting funky, with great wine-and-dine monthly specials with electronic sounds at Barsu, in the Sheraton Grande, and fashion shows and film nights at Met Bar, in The Metropolitan Hotel.

Live music

Front-line international acts of many genres stop off at Bangkok on Asian tours. Recent visits include Queen (featuring Adam Lambert), Scorpions, Morrissey and Big Bang. .

Local music in bars varies tremendously. The huge Tawandaeng German Brewhouse on Thanon Narathiwat features local band Fong Nam, led by American classical avant gardist Bruce Gaston. They fuse a traditional Thai *phiphat* orchestra with rock in a quirky, highly costumed night of cabaret. Thai rock and country (see box) features in barn-like venues, usually on the outskirts of town, and there's a good helping of R&B, blues, rock and jazz (see page 86), by local, visiting and expat musicians all over the city. Good live jazz and blues venues include Adhere and Saxophone; axe-hero rock appears at Overtone, on RCA; while Brick Bar, on Khao San Road, stages rock, ska and reggae.

T-pop (Thai pop music), like its Western counterpart, is a PR-heavy package of cute faces and bubblegum tunes, often fronted by *luk kreung* (half-Thai, half-Western) stars like Tata

Live jazz at Saxophone.

The spectacular view from Dome at the State Tower.

Young. Indie labels like Hualampong Riddim and Panda Records provide recording opportunities outside the mainstream, and their bands play regular gigs. Look out, too, in the local press for Indie promoters Mind the Gap, who hold regular events featuring various genres like electronica, thrash and grunge around the city. Every November, Bangkok's coolest radio station, Fat Radio (104.5FM), stages its two-day Fat Festival at various venues.

Bars and pubs

Upmarket bars with international sensibilities are found all over central Bangkok. Try

BLUE-BLOODED JAZZ PLAYER

King Bhumibol was a keen sax player and jazz composer – he jammed with virtually all the jazz musicians who visited Bangkok, including Stan Getz and Benny Goodman – and the city organises jazz festivals each year to commemorate his birthday. Regular gigs around town include Saxophone and the Living Room (Sheraton Grande hotel), both of which attract fine resident bands and visiting guests like sax player James Carter. The Oriental Hotel's Bamboo Bar has an excellent Russian jazz quartet which backs foreign singers.

sky-high champagne and caviar (both in price and altitude) at the rooftop Sky Bar and Distil, both with astonishing views of the city, in the State Tower on Thanon Silom, or cocktails at the exquisite modern Thai restaurant Mahanaga (Sukhumvit Soi 29) or Face Bar (Sukhumvit Soi 38). The Conrad Bangkok has one of the coolest hotel lobby bars imaginable in the Diplomat Bar, while the Sofitel Silom offers reasonably priced bottles of wine with 37th-floor city panoramas at V9. And, as high fliers sip their fine champagne and cocktails, lo-sos head for Cheap Charlie's – nothing more than a bar (no roof, no walls, no toilet…) – on Sukhumvit Soi 11. The hip Thai scene constantly shifts with the whims of local image mavens, but increasingly centres on Soi Thonglor, in venues like Demo and Escobar.

The English and Irish pub scene is mainly concentrated on Thanon Silom and Thanon Sukhumvit, with notable venues being the The Dubliner (Sukhumvit Soi 33) and Molly Malone's (Soi Convent, off Thanon Silom). There are also a few American-style sports bars, such as The Roadhouse (Thanon Surawong), which has great Buffalo wings, and microbreweries like the Londoner Brew Pub (recently moved to the corner of Pattanakarn). All these places have variations on the usual pub grub and games formula.

The Soi Cowboy red-light district, lined with go-go bars and nightclubs.

Increasingly bars, promoters and record companies are massaging the creative forces of Bangkok's non-mainstream musicians. Electro, grunge and metal bands are plugging in all over town.

The gay scene

Whether tolerance towards gays and lesbians is increasing or decreasing in Thailand often depends on the nuances of context, but either way the scene is thriving and very visible. Clubs and bars around Silom Soi 2 and Soi 4 cater to a variety of gay tastes, be it quiet drinking and Thai dining at Sphinx (Soi 4), boozy cruising at Balcony (Soi 4) or hard dance at DJ Station (Soi 2). Soi 2 has a pretty much exclusively gay crowd, while Soi 4 is more of a free-for-all, its street-side tables hosting people of varying sexual inclinations watching the world go by. Gay sex shows and gay pick-up joints with go-go boys are located around Thanon Surawong, particularly on Soi Tawan and Duangthawee Plaza. Gay Pride has been transformed in recent years to mirror the Songkran festival events in the Silom area, so now it is less about Gay Pride and more about a bolt-on party for Songkran.

Red-light entertainment

As titillating foreign press headlines so readily paint Bangkok as a city of sleaze, it surprises visitors to find how small the red-light zone really is. The go-go bars that cater to *farang* (foreigners) in Patpong 1 and Patpong 2, and Nana Entertainment Plaza and Soi Cowboy on Thanon Sukhumvit, are largely neon-lit strips with a (usually) gentle hustle from girls hanging

Kathoey performers getting ready for their show.

Cabaret performances vary in genres.

outside. Transsexual "ladyboys" (*kathoey*) can be more aggressive, particularly after hours around Soi Nana. Tourists who prefer more discreet adult entertainment seek out the bars along Sukhumvit Soi 33. Asian men often make a beeline for the massage parlours of Thanon Ratchadaphisek and Thanon Petchaburi; Soi Thaniya in Silom caters largely to the Japanese.

Most bars feature pole-dancing girls gyrating in bikinis, although a few illegal "upstairs" shows offer full nudity and sex acts, either simulated or real. The infamous shows where girls use their genitalia for assorted juggling of bananas, darts and ping pong balls still appear on menu cards handed out in Patpong. Often 'clip' joints which can cause tourists major issues if caught up in the scams, they are best avoided.

Prostitution, however, extends beyond the borders of these places; most clubs and bars around town will have freelance working girls (and boys) roaming the dance floors.

Kathoey cabaret

Thailand's famous transsexual cabaret shows have become an international staple, as these entertaining acts now travel to global events like the Edinburgh Festival. Mambo, on Thanon Rama III, and New Calypso Cabaret at Asia Hotel, on Thanon Phayathai, are the main Bangkok venues. The shows feature saucy (and sometimes risqué) lip-synching song and dance routines performed by a revue of sequinned and feather boa'ed artistes at various stages of sex-change surgery.

Theatre and dance

Thespian Patravadi Mejudhon stages modern dance and drama that is often inspired by traditional and Buddhist themes at her open-air Patravadi Theatre in Thonburi. Performances are usually in Thai, but as they are music and dance oriented, they are often accessible to foreigners.

There are short performances of the classical khon dance-drama at tourist venues and restaurants, while more serious performances are held at Sala Chalerm Krung Theatre each weekend.

The Aksra Theatre and Joe Louis Theatre, at Asiatique, which has won many international awards, both stage *hun lakhon lek*, a traditional puppet theatre based on the *khon* dance-drama.

Opera and classical music

Multi-talented Cambridge graduate Somtow Sucharitkul, who has written Hollywood horror scripts and several books in English, including the excellent *Jasmine Nights*, set up the Bangkok Opera in 2002. Among its three or four yearly productions of classics, like *The*

> Kathoey, or ladyboy, cabaret shows are now taking their sequins and lip-synching routines to international festivals, but two of the best companies, Mambo and New Calypso Cabaret, entertain every night in Bangkok.

Magic Flute, are Somtow's own works (written in English) such as *Mae Naak*, which is based on a Thai ghost story. Among their ambitious projects they intend to complete the entire Ring Cycle over the next few years. The concerts are mainly staged at the Thailand Cultural Centre, off Thanon Ratchadapisek.

The Bangkok Symphony Orchestra, as well as providing many of the musicians for the Bangkok Opera, plays regular concerts throughout the year,

A Thai Marilyn.

A frenetic bout of muay thai.

also at the Thai Cultural Centre and on Sundays during the cool season in Lumphini Park.

The International Festival of Dance and Music brings international acts for a season of opera, classical music, contemporary dance and ballet every September to October.

Night-time sports

Bangkok at night isn't all booze and boogie. You might want to try disco bowling – to music and flashing lights – at several bowling alleys in the city, or RCA has an indoor go-kart track. There's even night golf, and snooker clubs that open into the small hours.

Nobody who comes to Thailand should miss the sport of *muay thai*, frenzied kickboxing accompanied by the wailing of traditional music and animated betting on the outcome. Lumphini Stadium remains the world mecca of *muay thai*, which has been relocated to Thanon Ramintra in Bangkok's suburbs (close to the low-cost airport). Another venue at which to watch the sport is the Art Deco Ratchadamnoen Stadium in the Dusit area.

SPAS AND WELLNESS CENTRES

One of the world's great spa centres, Thailand has a penchant for pampering rooted in its ancient history of traditional Thai massage. And Bangkok is packed with plush spas to relax both body and mind.

Stress-relieving yoga meditation at Devarana Spa.

Thailand is renowned as the spa capital of Asia, and with good reason. Many treatments we now associate with modern spa "pampering" have their origins in the ancient healing methods brought to Thailand as part of Buddhist philosophy. They have existed here for nearly 2,000 years, so Thai therapists have a knowledge of practices that have been handed down through generations. Thai massage is one of the great pleasures of visiting Thailand, and it is available cheaply at small shophouses all over Bangkok, although signs offering services such as "soapy massage" promise a very different kind of experience. These days, of course, you can also opt for a more luxurious environment and a wider choice of treatments at hotel spas.

The spas draw on natural healing practices such as traditional Thai massage, herbal compresses and herbal steams and baths that have long been provided in the country's temples, which served as doctor and hospital to local communities.

The famed warmth of Thai people extends to masseuses and therapists, so the spa visit here tends to be not only gentle and relaxing, but also a highly personalised experience. In fact there is a Buddhist concept of giving on the part of the masseur that, in the best instances, ensures this personal connection.

Traditional Thai massage

Perhaps the most unique spa treatment for visitors to Thailand is the traditional Thai massage, or *nuad paen boran* (ancient massage), which is as old as the name suggests. Buddhist monks brought the practice with them from India when they arrived in Thailand in the 2nd or 3rd century AD. They taught that Shivakar Kumar Baccha, the Buddha's personal medical advisor, developed it from Indian Vedic treatments. Temples were traditional places of healing as well as worship, and as Buddhism spread through Thailand, so did Thai massage.

Thai massage technique is linked to the ancient Indian yoga philosophy which holds that our life energy is supplied along 72,000 meridian lines that run through our bodies. This is why some of the stretching actions of

The sumptuous River Private Spa suite at the Bangkok Peninsula Hotel.

Thai massage resemble the stretching poses of yoga. Thai massage focuses on 10 key energy lines (*sip sen*), and uses pressure to release the blocked energy along those lines.

> *The ancient healing art of Thai massage was initially considered a spiritual practice, a meditative application of loving kindness. It is based on the concept of invisible energy lines that run throughout the body.*

There is also a spiritual element to Thai massage. It is believed that the masseuse is healing the recipient by offering loving care through his or her hands. In ancient times, the masseuse would say a prayer to centre the mind in a meditative mood before performing a healing massage, and some will still do this today. This meditative awareness enables the masseuse to sense the energy flow and blockages in the recipient's body, thus providing optimum healing to the affected areas. When done properly, the masseuse should feel as relaxed as the recipient, because Thai massage is supposed to be a spiritual act that nourishes both the giver and the recipient.

Unlike Western massage, Thai massage does not make use of oils or lotions, apart from occasional heating balms on areas of particular tightness, and the recipient remains fully clothed. The client is supplied with loose-fitting cotton pyjamas and the massage is done on a mattress laid on the floor. The masseuse uses his or her thumbs, arms, elbows, knees and feet, and may climb all over your body and even walk on your back.

The masseuse uses a combination of pressure and stretching techniques, done in a rhythmic and rocking motion that usually lasts for between one and two hours. The deep tissue kneading can be initially painful and towards the end of the massage, expect to be twisted and stretched into yoga-like poses.

Shophouse operations all over Bangkok, particularly in tourist areas, offer Thai massage from around B200 an hour with little more than a mattress and a curtain as decor. In hotels and, increasingly, independent urban spas the treatment has

HOTEL AND DAY SPAS IN BANGKOK

For the ultimate in pampering, head for **The Mandarin Oriental Spa** in the Oriental Hotel. It is the pioneer of Thai spas and is designed in the style of a Thai teak house (48 Oriental Avenue; tel: 0-2233 9630; www.mandarinoriental.com). A few doors down is the equally stunning **Peninsula Spa** in the Peninsula Hotel (333 Thanon Charoennakorn; tel: 0-2861 2888; www.bangkok.peninsula.com). In the Business District, try the exquisite Thai-style **Devarana Spa** at the Dusit Thani Hotel (946 Thanon Rama 4; tel: 0-2636 3600, ext. 7006; www.devarana.com), which is imbued with the feeling of a light and airy Thai temple, or the **Shambala Spa** at the ultra-chic Metropolitan Hotel (27 Thanon Sathorn Tai; tel: 0-2625 3357; www.metropolitan.com.bz). Equally tempting is the exotic **Chi Spa** at the luxury Shangri-La Hotel (89 Soi Wat Suan Plu; tel: 0-2236 7777; www.shangri-la.com).

Bangkok's growing number of day spas are located all over town, often in renovated old houses. Popular is the **Divana** spa chain (8 Sukhumvit Soi 35, tel: 0-2661 4818; 7 Sukhumvit Soi 25, tel: 0-2261 6784; 103 Soi Thonglor 17, tel: 0-2712 8986; www.divana-dvn.com). Or try **Rasayana Retreat** (57 Soi Sukhumvit 39; tel: 0-2662 4803-5; www.rasayanaretreat.com), which also has Thailand's only raw-food restaurant offering organic meals.

gone upmarket, joining the likes of Swedish massage and reiki on wide-ranging, pampering menus that can cost thousands of baht. If you want to take things further, Wat Pho Thai Traditional Massage School (2 Thanon Sanam Chai; tel: 0-2622 3550; www.watpomassage.com; daily 10am–6pm) teaches traditional massage and meditation for those who want to learn the art.

The River Private Spa at the Bangkok Peninsula Hotel is one of the city's most luxurious spas.

Steams, saunas and compresses

A number of other treatments offered in Thai spas stem from the same ancient healing tradition. The use of heat therapies combined with herbal ingredients is a distinguishing trait of traditional Thai healing practices. One of the most popular is the Thai herbal steam or sauna. Their healing secret lies in the use of indigenous Thai herbs like turmeric, *prai*, lemongrass, camphor and kaffir lime. Aside from providing an overall health and skin booster, practitioners claim that Thai herbal steam can

Relaxing massage at Divana spa.

An energetic yoga workout.

result in weight loss if done consistently over an extended period of time.

Another ancient Thai healing therapy is the use of hot herbal compresses made of medicinal herbs wrapped in a tight bundle, steamed for several hours, and then pressed against trouble areas of the body, like tense shoulders or rheumatic joints. The key to healing lies in the combination of medicinal herbs and heat.

MEDICAL SPAS

The centrally located **S Medical Spa** is chic and well thought out. It has physicians, dermatologists, and even psychiatrists on site for clients. A wide choice of treatments is available, and includes use of steam rooms, hydrotherapy pools, jacuzzi and other facilities (2/2 Phakdi Building, Thanon Withayu; tel: 0-2253 1010; www.smedspa.com).

The **Dermaster Wellness & Aesthetic Institution** (342 Ekkamai Road Klongton Nua, Wattana; tel: 0 8075 42200; www.dermaster-thailand.com) puts the focus on beauty, with a dermatology clinic offering laser surgery, plus spa rooms for sessions of pampering body massages, scrubs and reflexology treatments.

Spa options

While Thailand is well known for its self-contained resort spas complete with accommodation and set in scenic areas, Bangkok also offers a bewildering number of spas that are popular with visitors as well as locals. The most luxurious establishments are hotel spas. These welcome the public as well as hotel guests, and usually spare no expense on design and fittings – with prices to match. Less extravagant but with a charm of their own are the many day spas around Bangkok, usually located in renovated old houses and set among well-tended gardens. Day-spa prices veer towards the mid-price range, and the treatments are just as good as hotel spas.

New on the scene is the medical spa, combining hospital health services with holistic spa therapies. Here, Western health practices such as medical check-ups and laser cosmetic surgery are offered in the same place as traditional Thai massage and Chinese acupuncture – to both fix and pamper your body at the same time. Patients can select from a variety of slimming, rejuvenation and detox fasting programmes, tailored to individual needs.

A seller at the Damnoen Saduak Floating Market.

The bright lights of Chinatown.

Street food stands in Chinatown.

INTRODUCTION

A detailed guide to the entire city and its
surroundings, with principal sites numbered
and clearly cross-referenced to the maps.

Modern Bangkok, much of which just 70 years ago was empty land,
has grown rapidly and largely unplanned. As a result, Thailand's
capital can seem a bewildering maze of old and new, exotic and
humdrum. But there are recognisable areas, each with its own character.

The city's layout began when King Rama I
dug a canal at a bend in the Chao Phraya river
to form the artificial island of Rattanakosin.
Its glittering highlights, including the Grand
Palace and Wat Pho, are an essential part of
any tour.

Surrounding Rattanakosin, but still within
the capital's original walls, is the Old City,
with important temples like Wat Suthat,
and shops devoted to religious materials,
frequented by monks. Also part of the Old
City is Banglamphu, a
hub for budget travel-
lers, especially around
Thanon Khao San and the Khao San Road.

Bot of the Emerald Buddha.

In the 20th century, the monarchy moved north to
Dusit, where the Ananta Samakom Throne Hall is the
centrepiece of several European-influenced palaces
around royal Dusit Park.

East of Rattanakosin, along the river, are the enclaves
where foreigners originally settled: Chinatown and
Bangrak, an early home to the European community.
Thanon Silom and Thanon Sathorn dominate Bangrak
today, and comprise the main business district. The infamous Patpong red-light area is at Silom's eastern end.

Night-time skyline.

North of here are the shopping malls of Pathumwan, where Thanon Rama
I continues east to Sukhumvit, a major middle-class residential area full of
nightlife and restaurants.

All of these are along one bank of the Chao Phraya river. On the opposite,
southern bank is Thonburi, which was briefly the royal capital. While it too
is an ill-considered urban sprawl, it has the attraction of canals that thread
past old wooden houses and temples to give a glimpse of a traditional life
perhaps less confusing than that of today.

Chatuchak Park   Ayutthaya

| 0 | 500 m |
| 0 | 500 yds |

S Skytrain BTS
M Metro MRT

PHA YA THAI
Sanam Pao

Th. Mit Maitri

2nd State Expressway

Thanon Ratchawithi   Samsen

Din Daeng Sports
Complex & Auditorium

Thanon Phahon Yothin   Soi Yothin 3

Soi Phahon   Thanon Sa Nam Phao   Soi Phra Nang   Soi Atthawimon

Thanon Wiphawadirangsit

Din Daeng   Thanon Prachasongkhro

Mineral
Research
Museum

Thanon Yothi

Anutsawari
Chaisamoraphum
(Victory Mon.)

Victory
Monument S

Soi Setsirak

Th. Phaya Thai

Soi Wattana
Yothin

Soi Chai
Samoraphun

Th. Asok
Din Daeng

Thanon Asok Din Daeng

Thanon Din Daeng 1

Soi Bun Chu

Thanon
Mit Maitri 1

Soi Sutthiphon

RATCHATHEWI

Thanon Sri Ayutthaya

Soi Man Sin 4

Th. Phaya Thai   Phaya
Thai S

Th. Rang Nam

Soi Loet
Panya

Soi Thep
Watsadu

Th. Sri Ayutthaya   Soi Si
Ayutthaya

Chalerm Mahanakhon Expressway

Bangkok Doll
Factory & Museum

Th. Asok Din Daeng

Samsen

Soi Mae
Phra Fatima

Soi
Sutthiphon 2

Soi Phothiprang   Soi Songprang

Th. Phetchaburi   Darun
Amam

Soi Phetchaburi   Thong

Ratchathewi
Tower

Soi 11
Soi 13
Soi 15
Soi 17

PRATUNAM

Suan
Pakkad
Palace

Baiyoke II
Tower

Pratunam
Market

Wongwian
Makkasan

Soi Watthanawong

Soi Watthanasin

Makkasan
Railway Station

Bung Makkasan

2nd State Expressway

Chonburi

21

ya Nak

Wongwian
Ratchathewi

Soi 12

Thanon Phetchaburi

Ratchathewi S

Jim
Thompson's
House

Soi Barthit

Th. Phaya Thai

Saen Saep   Panthip
Plaza

Soi 25
Soi 27

Soi 33
Soi Petchakit

Soi Ratchaprarop

Th. New Phetchaburi

Th. Nikhom Makkasan

Hope of
Bangkok

Th. New Phetchaburi   Phetchaburi M

Th. Rama I   Soi Ka Sem   Soi 2   Soi Kasem
San 1   San 2   San 3

thai   kon

Srapathum
Palace

Wongwian
Pathumwan

Siam
Centre

Siam
Paragon

Central
World

Th. Rama I

Wat
Pathum-
wanaram

Narayana Phand
(Handicrafts Store)

Gaysorn Plaza

Soi 32

Soi Chitlom

Thanon Withayu

Chit Lom S

Soi Tonson

Nai Loet

Soi Nana Nua

Saen Saep

Soi Sukhumvit

SUKHUMVIT

Soi 7

Soi Sukhumvit 11   Soi Sukhumvit 15

Sukhumvit

 national
adium

National
Stadium S   Siam S

Mahboonkrong
Shopping Centre

Siam
Square

S. Chulalongkoen 64

PATHUMWAN

Th. Ratchadamri

Erawan
Shrine

Th. Phloenchit

Phloen Chit S

Soi Sukhumvit 3

Watthana

Soi Sukhumvit 23

ulaongkorn 7   Soi Chulalongkorn 9

12   Chulalongkorn 62

Henri Dunant

Royal
Bangkok
Sports Club
(R.B.S.C.)

Ratchadamri S

Peninsula
Plaza

Soi Lang
Suan 1

Soi Lang
Suan

Soi Ruam Rudi

Nana
Entertainment
Plaza (NEP)

Nana S

Jai
Smarn

Soi Sukhumvit 4

Kamthieng
House
(Siam Society)

Asok S

Th. Sukhumvit

8   Chulalongkorn
42   Soi 50

na IV

National History
Museum

Imaging Technology
Museum

Chulalongkorn
University

Soi Lang
Suan 6

Thanon Sarasin

SUAN
LUMPHINI

Th. Ratchadamri

Thanon
Withayu

Soi Ruam Rudi

Holy
Redeemer

Soi
Sama
Han

Soi Sukhumvit 8

Calvary
Baptist

Soi Sukhumvit 10   Soi 12

Sukhumvit

Emporium

Soi Sukhumvit 16

Th. Ratchadaphisek

Sam Yan

Praya

Queen Saovabha
Memorial Institute
(Snake Farm)

Charn
Issara
Tower

Rama VI

Sanam
Khli

Thailand
Tobacco
Monopoly
(under
redevelopment)

Ratchada

BENJAKITTI
PARK

KHLONG TOEY

Santi Phap   Soi
Santi
Phap

PATPONG

Suriwong   Patpong

Si Lom

Wongwian
Saladaeng   Th. Rama IV

Thanon Rama IV

Chalerm Mahanakhon Expressway

Joe Louis
Puppet Theatre   S. Plukchit 2

Queen Sirikit
National
Convention
Centre

Queen Sirikit
Nat. Convention
Centre

Chonburi, Pattaya

son
ary
ma
mple
(saek)

Boonmitr
Bldg

Xavier

Chong Nonsi S

CP
Tower

Sala
Daeng S

Th. Silom

Th. Convent

Soi Phiphat 2

Soi Sala
Daeng

Soi Sala Daeng

Wongwian
Lumphini

Lumphini
Boxing Stadium

Goethe
Institute

Lumphini M

Thai-Belgium Br.

Soi Ngam Duphli

Soi Sap.

Soi San Chao

Soi Sukhumvit 18

Th. Ratchadaphisek

Soi 18

Chong
Nonsi

Soi Si Phraya

Thanon Silom

Soi Phiphat

Thanon Silom   Soi 7

Thanon Narathiwat Rajanakarin

Th. Phra
Phinij

Bhirasi
Institute of
Modern Art

Goethe

Chalerm Mahanakhon Expressway

Ruam
Chitt

Khlong Toei M

Thanon

Soi Phai
Singto

Soi Charoensuk

Rama IV

an Thawong
of Christ

Anuman Rajdhon

Thanon Sathorn Nua

Thanon Sathorn Tai

SATHORN

MR Kukrit
Pramoj's
Heritage Home

S. Suanplu

Thanon Sathorn Nua   Thanon Sathorn Tai

S. Nantha

S. Suanplu

Soi Ngan

Th. Pridi

S. Sathorn

S. Bamplen

S. Akin

Yen Akat

The striking Phra Si Rattana Chedi at Wat Phra Kaew.

RATTANAKOSIN: ROYAL BANGKOK

Thailand's kings built Rattanakosin as a royal city within a city, a host of extravagant palaces and temples. Today, it remains a treasure trove of cultural clues to the identity of the capital and its people.

Rattanakosin is the man-made island that forms the royal centre of the original Old City, called Phra Nakorn. It was designed in 1782 when Bangkok was installed as the new capital of Thailand. For more than a century, Rattanakosin, just a boat ride across from the earlier capital at Thonburi, was the pulse of the city, and was where the seeds of the modern kingdom were planted.

The foundations of Bangkok's new strategic powerhouse were based on the former capital of Ayutthaya, which was abandoned after being ransacked by the Burmese army in 1767. The area was located at the edge of the Chao Phraya river with the majestic Grand Palace as its epi-centre. As the palace took shape, to mirror the island layout of Ayutthaya, defensive moats were dug by extend-ing canals. Walls formed a protective stronghold around Phra Nakorn, and more canals were created to transport people across marsh and swampland.

Rattanakosin brims with architec-tural grandeur, its series of palaces and temples filled with important religious artefacts installed to indi-cate the strength of the re-unified nation. Even today, the district con-tains many government offices and

two of Thailand's most respected uni-versities (Thammasat and Silpakorn), in addition to being the religious nucleus of the nation. Ceremonies, festivals and parades are frequently held in this quarter.

Rattanakosin is best explored on foot. While most visitors attempt to cram all its sights into a day, two full days allow for greater appreciation of its more secluded treasures. The area's proximity to the river means that it can be conveniently accessed by water transport, and the famous backpacker

Main Attractions

Wat Phra Kaew and Grand
  Palace
Lak Muang
Sanam Luang
The National Gallery
The National Museum
Wat Mahathat
Wat Pho
Siam Discovery Museum
Wat Ratchapradit
Wat Ratchabophit

Maps

Pages 106, 109

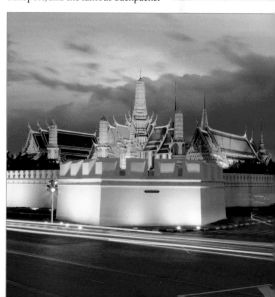

Outside the high walls of the Grand Palace and Wat Phra Kaew.

Rattanakosin: Royal Bangkok

Phra Mondop with its splendid exterior.

haven of Thanon Khao San (see page 141) is just a short stroll away. A project called the Krung Rattanakosin Plan that aimed to reorganise the district by relocating residents to form a historical park has largely been shelved, although there are still periodic announcements of tentative schemes for development.

WAT PHRA KAEW AND GRAND PALACE COMPLEX

Jostling among throngs of snap-happy tourists may not be the best context for viewing exotic Thailand, but the dignified splendour of two of Bangkok's principal attractions – the Wat Phra Kaew and the Grand Palace – is breathtaking nevertheless. The structures in this complex are an arresting spectacle of form and colour, with glistening golden *chedi*, glass mosaic-studded pillars, towering mythological gods, and fabulously ornate temple and palace structures piercing the sky.

Construction on the site, which originally spread over 160 hectares

(65 acres), was begun in 1782 at the command of King Rama I. He wanted not only a palace befitting the new capital, but somewhere to house the Emerald Buddha, the country's most revered religious image. The entire compound is surrounded by high crenellated walls, securing a once self-sufficient city within a city.

Wat Phra Kaew and Grand Palace complex ❶

Address: Thanon Na Phra Lan, www.palaces.thai.net
Tel: 0-222 8181
Opening Hrs: daily 8.30am–3.30pm
Entrance Fee: charge (includes entry to Vimanmek and several other sights in Dusit)
Transport: Tha Chang pier

The only entrance (and exit) to the complex is along Thanon Na Phra Lan to the north. An early morning visit is recommended, preferably when bright sunlight illuminates the buildings to their dazzling best. Make sure you are dressed appropriately (see margin tip) and disregard touts who linger outside the complex telling you that it is closed.

The complex is loosely divided, with Wat Phra Kaew encountered first to the left and the Grand Palace and its peripheral buildings to the right. At least two hours are needed for a full appreciation, with most people lingering within Wat Phra Kaew. The interiors of the Grand Palace buildings – but not Wat Phra Kaew – are closed to the public on Saturday and Sunday. It's worthwhile hiring the informative audio guide. If you prefer, official guides are also available near the ticket office.

Wat Phra Kaew

Wat Phra Kaew (Temple of the Emerald Buddha) serves as the royal chapel of the Grand Palace. The compound is modelled after palace chapels in the former capitals of Sukhothai and Ayutthaya, and contains many typical monastic structures, although, because of its royal function, it does not have living quarters for monks.

At the main entrance is the statue of Shivaka Kumar Baccha, who was reputed to be the Buddha's private physician, and on the upper terrace to the left are the gleaming gold mosaic

TIP

The dress code for Wat Phra Kaew and the Grand Palace is strict. Visitors must be dressed smartly – no shorts, short skirts or revealing tops, sandals or flip-flops. Suitable clothing may be borrowed from an office near the Gate of Victory, but unless you want to don stale rubber slip-ons and a gaudy sarong, dress conservatively.

Prasap Phra Thep Bidom, the Royal Pantheon.

TIP

For an explanation of the architectural features of Thai temples, see Temple Art and Architecture, page 56.

tiles encrusting the Sri Lankan-style circular **Phra Si Rattana Chedi** . Erected by King Mongkut (Rama V), the *chedi* is said to enshrine a piece of the Buddha's breastbone.

In the centre is **Phra Mondop** Ⓑ (Library of Buddhist Scriptures), surrounded by statues of sacred white elephants (the white elephant is the symbol of royal power). The library was erected to hold the holy Buddhist scriptures called *Tripitaka*. The original library was destroyed by fire, ignited by fireworks during festivities to celebrate its completion. Phra Mondop is a delicate building, studded with blue and green glass mosaic, and topped by a multi-tiered roof fashioned like the crown of a Thai king.

Adjacent to it is the **Prasat Phra Thep Bidom** Ⓒ (Royal Pantheon), This contains life-sized statues of the Chakri kings and is open to the public only on Chakri Day, 6 April. Around the building stand marvellous gilded statues of mythological creatures,

Worshipper outside the Bot of the Emerald Buddha.

Gilded garuda images encircle the exterior of the Bot of the Emerald Buddha.

including the half-female, half-lion *aponsi*. The original pantheon was built in 1855, but was destroyed by fire and rebuilt in 1903. Flanking the entrance of the Prasat Phra Thep Bidom are two towering gilded *chedi*.

Behind Phra Mondop is a large, sandstone model of the famous Khmer temple of Angkor Wat in Cambodia. The model was built during King Rama IV's reign when Cambodia was a vassal Thai state. Just behind, along the northern edge of the compound, is the **Viharn Yot** (Prayer Hall), flanked by the **Ho Phra Nak** (Royal Mausoleum) on the left and **Ho Phra Montien Tham** (Auxillary Library) on the right.

The walls of the cloister enclosing the temple courtyard are painted with a picture book of 178 murals telling the *Ramakien* epic, the Thai version of the Indian *Ramayana*. Originally painted during the reign of King Rama III (1824–50), they have been meticulously restored.

Around the cloisters, six pairs of towering stone *yaksha* (demons), again characters from the *Ramakien*, stand guard, armed with clubs, protecting the Emerald Buddha. At the complex's eastern edge are eight *prang* structures, which represent Buddhism's Eightfold Path.

The Emerald Buddha

Finally you come to Wat Phra Kaew's most sacred structure, the **Bot of the Emerald Buddha** . Outside this main hall, at the open-air shrine, the air is always alive with the supplicants' murmured prayers and heavy with the scent of floral offerings and joss sticks. Remove your shoes before entering the hall.

At the top of the elaborate golden altar, in a glass case and protected by a nine-tiered umbrella, sits the country's most celebrated image, the diminutive 75cm (30ins) tall **Emerald Buddha**, which, surprisingly, is not made of emerald but carved from a solid block of green jade. Many non-Buddhists may be disappointed by the size of the Emerald Buddha statue, but the belief in its power and importance are apparent from the demeanour of the pilgrims inside the hall. This gets particularly busy on weekends and holidays when worshippers fill the main sanctuary, prostrating themselves on the marble floor before the temple's 11-metre (36ft) -tall altar. Photography is forbidden and it's hard to get a clear view of the statue from ground level.

Three times a year, at the beginning of each new season, the Thai

Night-time traffic outside the Grand Palace walls.

Wat Phra Kaew and Grand Palace

Main Entrance — Thanon Na Phra Lan

Gate of Victory

0 — 100 m
0 — 100 yds

Ho Phra Nak (Royal Mausoleum)
Viharn Yot (Prayer Hall)
Ho Phra Montien Tham (Auxiliary Library)

Angkor Wat Model

Phra Si Rattana Chedi **A**
Phra Mondop (Library) **B**
Prasat Phra Thep Bidom (Royal Pantheon) **C**

Sunday Entrance

Wat Phra Kaew

Tickets   Entrance
Coins & Decorations Museum **J**

Bot of the Emerald Buddha **D**

8 Prangs

Wat Phra Kaew Museum **I**

Thanon Maharat

Thanon Maharat

Grand Palace   Exit

Arporn Phimok Prasat (Disrobing Pavilion)

Dusit Maha Prasat (Dusit Hall) **H**

Amarin Vinitchai Throne Hall **F**

Borombhiman Hall **E**

Chakri Maha Prasat (Grand Palace Hall) **G**

Thanon Sanam Chai

A Mythical Zoo

All around Bangkok are images of strange creatures that have migrated from the tales of Hindu mythology to the stuff of everyday life. These are the most common:

Garuda: Considered the most powerful creature of the Himaphan Forest, this half-eagle, half-man demigod is the mount of the Hindu god Vishnu. *Garuda* is the sworn enemy of the magical water serpent *naga*. *Garuda* is often depicted with *naga* caught in his talons. Since Ayutthayan times the *garuda* has been a symbol for the Royal Seal, and today, brightly coloured representations are emblazoned across official documents as well as the facades of royally approved banks and corporations.

A five-headed naga at the Prasat Phra Thep Bidom.

Naga: Brother and nemesis of *garuda*, the *naga* is a semi-divine creature with multiple human heads and serpent tails. The snake has special symbolism to most of the world's faiths and cultures, and in Buddhism a great *naga* is said to have provided shelter to the meditating Buddha. A resident of the watery underworld, the *naga* is associated with water's life-giving force, as well as acting as a bridge between the earthly and divine realms. *Naga* are typically represented along steps leading into temples.

Erawan: The magical elephant *erawan* was the steed for Indra, the Hindu king of the gods. The gigantic pachyderm has 33 heads, each with seven tusks so long that thousands of angels live inside them. Obviously, with such a gargantuan beast, a more modest three-headed version is usually represented. For proof of *erawan*'s importance to Thais, head to Erawan Shrine (see page 158) at one of Bangkok's busiest intersections, where wooden elephants are presented as offerings.

Kinnaree and **Aponsi:** This exotic looking belle has the head and body of a woman with the tail and legs of a swan. Known for her talent in song and dance, beautifully crafted *kinnaree* sculptures can be seen at Wat Phra Kaew. Perhaps a distant relative, *aponsi* is similarly portrayed as half-female, half-lion. The Golden Kinnaree is the Thai film industry equivalent of the Oscar.

Hongsa: This bird-like creature has similarities to the swan and goose, and is a prevalent motif in traditional arts and crafts. In Hindu mythology, the *hongsa* is the mount of Brahma, the god of creation. Take a drive along Utthayan Avenue in Bangkok's southern suburb of Puttha Monthon, and you will see some 1,000 golden *hongsa* birds decorating the tops of lampposts.

Yaksha: These giant half-demon, half-god creatures, which appear so forbidding as they guard the entrances to the temple structures at Wat Phra Kaew and Wat Arun, are actually protectors of earthbound wealth. Led by Kuvera, they are worshipped as symbols of fertility and are also believed to protect newborn infants.

king presides over the changing of the Emerald Buddha's robes: a golden, diamond-studded tunic is used for the hot season, a gilded robe flecked with blue for the rainy season, and a robe of enamel-coated solid gold for the cool season.

According to legend, the Emerald Buddha was carved in India, but stylistically its design is 13th- or 14th-century Thai. It was discovered in 1434 in Chiang Rai, where, for unknown reasons, it had been hidden in a *chedi* in a temple also known as Wat Phra Kaew, until the *chedi* was struck by lightning during a storm. In the mid-16th century, the invading Lao army took the figure to Vientiane, Laos. It was seized back by the Thais in 1779. King Rama I eventually brought the statue to Bangkok from Thonburi in 1784 after the city was established as the new capital. The Emerald Buddha is claimed to bestow good fortune on the kingdom that possesses it.

The Grand Palace

Adjoining Wat Phra Kaew is the **Grand Palace**. Embodying Thailand's characteristic blend of temporal and spiritual elements, the Grand Palace has been added to or modified by every Thai king, so that today the complex is a mélange of architectural styles, from traditional Thai, Khmer and Chinese to British, French and Italian Renaissance. In the early 20th century, the royal abode shifted to the more private Chitralada Palace in Dusit district (see page 142), with the Grand Palace now reserved for special ceremonies and state visits.

Palace buildings

Exit from Wat Phra Kaew. On your left and tucked behind a closed gate guarded by sentry is the French-inspired **Borombhiman Hall** ❺. It was built in 1903 as a residence for King Rama VI but is now reserved as a state guesthouse for dignitaries.

To the right lies the **Amarin Vinitchai Throne Hall** ❻, part of the three-building Phra Maha Montien complex. Originally a royal residence, it contained the bedchamber of Rama I, with the main audience hall beyond. Today, the audience

Chakri Maha Prasat Hall, Grand Palace.

Sentry guard on duty outside the Chakri Maha Prasat.

Chinese-style statue outside the Dusit Maha Prasat.

Thai national flag and coat of arms, Grand Palace complex.

where the king receives foreign ambassadors on a niello throne under a nine-tiered white umbrella, originally made for King Chulalongkorn. Outside, the courtyard is dotted with ornamental ebony trees pruned in Chinese *bonsai* style. Beside the hall, a closed-off door leads to the **Inner Palace**, where the king's many wives once lived. The king himself was the only male above the age of 12 allowed to enter the area, which was guarded by armed women.

The next building of interest is the **Dusit Maha Prasat** N (Dusit Hall), built by King Chakri (Rama I) in 1789 to replace an earlier wooden structure. A splendid example of classical Thai architecture, its four-tiered roof supports an elegant nine-tiered spire. The balcony on the north wing contains a throne once used by the king for outdoor receptions. Deceased kings and queens lie in state here before their bodies are cremated on Sanam Luang.

To its left stands the exquisite **Arporn Phimok Prasat** (Disrobing Pavilion). It was built to the height of the king's palanquin, so that he could alight from his elephant and don his

hall is used for coronations and special ceremonies. By tradition, each new king also spends the first night after his coronation here.

Next to it in a large courtyard stands the triple-spired royal residence – and the grandest building in the complex – the **Chakri Maha Prasat** N (Grand Palace Hall). This two-storey hall set on an elevated base was constructed during King Chulalongkorn's reign (1868–1910) to commemorate the 100th anniversary of the Chakri dynasty in 1882. An impressive mixture of Thai and Western architecture, the building was designed by British architects. The Thai spires, however, were added at the last moment, following protests that it was improper for a hallowed Thai site to be dominated by a European-style building.

The top floor contains golden urns with ashes of the Chakri kings; the first floor still functions as an audience chamber for royal banquets and state visits, while the ground floor is now a **Weapons Museum**.

The central hall contains the magnificent **Chakri Throne Room**,

PARK LIFE

Contemporary accounts record that when King Rama I was cremated at Sanam Luang in 1809, the congregation included 10,000 monks and the atmosphere resembled a festival. Alongside the solemnity there were theatre performances, fireworks and boxing matches and the crowds was showered with money buried in limes. Today, one of the most important events is the Royal Ploughing Ceremony each May. This Brahman festival, which dates to the Sukhothai era nearly 1,000 years ago, sees a pair of sacred cows led to a choice of seven foodstuffs, such as rice, green beans and liquor. Whichever they consume first prophesises what kind of harvest farmers will have that year.

ceremonial hat and gown before proceeding to the audience hall.

Opposite, do not miss the superb collection of small Buddha images made of silver, ivory, crystal and other materials at the **Wat Phra Kaew Museum ❶**. On the way out, next to the ticket office is the **Coins and Decorations Museum ❶**. It has a collection of coins dating from the 11th century and also royal regalia, decorations and medals made of gold and precious stones.

Lak Muang ❷

Address: Thanon Sanam Chai
Tel: 0-222 9876
Opening Hrs: daily 5am – 7pm
Entrance Fee: free
Transport: Tha Chan pier

Every Thai city is supposed to have a foundation stone, around which the city's guardian spirits gravitate, protecting and bringing supposed good fortune to worshippers and the municipality. Bangkok was officially born into the world in 1782, when King Rama I erected the **Lak Muang** (City Pillar), to mark the official centre of the capital.

Located just across Thanon Sanam Chai from the eastern wall of the Grand Palace, this is a gilded wooden pillar sheltered by a Khmer-style *prang*. Resembling the Hindu Shiva *lingam*, which represents potency, it is accompanied by the taller Lak Muang of Thonburi, which was moved here when the district (and former capital) became part of Bangkok. The pillar is considered the city's spiritual core, and is watched over by a pavilion containing several golden spirit-idols. Devotees thankful their prayers have been answered usually hire resident classical *lakhon* dancers to perform here.

Museum of Old Cannons ❸

Clearly visible across the street from the Lak Muang is a battalion of antique armoury that menacingly protects the imposing Ministry of Defence. Of passing interest to those with a military bent is the **Museum of Old Cannons** (daily 24 hours; free). On the lawn in front of the 19th-century European-style former barracks are displays of battle-worn and bulky cast-iron cannons.

Relaxing in the grounds of Sanam Luang.

Mae Toranee, or the Earth Goddess, was one of the protectors of the meditating Buddha.

Inside the Thai National Museum.

National Museum exterior.

of the coming harvest. When not in official use, the field becomes a general recreation and market stall area, also used by fortune tellers. It is also where the homeless find a place to lay their heads, but are unobtrusive and can be rather helpful if engaged in conversation – most even offering up a smattering of information about the area in broken English.

Previously, Sanam Luang was a racecourse, a golf course and home to a Sunday market, until it moved to Chatuchak in 1982 when the grounds were prepared for the Bangkok Bicentennial.

Northeast of Sanam Luang, opposite the Royal Hotel, is an elaborate public drinking fountain in the shape of **Mae Toranee** (Earth Goddess). Erected by King Chulalongkorn in the late 19th century, the ornate statue depicts the goddess wringing torrents of water out of her hair to wash away evil spirits trying to corrupt the meditating Buddha. It is an apt symbol, perhaps, in a city that is still sometimes flooded by overflowing waters from the monsoon-swollen Chao Phraya river.

Sanam Luang ❹

North of the Wat Phra Kaew and Grand Palace, the large oval turf of **Sanam Luang** (Royal Field) is where royal cremations and important ceremonies are held. It is particularly lively on royal birthdays; during the Songkran festival; the kite-flying competition season (Feb–Apr) – which attracts contestants from all around the country and abroad – and for the Ploughing Ceremony, a Brahman ritual held in May to predict the state

National Theatre ❺

North of Sanam Luang, next to the traffic-clogged Saphan Phra Pin Klao bridge along Thanon Rachinee is the **National Theatre** (tel: 0-2244 1342; open only during performances). Unfortunately, this large white modern Thai edifice does not open its doors as frequently as it used to. It has weekly and monthly performances of folk and classical Thai music, dance and drama. Occasionally it showcases highbrow concerts and theatre from abroad. Call ahead for schedules.

National Gallery ❻

Address: Thanon Chao Fa
Tel: 0-2281 2224
Opening Hrs: Wed–Sun 9am–4pm
Entrance Fee: charge
Transport: Phra Athit pier

On the opposite side of the Saphan Phra Pin Klao bridge is the **National Gallery**, which has seen better days as an exhibition space, with little renovation since the 1970s. Situated within a fine old colonial-style building that used to function as the Royal Mint, the gallery's permanent collection of traditional and contemporary Thai art isn't particularly outstanding. However, the annexe on both sides of the gallery holds interesting monthly exhibitions, mainly by local groups, veteran Thai artists or the odd cutting-edge youngster, and occasional international exposes.

National Museum ❼

Address: Thanon Na Phra That, www.finearts.go.th/museumbangkok
Tel: 0-2224 1333
Opening Hrs: Wed–Sun 9am–4pm
Entrance Fee: charge (guided tours at 9.30am Wed and Thur)
Transport: Phra Athit pier

Schoolboy studies a mural in the Thai National Museum.

Statue of Dr Pridi Banomyong, founder of Thammasat University.

To the west of Sanam Luang is the **National Museum**. Besides housing a vast collection of antiquities from all over Southeast Asia, the museum has an interesting history of its own (see page 122). Its grounds and some of the principal rooms were part of the former Wang Na (Front Palace) of the king's second-in-line, the Prince Successor, a feature of the Thai monarchy until 1870.

The oldest buildings in the compound date from 1782, including the splendid **Buddhaisawan Chapel**. Built by the Prince Successor as his private place of worship within the palace, it contains some of Thailand's most beautiful and best-preserved murals, depicting 28 scenes from the Buddha's life and dating from the 1790s. Above the windows, five bands of angels kneel in silent respect to Thailand's second most sacred Buddha image, the famous Phra Buddha Sihing. According to legend, the bronze image came from Ceylon, but art historians attribute it to 13th-century Sukhothai. The image is paraded through the

TIP

Arts buffs should visit the Silpakorn University Gallery (Mon–Fri 9am–7pm, Sat 9am–4pm; free). It displays interesting works of art by both teachers and students as well as those by visiting artists.

SHOP

Amulets are associated with fortune, both good and bad, so in the lanes around the Wat Mahathat amulet market you'll also find astrologers working in palmistry, Thai astrology and tarot. There are several more at Pra Chan pier.

streets of Bangkok each year on the day before Songkran.

To the left of the entrance is the **Sivamokhaphiman Hall**, originally an open-sided audience hall that now houses a prehistoric art collection. It displays bronzes and some of the painted earthenware jars found in northeast Thailand. The front of the building is devoted to the Thai History Gallery, documenting the country's history from the Sukhothai period (13th century) to the present Rattanakosin period (1782 onwards). Most of the exhibits are weak on contextual information, so buy a copy of the museum guidebook.

Also on site is the **Red House** (Tamnak Daeng), an old golden teak dwelling that once belonged to King Rama I's elder sister. Built in the Ayutthaya style, the house has an ornate wood finish and elegant early Bangkok-style furnishings.

The central audience hall of the Wang Na is divided into rooms containing various ethnological exhibits of elephant *howdah*, wood carvings, ceramics, palanquins, royal furnishings, weapons, *khon* masks, musical

Wat Mahathat detail.

instruments and other artefacts. Temporary exhibits are displayed in the Throne Hall.

Adding to the museum's ambience are the inner courtyards, embellished with ponds and shady trees, providing spots for reflection. Mingling among armies of curious young local students, the museum feels more inviting than more austere museums elsewhere.

Thammasat University ❽

Adjoining the National Museum at Thanon Phra Chan is **Thammasat University**, Thailand's second most prestigious educational establishment (after Chulalongkorn University). The university was founded in 1934 to educate people in the new political constitution, which had been introduced two years earlier. Thammasat scholars have a reputation for being vocal in their strong political beliefs and in the past have been labelled as radicals.

The university's darkest days came in October 1973 and 1976, when students peacefully protesting for greater democracy were brutally suppressed by the military, police and rightist thugs. Hundreds of innocent students were slain. Inside the university

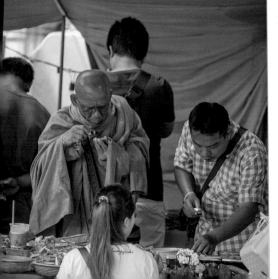

Monk at Wat Mahathat's amulet market.

gates are a number of small but pertinent memorials to these bloody crackdowns and other major events in Thailand's modern political struggles, hidden reminders of Thailand's chequered past and the continuing might of the Thai military.

Silpakorn University ❾

North of the Grand Palace and Wat Phra Kaew complex is **Silpakorn University**. The oldest and most prestigious art institution in Thailand, Silpakorn was originally the site of Tha Phra Palace, once occupied by the royal grandchildren. A few of the old buildings still stand, now part of the university campus.

The art school is attributed to the vision of Italian sculptor Corrado Feroci, known as Silpa Bhirasri to locals and dubbed "the father of Thai modern art". During the 1920s, Feroci was invited to work as a sculptor in Thailand, where he executed key public commissions like the design for the Democracy Monument.

The university's Fine Arts Department operates a **Hall Of Sculpture** (Mon–Fri 8.30am–4.30pm; free). It displays a collection of original plaster casts of statuesque monuments to royal, religious and other important dignitaries, whose originals stand tall throughout the kingdom. The university galleries also hold decent monthly exhibitions by students, teachers, alumni and visiting artists.

Wat Mahathat ❿

Address: Sanam Luang
Opening Hrs: daily 7am–8pm
Entrance Fee: free
Transport: Tha Chang pier

Nestled between Silpakorn and Thammasat universities is **Wat Mahathat**. You will enter through the gates of the earth-toned Thawornwatthu building, a former royal funerary hall donated to the temple as a library for monks. Compared to other sites in the vicinity, Wat Mahathat, although an important temple, has little visual appeal to capture tourist attention. Founded

Wat Mahathat Buddha statues.

Amulets come in myriad forms and serve a variety of purposes, from religious or spiritual to the more practical, such as ensuring sexual potency.

The giant Reclining Buddha's head.

The giant Reclining Buddha in its full glory.

in the 1700s, the temple houses the **Maha Chulalongkorn Rajavidyalaya University**, one of the two highest seats of Buddhist learning in the country, and where King Rama IV spent almost 25 years studying as a monk before taking the throne in 1851.

Wat Mahathat exudes a more genuine, working-temple atmosphere compared to the more ceremonial temples in the area, with locals swarming here to receive spiritual tutelage. Apart from an outdoor herbal medicine market, an **amulet market** has stalls along Trok Silpakorn, an alley between the temple and Silpakorn University, all the way to the riverside Thanon Mahathat.

You might also be able to get in tune with your inner self at the temple's **International Buddhist Meditation Centre**, which conducts regular classes in English (tel: 0-2623 5881; www.mcu.ac.th/ibmc).

Wat Pho ⓫

Address: Thanon Thai Wang
Tel: 0-2222 5910
Opening Hrs: daily 8am–5pm
Entrance Fee: charge
Transport: Tha Tien pier

South of the Grand Palace and Wat Phra Kaew complex is the much visited **Wat Pho**, Bangkok's largest and oldest surviving temple. The site retains a more casual ambience than the younger and more dominant Wat Phra Kaew. Apart from its historic significance, visitors come to Wat Pho for two things: to pay homage to the monumental Reclining Buddha, and to unwind at the city's best traditional massage centre.

Also known to Thais as Wat Phra Chetuphon, the temple dates back to the 16th century. However, it did not achieve real importance until the establishment of Bangkok as the capital. Wat Pho was a particular favourite of the first four Bangkok kings, all of whom added to its treasures. The four towering coloured *chedi* to the west of the *bot* (ordination hall) are memorials to the monarchs, and around the hall are 90-plus other *chedi*. The temple cloisters contain 394 bronze Buddha images, retrieved from ancient ruins in Sukhothai and Ayutthaya. One of the most important was the Reclining Buddha, added by

King Rama III in 1832. This king also converted the temple into the country's earliest place of public learning and instructed that the walls be inscribed with lessons on astrology, history, morality and archaeology, leading locals to fondly call it the kingdom's first university.

Wat Pho's gigantic **Reclining Buddha**, 46 metres (150ft) long and 15 metres (50ft) high, and made from brick, plaster and gilded in gold, depicts the resting Buddha passing into nirvana. The flat soles of the Buddha's feet are inlaid with mother-of-pearl designs, illustrating the 108 *laksana* (distinctive marks of a Buddha). Also numbering 108 are the metallic bowls that span the wall; a coin dropped in each supposedly brings goodwill to the devotee. With the building's pillars preventing full view, the head and feet are the best vantage points.

The temple's main hall is considered to be one of Bangkok's most beautiful. Girding its base are superbly carved sandstone panels depicting scenes from the *Ramakien*.

Wat Pho.

The striking doors are also devoted to *Ramakien* scenes, brilliantly rendered in some of the finest mother-of-pearl work found in Asia. The ashes of Rama I are interred in the pedestal base of the hall's principal Buddha image. Standing beside the inner doorways, pairs of large stone *farang* (foreigner) guards are striking for their Western characteristics.

Wat Pho massage school
Address: Thanon Thai Wang, www.watpomassage.com
Tel: 0-2221 2974
Opening Hrs: daily 10am–6pm
Entrance Fee: charge
Transport: Tha Tien pier

Wat Pho became, and still is, the place to learn about traditional medicine, particularly massage and meditation. The medicine pavilion displays stone tablets indicating beneficial body points for massage. Skirting the temple grounds are several small rock gardens which contain statues of hermits striking poses; these were used as diagnostic aids. Many of the old shophouses that fringe the temple

The walls of Wat Ratchabophit are decorated with brightly patterned Chinese ceramic tiles called bencharong.

Wat Ratchabophit.

Hanging art in the Siam Discovery Museum.

walls today still peddle a range of traditional herbal remedies.

Traditional Thai massage is based on Indian yoga philosophy, and originated from millennia-old Indian therapies that aim to release blocked energy. In Thai massage, strong thumbs dig deep into tense muscles and the body's energy points. The masseurs also bring their full body weight to bear as they stretch the recipients' bodies into yoga-like poses. The **Wat Pho Thai Traditional Massage School** offers cheap hour-long massages, and also offers courses for those wanting to learn the art. Many masseurs around the country claim to have received tuition here, and the hands-on training has proved a staple career option for many of Thailand's blind population.

Siam Discovery Museum ⓬

Address: Thanon Sanam Chai
Tel: 0-2622 2599
Opening Hrs: Tue–Sun 10am–6pm
Entrance Fee: charge
Transport: Tha Tien pier

Southeast of Wat Po, the interactive multimedia displays and tableaux at the **Siam Discovery Museum** explain what it is to be "Thai". Starting from the ancient ethnic groups that populated the Southeast Asian region 2,000 years ago, when it was known as Suvarnabhumi (Golden Land) – the name adopted by Bangkok's main airport – the exhibits run through historical periods and population shifts, including the periods of Khmer, Sukhothai and Ayutthayan dominance. The museum is housed in a handsome listed building that was previously the Ministry of Commerce.

Wat Ratchapradit ⓭

Address: Thanon Saranrom
Tel: 0-2223 8215
Opening Hrs: daily 5am–10pm (chapel 9–9.30am, 5–7pm)
Entrance Fee: free
Transport: Tha Tien pier

Wat Ratchapradit, located next to Saranrom Park on Thanon Saranrom, is less grand than many other temples in this royal district, but it offers a more intimate appreciation of a monarch's connection with religious buildings. King Mongkut ordered its construction on a reclaimed coffee

Modern exhibits in the Siam Discovery Museum.

plantation in 1864, and some of its unusual interior murals depict the king, an avid astronomer, observing a solar eclipse in 1868 in the fishing village of Wa Kor, south of Bangkok. On the trip, the king contracted malaria and later died. His remains are held beneath the main Buddha statue here. The quaint grey marble-clad temple is an example of his, and later King Chulalongkorn's, interest in mixing Thai and Western architecture.

Saranrom Park ⓮

Just behind Wat Ratchapradit, the manicured landscape of **Saranrom Park** (daily 5am–8pm; free) is the perfect place to wind down after a full day of palace and temple tours. The park was originally a garden attached to Saranrom Palace, which was supposed to have been the retirement retreat for King Mongkut. However, he passed away before the palace was completed. Enhanced by bridges, ponds, a European-style cherub-spouting fountain and a Chinese pagoda, this green space has been open to the public since the 1960s. At the park's centre is a memorial erected by King Chulalongkorn for his wife Queen Sunanda, who tragically drowned in a boating accident in 1880. At the park's main gates, drink vendors sell freshly-squeezed juice to the legion of joggers – so grab a seat on a park bench and cool off with a drink.

Wat Ratchabophit ⓯

Address: Thanon Fuang Nakhon
Tel: 0-2222 3930
Opening Hrs: daily 5am–8pm (chapel 9–9.30am, 5.30–6pm)
Entrance Fee: free
Transport: buses 1, 508

Although it is located on the opposite bank of Khlong Lord canal and Rattanakosin, **Wat Ratchabophit** is easily accessed from Saranrom Park. This infrequently visited sanctuary is recognisable for its characteristic amalgamation of local temple architecture and period European style. It has an unusual design that places the main circular *chedi* and its circular cloister in the centre. Started in 1869 by King Chulalongkorn (Rama V), the complex took well over two decades to complete.

The *bot* (ordination hall), built into the northern side of the yellow tile-clad cloister, is covered in brightly patterned Chinese ceramic tiles, known as *bencharong*. The windows and entrance doors to the hall are exquisite works of art, with tiny pieces of mother-of-pearl inlaid in lacquer, in an intricate rendition of the insignias of the five royal ranks. The doors open into one of the most surprising temple interiors in Thailand, with a Gothic-inspired chapel of solid columns that looks more like a medieval cathedral than a Thai temple. The courtyard doors are carved in relief with jaunty-looking soldiers wearing European-type uniforms. Wat Ratchabophit was built before King Chulalongkorn made his first trip to Europe, so its design is all the more remarkable.

THE NATIONAL MUSEUM

Bangkok's National Museum, one of the largest in Southeast Asia, is a good place to learn more about Thailand's history and culture.

The National Museum's three main galleries are spread over a handful of old and new buildings. Thai history from the Sukhothai period (13th–14th centuries) to the Rattanakosin period (1782–the present) is covered in the Sivamokhaphiman Hall, while behind the hall, the Prehistoric Gallery has 5,000 year-old exhibits from the Ban Chiang archaeological site in the northeast. The south wing exhibits Buddha images and artefacts from the Srivijaya and Lopburi periods, while the north wing displays exhibits from the Lanna, Sukhothai, Ayutthaya and Rattanakosin periods. The rooms in the Wang Na, or Front Palace, display fine art masterpieces, mostly from the Rattanakosin period, with treasures in the form of gold, carvings, enamelware, musical instruments, ceramics, clothes, weapons and palanquins.

In front of the old palace is the Buddhaisawan Chapel, once the private chapel of the Prince Successor and a good example of Rattanakosin architecture. Today, it houses the second holiest image in Thailand, Phra Buddha Sihing, a Sukhothai-style Buddha image. Beautiful murals cover the wall of this chapel.

A chariot fitting of a bronze Garuda holding a Naga. In Hindu and Buddhist mythology, Garudas are half-man half bird mounts of Vishnu; Nagas are serpents.

Puppets used in the now disappearing art of hun lakhon lek, which recounts legends from the Thai epic The Ramakien, based on the Indian Ramayana.

THE ESSENTIALS

Address: Thanon Na Phra That, www.finearts.go.th/museumbangkok
Tel: 0-2224 1333
Opening Hrs: Wed–Sun 9am–4pm
Entrance Fee: charge (guided tours at 9.30am Wed and Thur)
Transport: Phra Athit pier

The murals in the Buddhaisawan Chapel surround the Phra Buddha Sihing, Thailand's second most sacred Buddha image.

THE FIRST THAI MUSEUM

King Chulalongkorn was Thailand's great moderniser. He introduced railways, mapping and the postal service, and reformed education and health care.

King Chulalongkorn, or Rama V established the country's first public museum in 1874 in the Grand Palace. The collections were based on those of his father, King Mongkut (Rama IV). In 1926 the museum was moved to what was the Wang Na (Front Palace), the abode of the second-in-line to the throne, called the "second king" or the Prince Successor. This vast palace, dating from 1782, once extended across Khlong Lot up to the Grand Palace park. When his heir-apparent attempted a violent overthrow, Chulalongkorn abolished the office in 1887 and tore down most of the buildings. The Wang Na is one of the remnants of the original palace and today it houses a variety of artefacts in Rooms 4–15. Room 6 contains a beautifully carved *howdah*, or elephant seat, made of ivory.

Chulalongkorn's statue can be found in the Issaretrachanusorn Hall, which also exhibits the beds of Phra Pin Klao, the thrones of King Chulalongkorn and King Vajiravudh, and intricate Chinese and European-style furniture.

A statue of the reclining Buddha. It represents the moment the Buddha ascends into Nirvana, having completed the cycle of birth and rebirth and attained Enlightenment. The event is celebrated on Visakha Bucha Day.

The new exhibition space dedicated to southeast Asian sculpture.

Wat Arun.

THONBURI

Thonburi had a brief moment of glory as the country's capital in the 18th century, and the royal connection left a legacy of important temples. Some are still best reached via winding canals, which offer respite from the hustle of the modern city.

fter the fall of Ayutthaya in 1767, King Taksin established Thonburi as Thailand's third capital, which it remained for 15 years until Bangkok's ascendance in 1782. Taksin spent most of his reign fighting rebel factions that coveted the throne, leaving time only late in his reign to embellish his city.

Thonburi, which means "Town of Riches", remained a separate town until 1971, when it was incorporated into the Bangkok Metropolis. You can reach it by numerous bridges, the oldest of which is **Memorial Bridge** (Phra Buddha Yodfa). The area has only recently seen the growth of riverside condos and it has only a few high-end hotels, although these benefit from having views to the city across the river. Its tourist attractions are largely confined to the areas close to the old palace grounds. One of the most pleasing activities in Bangkok is a tour of Thonburi's canals (see page 130).

The canals worth exploring include **Khlong Bangkok Noi**, which winds into **Khlong Bangkok Yai** downstream, as well as connecting to **Khlong Om** upstream. Once a source of fresh produce for local communities, the floating markets

at **Wat Sai** and **Taling Chan** now function mainly as tourist souvenir stops, so much so that several similar markets have been revived in Bangkok. The further down the canals you venture, the narrower and calmer the waterway becomes. With rickety teak houses, vendors selling produce from boats, fishermen dangling rods out of windows and kids frolicking in the water, the sights along Thonburi's canals are reminiscent of a more peaceful bygone era.

Main Attractions
Wat Arun
Wat Rakhang
Museum of Forensic Medicine
National Museum of Royal Barges
Wat Suwannaram
Wat Kalayanamit
Santa Cruz Church

Map
Page 126

Riverside food stall.

Canal and river cruising

The major canals are serviced by public **longtail boats** (see box). But as the experience can be hectic at certain times of the day – most commuters travel into the city in the mornings and return in the afternoons – it might be better to hire your own private longtail boat for a more leisurely exploration.

Getting from pier to pier along the Chao Phraya river is best on the **Chao Phraya Express** boats, which operate from the southern outskirts up to Nonthaburi in the north. For shuttling from one side of the river to the other, make use of the cheap **cross-river ferries**, which you can board at the many jetties close to the Chao Phraya Express boat piers (see page 233).

Wat Arun ❶

Address: Thanon Arun Amarin
Tel: 0-2891 2185
Opening Hrs: daily 8.30am–5.30pm
Entrance Fee: charge

Detail of a porcelain-encrusted prang of Wat Arun.

Transport: Wat Arun pier

Also known as The Temple of Dawn, this temple gets its confusing nickname – the sun actually sets, not rises, behind the temple – from the arrival of King Taksin, who led the remnants of the Siamese armies here in 1767 after their defeat by the Burmese in the siege of Ayutthaya. The king first viewed **Wat Arun**, at dawn, and chose the area, Thonburi, as the new capital of Siam.

Taksin incorporated the temple – then called Wat Magog – into his palace compound, renamed it Wat Jaeng (Temple of Dawn), and housed the greatly revered Emerald Buddha here. King Rama I later moved it to Wat Kaew, near the Grand Palace. Rama II (1809–24) officially changed Wat Arun's name to Wat Arunratchatharam, and Rama IV (1851–68) later chose Wat Arunratchawararam.

After renovations of the temple by several kings of the Chakri

LONGTAIL BOAT TOURS

Some of the sights in this chapter are best visited by private longtail boat. Longtail boat operators (found at major piers like Tha Thien and Tha Chang) are notorious for overcharging tourists, so be prepared to bargain hard and set a price before embarking; B700–1000 an hour (per boat) is a rough guide. Discuss beforehand where you want to visit and how much time you want to spend at each place. Bear in mind that once underway, it may be difficult to switch itineraries as boat drivers speak little or no English. Ask for a slow ride so that photos can be taken and the scenery enjoyed. Sit near the front of the boat, away from the noisy rear engines.

dynasty, the main Khmer-style *prang* (spire) now stands at 79 metres (259ft). Rama III introduced the colourful fragments of porcelain that cover most of the temple's exterior, recycling piles of broken ceramic that was leftover ballast from Chinese merchant ships. When builders ran out of porcelain the king asked his subjects to contribute broken crockery to complete the decoration. Artisans fashioned the pieces into flowers or used them to embellish the costumes of the gods and mythical figures that ring each tier.

The great *prang* represents the Hindu–Buddhist Mount Meru, home of the gods, with its 33 heavens. It is topped by a thunderbolt, the weapon of the Hindu god Indra. Four smaller *prang* stand at each corner of the temple, each with niches containing statues of Nayu, god of the wind, on horseback. Between the minor *prang* are four beautiful smaller towers, or *mondop*. In niches at the foot of each stairway, Buddha images portray the four key events of his life: birth, meditation (while sheltered by a seven-headed *naga* serpent),

preaching to his first five disciples, and death/enlightenment. Mythical giants called *yaksha*, similar to those that protect Wat Phra Kaew, guard the complex.

Wat Rakhang ❷

Address: Thanon Arun Amarin
Tel: 0-2411 2255
Opening Hrs: daily 8.30am–5.30pm
Entrance Fee: charge
Transport: Sirirat pier

Further upriver, directly across from the Grand Palace complex, this temple has a lovely collection of bells. King Taksin liked the chime of the original temple bell and had it moved to Wat Phra Kaew, donating five bells as replacement.

Hidden at the rear of Wat Rakhang is the red-painted *ho trai* (wooden library), a three-part stilted building that King Rama I lived in as a monk before becoming king and when Thonburi was the capital. The late 18th-century building is considered

Numerous small bells hang from Wat Rakhang's temple towers and gently chime in the afternoon breeze, adding a musical ambience to this riverside temple.

Wat Rakhang's Buddha statue.

Between the Museum of Royal Barges and Wat Suwannaram, ask your boatman to stop at Ban Bu, where a short alley leads to a workshop making hand-beaten alms bowls called *khan long hin*. You can watch the process and buy these beautiful bronzeware items from around B700.

Seven-headed naga, or serpent, adorning the prow of the Anatana-ganaj barge at the Museum of Royal Barges.

an architectural gem and is decorated with murals from the *Ramakien*.

The Museum of Forensic Medicine ❸

Address: 2/F, Adulaydejvigrom Building, Siriraj Hospital, 2 Thanon Phrannok
Tel: 0-2419 7000
Opening Hrs: Mon–Fri 8.30am–4.30pm
Entrance Fee: charge
Transport: Sirirat pier

To the north of Wat Rakhang, several museums are located within the Siriraj Hospital complex, the best known of which is this one. Green arrows point the way from the hospital grounds to the museum, located on the 2nd floor of the Forensic Department. The stomach-churning exhibits are definitely not for the queasy. Mummified corpses of Thailand's most notorious criminals, deformed foetuses in formaldehyde and a gallery of disturbing post-mortem photographs are among the exhibits here.

National Museum of Royal Barges ❹

Address: Khlong Bangkok Noi, off Chao Phraya river, Thanon Arun Amarin
Tel: 0-2424 0004
Opening Hrs: daily 9am–5pm
Entrance Fee: charge (photography fee extra)
Transport: longtail boat to museum pier

On the north bank of the Khlong Bangkok Noi canal is the **National Museum of Royal Barges**. A crammed canal bank community nearby provides a stark contrast to the regal opulence of the wooden barges. The dry-dock warehouse displays eight vessels from a fleet of over 50 that are only put to sail on auspicious occasions.

Their last outing – to celebrate the king's 80th birthday in 2007 – saw 2,000 oarsmen, musicians and guards in traditional dress sailing in a 52-barge procession to Wat Arun for a *khatin* ceremony, in which robes are presented to monks. Of the six barges displayed in dry dock here, pride of place goes to *Suphannahongse* (Golden Swan), named after the mythical steed of the Hindu god Brahma and in which the king travels on a gold-coloured throne. It's 50 metres (164ft) long – the largest vessel in the world to be crafted from a single piece of wood. Barge processions date to the Ayutthaya period, but the original *Suphannahongse* was built in the reign of King Rama I (1782–1809). King Rama VI launched the current version in 1911.

Also displayed are old figureheads from boats damaged by World War II Allied bombs aimed at the nearby

Santa Cruz Church.

Bangkok Noi Railway Station, which the Japanese used to ship supplies to and from western Thailand via the infamous Death Railway (see page 195). Around the museum are glass cases with models of traditional canal transport, Ayutthaya-era drawings, photos of barge construction and gold ornamental cloths that adorn the barges.

Wat Suwannaram ❺

Address: 33 Charan Sanit Wong Soi 32
Tel: 0-2434 7790
Opening Hrs: daily 6am–5pm
Entrance Fee: free
Transport: longtail boat to wat's pier

From the museum pier, it's a five-minute boat journey up Khlong Bangkok Noi canal to this historic temple on the opposite bank to the museum. Have a look at the grand murals contained within **Wat Suwannaram's** main building. If the building is locked, look for a monk, who may open the doors and windows to reveal the magnificent, if slightly deteriorated, paintings that tell the story of the Buddha's previous 10 lives. The intricate artwork, which adorns every corner of the temple's interior, was commissioned by King Rama III and is considered to be among the finest examples of 19th-century painting.

Wat Kalayanamit ❻

Address: 371 Soi Wat Kanlaya
Tel: 0-2466 5018
Opening Hrs: daily 8am–5pm
Entrance Fee: free
Transport: Wat Arun pier

South of Wat Arun, at the mouth of Khlong Bangkok Yai canal, are two sights worth visiting. The first is this 19th-century temple with Chinese-style embellishments. Built at the behest of Rama III, the tall main *viharn* (sermon hall) contains an impressive seated Buddha image. This is the largest of its kind in the country, as is the large bronze bell in the grounds.

Santa Cruz Church ❼

Address: 112 Thanon Thetsaban Soi 1
Opening Hrs: Mon–Sat 5–8pm, Sun 9am–8pm
Entrance Fee: free
Transport: Santa Cruz Church pier

From the temple head for **Santa Cruz Church**, the spire of which is visible from a couple of streets away. The pastel-coloured church, topped by an octagonal dome, has been rebuilt twice since it was first constructed in the 18th century. The present edifice dates from 1913. The neighbourhood surrounding the church was once part of a flourishing Portuguese district that migrated here after Ayutthaya was abandoned.

Buddha image at Wat Kalayanamit.

LIFE ON THE CHAO PHRAYA RIVER

The river offers respite from Bangkok traffic, and gives an alternative view of a city that grew up along its banks.

Many people enjoy travelling on the Chao Phraya River, not only to escape the roads, for the cool breeze and the cleaner air, but because numerous sites are best seen from the water. The city grew up along the river, so its banks are full of interesting old buildings. In the east are beautiful colonial-style structures and early European churches, and drifting towards the Old City are temples such as Wat Arun, which rises atmospherically on the Thonburi side.

Many of the riverside wooden dwellings hark back 100 years; there are back doors to markets, where waterborne goods are still loaded from boats; and not very far north you are into the green countryside. The river is not just a means to get from A to B; it can be a very satisfying tour in itself and well worth an hour or two of your time. There is a variety of water transport, from express boats – which travel up and down the length of the river – to cross-river ferries and longtail taxi boats (which link from the river into the *khlongs*, or canals).

As old wooden houses in this rapidly developing city disappear, those on waterways offer the best glimpse of Bangkok's traditional dwellings.

In pockets of Bangkok, boats remain the prime means of transport. Some are floating shops, selling everything from rice and beer to postal services.

With few bridges and heavy road traffic, people rely on river ferries, both across river and along it.

The truly authentic Thai floating market is more or less a thing of the past. Head for the floating market at Damnoen Saduak (see page 192) keeping in mind that much of it is staged for tourists.

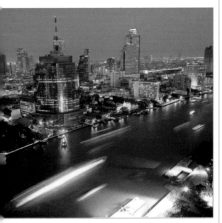

The rapidly developing river skyline is particularly fine at night, especially when the hotels coordinate firework displays.

HOW THE *KHLONGS* DEVELOPED

Canal life in 1893.

Bangkok's origins date back to the 16th century when a canal was dug across a loop of the Chao Phraya River to cut the distance between the sea and the then Thai capital at Ayutthaya, 85km (55 miles) north. Over the years, monsoon floods scoured the banks of the canal until it widened to become the main course of the river. On its banks rose two towns, Thonburi on the west and Bangkok on the east. The abandoned river loop became Khlong Bangkok Noi and Khlong Bangkok Yai, the principal canals that run through Thonburi. Bangkok's founding king, Rama I, established Rattanakosin as the nucleus of the new capital in 1782 by digging three concentric canals, turning it into an easily defensible island. Houses were built on bamboo rafts and people travelled primarily by boat. In the mid-20th century, Bangkokians began leaving boats for cars. Canals were filled in to make roads, and houses were built on land. The congested streets that are sweltering in the hot season become flooded in the monsoon season. Some canals, though, remain, and Khlong Saen Saep still ferries people right across town from the Old City to Bangkok's eastern fringes.

Chao Phraya River ferries operate every few hundred metres.

Buddha images lining the cloisters at Wat Suthat.

THE OLD CITY

Bangkok's Old City retains some of its historic calm and charm, and is one of the easiest areas to tour on foot. There are many temples and Buddhist shops, and to the north, lively Khao San Road is where backpackers party until dawn.

Dominated by the wide boulevard of Thanon Ratchadamnoen, the "Old City" contains all the peripheral buildings and temples that lie just outside Rattanakosin island. The area once marked the outskirts of the city, with the canals of Khlong Banglamphu and Khlong Ong Ang ferrying in supplies from the surrounding countryside. At the turn of the 20th century, hardly any roads cut into the landscape, with the neighbourhood occupied by traditional craftspeople and performing artisans. Devotional structures were the main protrusions on the skyline.

Time has drastically altered the area's visual appeal, yet there is still a strong sense of the past, making this one of the city's most pleasant areas to explore. Aside from tourist attractions, most foreigners head to the district of Banglamphu for cheap accommodation and entertainment in the well-known backpackers' haven of Thanon Khao San.

Thanon Bamrung Muang

Thanon Bamrung Muang, an old elephant trail, was one of the city's first paved tracks. This area is full of temples, and this street is typical for its shops selling accoutrements for Buddhist worship and funeral rites.

Monks in orange robes mingle with housewives and businessmen placing orders for ceremonial candles, tiered umbrellas, temple drums, bells and gongs, incense and sparkling lanterns, and it's not unusual to see pickup trucks driving around with 3.5-metre (12ft) gold Buddha statues strapped to the back.

Giant Swing ❶

Thanon Bamrung Muang intersects a large square with City Hall at its northern end and Wat Suthat and

Main Attractions
Wat Suthat
Pak Khlong Talad
Democracy Monument
Wat Bowonniwet
Loha Prasat
King Prajadhipok Museum
Golden Mount
Soi Ban Baat
Thanon Khao San

Map
Page 134

The Giant Swing.

The Democracy Monument.

the **Giant Swing** opposite. Bangkok's original Giant Swing (Sao Ching Cha), erected by King Rama I in 1784, was based on one in Ayutthaya that had been brought to Thailand by Brahman priests in the 16th century. It was used to observe Triyampawai, the Brahman New Year Ceremony, during which four young men in a gondola would swing ever higher trying to catch purses of gold hanging from poles. The ceremony was banned in 1931 after several accidents. The swing itself has been removed, leaving just the tall red-painted teak frame as a marker.

Wat Suthat ②

Address: 146 Thanon Bamrung Muang
Tel: 0-2224 9845
Opening Hrs: daily 8.30am–9pm
Entrance Fee: charge
Transport: buses 10, 12, 42

Standing tall behind the Giant Swing, this is one of the country's six principal temples. Begun by Rama I in 1807, it took three reigns to complete. The temple is notable for its enormous *bot*, or ordination hall, said to be the tallest in Bangkok, and for its equally large *viharn* (sermon hall), both of them surrounded by cloisters of gilded Buddha images.

The 8-metre (26ft) -tall Phra Sri Sakyamuni Buddha is one of the largest surviving bronze images from Sukhothai, and was transported by boat all the way from the former northern kingdom. The base of the image contains the ashes of King Ananda Mahidol (Rama VIII), older brother of the present king. The murals date from the reign of King Rama III; most intriguing are the depictions of sea monsters and foreign ships on the columns.

Accounts vary, but it is said that Rama II himself carved the ornate teakwood doors of the *bot*. Incised to a depth of 5cm (2ins), they follow the Ayutthaya tradition of floral motifs,

Detail of wall mural at Wat Suthat.

with tangled jungle vegetation hiding small animals. The temple courtyard is a virtual museum of statuary, with stone figures of Chinese generals and scholars, which came as ballast in 18th century rice ships returning from deliveries to China.

Devasathan ❸

West of the Giant Swing along Thanon Dinso is a row of three adjoining Brahman shrines called **Devasathan** (daily 9am–5pm, chapel Thur and Sun only 10am–4pm; free). Built in 1784 at the same time as the Giant Swing and recently renovated, the three chapels house images of Shiva, Ganesha and Vishnu. Although Thais are largely Buddhists, certain Brahman beliefs have been retained from historical ties with Angkor (see margin).

Rommaninat Park ❹

Southwest of Wat Suthat, a short walk along Thanon Siri Phong brings you to **Rommaninat Park** (daily 5am–9pm; free). Formerly the grounds of a prison built in 1893, this became a public park in 1992 to celebrate Queen Sirikit's birthday. The original watchtowers are still standing, and some of the former prison buildings now house the small **Corrections Museum**, with displays of old methods of punishment (Mon–Fri 8.30am–4.30pm; free). Other features include ponds, fountains, a children's play area, jogging tracks and a large bronze sculpture of a conch shell.

Pak Khlong Talad ❺

South of the park, on Thanon Chakraphet, the atmospheric **Pak Khlong Talad** (Flower Market) sits by the riverfront at the mouth of Khlong Lord. It's a convenient location for supplying funeral wreaths for use in the Old City temples. The market, busy 24 hours a day, spills from covered warehouses onto streets lined with stalls selling roses, carnations, sunflowers and myriad orchids. It is best visited after nightfall, when the surrounding area also heaves with the youthful clothes and accessory stalls of Saphan Phut Market.

The Devasathan shrine has strong Hindu influences.

The 14 October Monument is a shrine to the people who died in the 1973 demonstrations against Thailand's military dictatorship.

Roses at Pak Khlong Talad.

Democracy Monument 6

Moving north, the **Democracy Monument** lies beyond City Hall. Designed with four elongated wings by Italian sculptor Corrado Feroci (also known as Silpa Bhirasri), the 1939 monument is a celebration of Thailand's 1932 transition from absolute to constitutional monarchy. Almost every detail and measurement of the monument has symbolic relevance, and the central metal tray contains a copy of the original Constitution of the Kingdom of Thailand. A rallying point for civil discontent in October 1973 and May 1992, the monument became the scene of bloodbaths after the army violently suppressed peaceful demonstrations against military dictatorships. Officially nearly 200 protesters were killed during the two incidents.

14 October Monument 7

A short walk west from Democracy Monument, along Thanon Ratchadamnoen Klang, brings you to the **14 October Monument**. This chiselled granite edifice is a sombre memorial to the victims of the 1973 mass demonstrations against the dictatorship of the "Three Tyrants", led by Prime Minister Thanom Kittikachorn. A small amphitheatre surrounds the central spire, which has the names of 73 of the victims inscribed in Thai. Beneath are an exhibition room, meeting rooms and a mini-theatre. Given the government's past denial of this tragic event, it was a major victory for survivors and victims' families when this tribute was erected in 2002.

Wat Bowonniwet 8

Due north of the 14 October Monument along Thanon Tanao is **Wat Bowonniwet**, a modest-looking temple with strong royal bonds (daily 8am–5pm; free). Built in 1826 during the reign of Rama III, King Mongkut (Rama IV) served as abbot of the temple for a small portion of his 27 years as a monk. More recently the present King Bhumibol (Rama IX) donned saffron robes here after his coronation in 1946.

Home to Thailand's second Buddhist university, the temple is known for its extraordinary murals painted by innovative monk-artist Khrua In Khong. Krua had never travelled outside Thailand, but had looked

ARMED WITH AMULETS

The thriving amulet market in the forecourt of Wat Ratchanatda reflects the Thai belief in a mix of talismanic powers based on animism as well as Brahman and Buddhist beliefs. The market deals in amulets of all shapes and sizes, along with prayer beads, Buddha images and totems of revered monks. They are worn for religious or spiritual purposes or for more practical reasons, such as keeping the wearer safe or attracting fortune in love or money. Look out for wooden *palad khik* (phalluses), which are believed to ward off evil spirits. Many will have been blessed by monks for use in exorcism. There is another famous amulet market close to Wat Mahathat (see page 117).

The pointed metal spires of the Loha Prasat.

at Western art reproductions and understood the concept of perspective. Unlike the flat, two-dimensional paintings of classical Thai art, these recede into the distance and are characterised by muted, moody colours. Also interesting are the subjects: pre-Civil War American mansions, horse-racing tracks and people dressed in the fashions of 19th-century America.

Thanon Ratchadamnoen

Stretching all the way from the Grand Palace to the Dusit Park area, the wide **Thanon Ratchadamnoen** (Royal Passage) splits into three sections and is modelled after Paris's famous boulevards. Built at the turn of the 20th century, the tree-lined avenue has some of the city's widest and least cluttered pavements.

The somewhat austere-looking 1930s buildings that line both sides of Thanon Ratchadamnoen Klang have been given a lick of paint and public benches have been added along the pavements to offer rest for

the weary. On royal birthdays, the area is turned into a sea of decorative lights, flags and royal portraits. Don't be surprised if all traffic and pedestrians are abruptly halted by legions of police – it means a royal cavalcade is on its way.

Queen's Gallery

Towards the eastern end of Thanon Ratchadamnoen Klang, on the corner of Thanon Phra Sumen, is the modern, cream-coloured **Queen's Gallery** (tel: 0-2281 5360/1; www.queengallery.org; Thur–Tue 10am–7pm; charge). This five-floor gallery exhibits modern and contemporary paintings, predominantly by local artists.

Loha Prasat and Wat Ratchanatda ❾

Address: 2 Thanon Maha Chai
Tel: 0-2224 8807
Opening Hrs: daily 9am–5pm
Entrance Fee: charge
Transport: buses 2, 12, 42

Mahakan Fort, one of only two remaining watchtowers that guarded the old city walls of Bangkok.

During World War II, the Golden Mount served as a watchtower, with guards armed with signal flags to warn of enemy invaders.

The climb to the Golden Mount is rewarding for its views of the Rattanakosin area.

Just before the point where Thanon Ratchadamnoen Klang crosses Pan Fah Bridge over the canal and veers left into Ratchadamnoen Nok are several noticeable structures on the right. The **Loha Prasat** (Metal Palace), evocative of Burmese temple structures, is the main attraction in the grounds it shares with **Wat Ratchanatda**. The Loha Prasat is a step pyramid construction modelled on a Sri Lankan temple from the 3rd century BC. King Rama III ordered it built in 1846. Its 37 black spires, each topped with an umbrella embellishment called a *hti*, depict the virtues needed to attain enlightenment. You can climb a spiral staircase past corridors of meditation cells right onto the roof itself, where a tower holds a sacred bell. Dizzying views include the Golden Mount.

The *viharn* at Wat Ratchanatda has lovely murals depicting heaven and hell on its interior walls. Outside the entrance is a manicured forecourt with the **Mahachesdabodin Royal Pavilion**. The ornate wooden pavilion is actually just over a decade old, one of the first additions in a grand scheme to redevelop the area. Its rich, gleaming embellishments have made it an appropriate setting for special ceremonies. Just behind the temple is a thriving amulet market (see box).

Mahakan Fort ⑩

Across Thanon Maha Chai from Wat Ratchanatda is one of only two surviving remnants of the 14 original fortified watchtowers that once protected the old city wall. With development having consumed most of the wall and other towers, the white octagonal turret of **Mahakan Fort** survives along with Banglamphu's larger Phra Sumen Fort. The cannons here were only recently disarmed. The site is closed to the public.

King Prajadhipok Museum ⑪

Address: 2 Thanon Lan Luang
Tel: 0-2280 3413
Opening Hrs: Tue–Sun 9am–4pm
Entrance Fee: charge
Transport: buses 2, 12, 42

Over the bridge from Mahakan Fort, this museum tells something of the intrigue behind the end of absolute monarchy in 1932, when

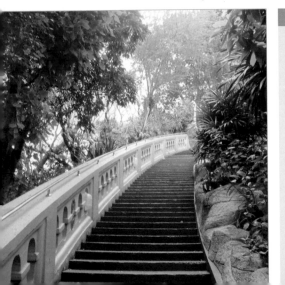

FUN OF THE FAIR

Bangkok's most famous temple fair (*ngan wat*) is held at Wat Saket each November. Temple fairs are an annual feature in many Bangkok communities and villages across the country, often lasting several days. They are raucous occasions that bring all ages together to enjoy a mix of market stalls, fairground games, fortune telling, theatre and comedy shows, and to raise money for the temple. Young girls enter beauty contests and their brothers, sometimes as young as seven, might start a fledgling career in Thai boxing. Bands play all kinds of music, often all at once, and the night brings romantic liaisons forged over rice wine and plates of spicy food to a soundtrack of thunderous disco.

Skilled artisans hammering out alms bowls for monks at Soi Ban Baat.

King Prajadhipok (Rama VII) was Thailand's ruler. It portrays the king's life before, during and after his reign through photos, official documents, personal effects and audio-visual displays. They cover his school days at Eton and his coronation, plus significant public works, such as the construction of Memorial Bridge. The king abdicated in 1935 and lived the rest of his life in England. The white neoclassical building, dated 1906, was originally the John Sampson Store, an early Bangkok purveyor of Western clothes.

Golden Mount ⑫

Address: 344 Thanon Chakraphatdi Phong
Tel: 0-2223 4561
Opening Hrs: daily 7.30am–5.30pm
Entrance Fee: charge
Transport: buses 2, 12, 42

Standing tall, south of King Prajadhipok Museum, is the elevated spire of the **Golden Mount** (Phu Khao Thong). Started by Rama III as a huge *chedi*, the city's soft earth made

it impossible to build and the abandoned site became an artificial hill overgrown with trees and shrubbery. In 1865, flat Bangkok got its then highest point when Rama IV added a golden *chedi* to the top, completing the 78-metre (255ft) high Golden Mount and giving it its name.

The *chedi*, a part of Wat Saket, is said to contain a Buddha relic from India. Visitors take the gentle climb past shrines, trees and rock gardens, ringing temple bells and enjoying 360-degree views of the city as the path spirals upwards. There's a refreshment stop halfway.

Wat Saket ⑬

At the bottom of the Golden Mount stands one of the capital's oldest temples, **Wat Saket** (daily 8am–5pm; free). Upon returning from Laos in 1782 with the Emerald Buddha, General Chakri stopped here and took a ceremonial bath before making his way back to Thonburi to be crowned King Rama I. The temple's name was later changed to Saket, which means "the washing of hair".

The temple is also associated with a more grisly history as it was used

Amulets for sale in the market behind Wat Ratchanatda.

TIP

Popular backpacker land Khao San Road has its own website, www.khaosanroad.com, packed chock-a-block with tips on cheap guesthouses, food and nightlife, as well as offbeat advice on how to wash your dreadlocks.

as the Old City's main crematorium. Disease epidemics broke out regularly during the 19th century, killing an estimated 60,000 people. The bodies of the dead were taken out of the city to the temple through the **Pratu Pii** (Ghost Gate) for cremation; if the families were too poor to pay for the ceremony, they were left for the vultures. Notable features are the fine murals in the main hall, and a beautiful wooden scripture library that dates to Rama I.

Monks' Bowl Village

Skirting the western edge of the Golden Mount is **Thanon Boriphat**, a street lined with timber merchants and wood carvers, chiselling away at doors, lintels and even birdcages. Further along the some road are the narrow alleyways that run off **Soi Ban Baat ⑭**. This area's name means Monk's **Bowl Village**. Although you still see monks carrying metal alms bowls (*baat*) around Bangkok's

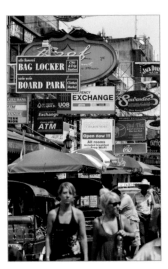

Khao San, a magnet for budget travellers.

streets to this day, they are now mainly machine-made, and there are just five families remaining of the original community that moved here from Ayutthaya in the 18th century to make hand-beaten bowls in the new capital.

Saffron-robed monks walk barefoot along the streets at dawn collecting food offerings from merit-seeking alms-givers. The bowls are crafted from eight pieces of metal, representing the eight spokes in the wheel of Dharma. Cashing in on the tourist market, the community has posted signs in English guiding you towards the tap-tap of distant hammers. Finished in enamel paint, the bowls sell from about B500.

Banglamphu

Called the village (*bang*) of the *lamphu* tree, the **Banglamphu** district was originally settled by farmers who fled the old capital of Ayutthaya after it was abandoned. The riverbank once held several princely mansions for nobles, a few of which survive on Thanon Phra Athit as offices of large

Streetside hair-braiding service at Thanon Khao San.

companies and international agencies like UNICEF.

The riverfront from Saphan Phra Pin Klao Bridge along the length of Thanon Phra Athit to **Santichai Prakan Park** is one of the city's few easily accessible river paths. It offers sweeping views up towards the Rama VIII Bridge. This lovely bankside park (daily 5am–10pm), always busy with activity of some sort, fringes the whitewashed octagonal **Phra Sumen Fort** ⑯, and has the only surviving *lamphu* trees in the neighbourhood. The fort, built in 1873 and restored in 1999, is one of two remaining defences of the old city wall. It is not open to the public.

Nearby **Thanon Phra Athit** is a lively street of art bars, some frequented by budding artists from nearby Silpakorn University. These colourful and cosy venues, which hold regular exhibitions and cultural events, are far less hectic than the backpacker-crammed watering holes just a stone's throw away on Thanon Khao San.

Thanon Khao San ⑰

Since the early 1980s, **Thanon Khao San** (or Khao San Road as it's popularly referred to) has been a self-contained ghetto for the backpacking globetrotter. Once a rather seedy gathering of cheap guesthouses, rice shops and pokey bars, as portrayed in Alex Garland's bestselling novel *The Beach*, Banglamphu's nerve centre has undergone a significant upgrade in recent years, with the arrival of boutique hotels like Buddy Lodge (www.buddylodge.com), sleek bars and international chains like Starbucks.

In the late 1990s, after local film and TV shows began using the street as a location, young Thais craving a sympathetic ambience for their own growing indie lifestyle started opening their own places to hang out in. The result is a mix of East and West 20-something culture that now stretches over several blocks and is among the most vibrant areas of the city.

All the needs of the "alternative" traveller are here – tattooists, hair braiders and body piercers, jugglers and buskers, tarot readers, used books and dealers in fake IDs. And of course a perpetual party atmosphere.

Alms bowls, or baat are used by monks to collect food from faithful Buddhists every morning.

Fried insects for sale on Khao San Road.

DUSIT

Bangkok's close-knit streets of fuming traffic are left far behind in royal Dusit, an expanse of wide parades and grandiose European architecture developed as a retreat by King Chulalongkorn. Museums galore sit in a tranquil park next to a zoo with boating on a lake.

The monarchy chose Dusit as the new area in which to build palaces and official buildings from the reign of King Chulalongkorn. The king was widely travelled and incorporated ideas he found abroad into all aspects of Thai life. Consequently, the royal quarter of Dusit is unlike any other area of Bangkok. The streets are modelled on the wide boulevards of Paris and the architecture rises in classical lines more associated with London or Rome.

Dusit Park

As Thanon Ratchadamnoen Klang leaves the Old City, it becomes Ratchadamnoen Nok, a pleasant, tree-lined boulevard leading to **Royal Plaza**, a broad square watched over by the bronze equestrian **Statue of King Chulalongkorn** (Rama V) **1**. Chulalongkorn was the first Thai monarch to venture to Europe and his travels left a lasting impression on the architecture and layout of this district, which was once a rustic royal retreat from the city and the Grand Palace.

The much revered king was also a great reformer and modern thinker. He abolished slavery and modernised many institutions, including the fields of medicine and education. People gather at the statue regularly, but particularly on 23 October, the anniversary of Chulalongkorn's death, to give offerings, including brandy, whisky or cigars which he particularly enjoyed, and wish luck for themselves in health, business and love. Royal Plaza hosts ceremonial occasions such as the Trooping of the Colour.

Ananta Samakhom Throne Hall **2**

Address: Thanon U-thong Nai
Tel: 0-2628 6300-9

Vimanmek Mansion.

Opening Hrs: daily 8.30am–4.30pm
Entrance Fee: charge (or free with Grand Palace entrance ticket)
Transport: buses 3. 72

Behind Chulalongkorn's statue is the monumental **Ananta Samakhom Throne Hall,** an Italian Renaissance-style hall of grey marble crowned by a huge dome. It is the tallest building within **Dusit Park,** which comprises a network of former royal gardens with canals, bridges, fountains and several small museums.

Built in 1907 by King Chulalongkorn as a grandiose venue for receiving visiting dignitaries, the hall is still used for state occasions. It was used for the first official meeting of the new parliament after Thailand became a constitutional monarchy in 1932. A Parliament House has since been built behind the throne hall. The highlights of the rich interior are frescoes on the domed ceiling depicting the Chakri monarchs from Rama I to Rama VI.

Vimanmek Mansion ❸

Address: 16 Thanon Ratchawithi, www.palaces.thai.net
Tel: 0-2628 6300
Opening Hrs: daily 9.30am–4pm
Entrance Fee: charge (free with Grand Palace entrance ticket); compulsory guided tours every 30 minutes; visitors dressed in shorts must wear sarongs that are provided at the door; shoes and bags have to be stowed in lockers
Transport: buses 18, 28, 110

Beyond Ananta Samakhom Throne Hall is the **Vimanmek Mansion,** billed as the world's largest golden teak building. Chulalongkorn had it built in 1868 as a summer palace on the east coast island of Ko Si Chang. However, he ordered the three-storey mansion dismantled and reassembled on the Dusit grounds in 1901. Made entirely from golden teak and without a single nail, the gingerbread fretwork and octagonal tower of this 72-room lodge looks more Victorian than period Thai. The king and his

Ananta Samakhom Throne Hall, which dates back to 1907, is more European than Thai in character.

Meerkats at Dusit Zoo.

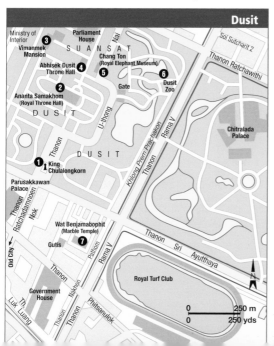

Dusit

Ministry of Interior ❸
Parliament House
Vimanmek Mansion
SUAN SAT
Chang Ton (Royal Elephant Museum) ❺
Abhisek Dusit Throne Hall ❹
Ananta Samakhom (Royal Throne Hall) ❷
Gate
Dusit Zoo ❻
Soi Sutcharit 2
Thanon Ratchawithi
DUSIT
U-thong
Khlong Prem Prachakon
Rama V
Thanon
Chitralada Palace
DUSIT
Thanon
King Chulalongkorn ❶
Parusakkawan Palace
Ratchadamnoen Nok
Wat Benjamabophit (Marble Temple) ❼
Gutis
Pathom
Rama V
Thanon Sri Ayutthaya
Old City
Government House
Thanon Nakhon
Thanon
Thanon
Th. Luk Luang
Thanon Phitsanulok
Royal Turf Club

0   250 m
0   250 yds

The Abhisek Dusit Throne Hall.

TIP

Be sure to keep your admission ticket to Wat Phra Kaew and the Grand Palace (see page 106). This allows you free access to many of Dusit's sights, such as the Ananta Samakhom Throne Hall, Vimanmek Mansion, Abhisek Dusit Throne Hall and the Royal Elephant Museum.

family lived here for only five years, during which time no other males were allowed entry. The mansion was occupied on and off during the next two decades before being abandoned and used as storage space. It was restored for the Bangkok bicentennial in 1982 and given a new lease of life.

Vimanmek (meaning "Palace in the Clouds") offers an interesting glimpse into how the royal family of the day lived. Only 30 of the rooms are open to the public and the tour is rather brief given the fact that there are so many treasures to see. A highlight is the king's bedroom, which has a European-style four-poster bed, and the bathroom, which houses what was probably Thailand's first bathtub and flushing toilet. The plumbing, however, was in its early days – the waste had to be carried out on a spiral staircase hidden beneath. Among the porcelain and hunting trophies are rare finds like the first typewriter to have Thai characters.

Free performances of Thai dance and martial arts are held every day at 10.30am and 2pm in the pavilion south of the mansion.

Abhisek Dusit Throne Hall ④

Address: 16 Thanon Ratchawithi
Tel: 0-2628 6300
Opening Hrs: daily 9.30am–4pm
Entrance Fee: charge (free with Grand Palace entrance ticket)
Transport: buses 18, 28, 110

In the garden east of Vimanmek is the **Abhisek Dusit Throne Hall**. Constructed in 1903 for King Chula-longkorn as an accompanying throne hall to Vimanmek, the ornate building is another sumptuous melding of Victorian and Moorish styles. The main hall is now used as a showroom-cum-museum for the SUPPORT foundation, a charitable organisation headed by Queen Dowager Sirikit, which helps preserve traditional arts and crafts. On view are examples of

jewellery, woodcarving, nielloware, silk and wicker products. Next to the museum is a shop selling the handi-work of village artisans.

Royal Elephant Museum ⑤

Further east is the **Royal Elephant Museum** or Chang Ton (daily 9.30am–4pm; charge, or free with Grand Palace entrance ticket). This is a former stable for white elephants, which, when found in the wild, automatically become the property of the king. It displays a large model of one of the present king's prized living pachy-derms, plus tusks and charms used by elephant handlers (*mahouts*), photos and articles about elephant capture and training, and a tableau of the Brahman ceremony conferring royal status on white elephants (see box).

Dusit Zoo ⑥

Address: 71 Thanon Rama V
www.dusitzoo.org
Tel: 0-2281 2000
Opening Hrs: daily 8am–6pm
Entrance Fee: charge
Transport: buses 18, 28, 110

Continuing east, across a small road is **Dusit Zoo**. Originally King Chula-longkorn's private botanical gardens,

WHITE ELEPHANTS

To the uninitiated, white elephants look nearly the same as everyday grey ones. It is only by a complicated process of examining skin colour, hair, eyes and genitalia that an elephant's albino traits can be determined. Historically in Southeast Asia, the number of white elephants a king owned was seen as a direct reflection of his wealth and power. But these rare animals had to be fed rare foods and housed in special quarters. If the king disliked a courtier for some reason, he might give him a white elephant. The courtier would go bankrupt trying to maintain it. Hence, the term "white ele-phant" denotes a gift that is less desirable than it seems.

it contains 300 animal species and a lake, with pedaloes for hire. Most of the animals are located around the park's edges, and include deer, gibbons, bears, hippos, lions, tigers and birds. The zoo is a favourite place for locals to hang out away from the heat and fumes of the city.

Chitralada Palace

Next to Dusit Zoo, a thick tree-shaded fence and moat protects the grounds of **Chitralada Palace**, the current king's permanent home. It was built in 1913 as a place where King Vajiravudh (Rama VI) found creative solitude away from court life at the Grand Palace. It is not open to the public, but keen observers might spot agricultural equipment along the fence perimeter, where King Bhumibol himself once conducted experiments in agricultural sustainability for the benefit of his people.

Opposite the palace on Thanon Sri Ayutthaya is the **Royal Turf Club** horseracing track. Races are held here every other week.

Wat Benjamabophit ❼

Address: 69 Thanon Rama V
Tel: 0-2282 7413

Opening Hrs: daily 8.30am–4.30pm
Entrance Fee: charge (free with Grand Palace entrance ticket)
Transport: buses 3, 72

Further west, on the corner of Thanon Rama V, the Marble Temple was the last major temple built in central Bangkok and the best example of modern Thai religious architecture. Started by King Chulalongkorn at the turn of the 20th century, the *wat* was designed by the king's half-brother Prince Naris and Italian architect Hercules Manfredi, and completed in 1911. They incorporated Western elements to dramatic effect, most notably in the walls of Carrara marble from Italy, the cruciform shape and the unique European-crafted stained-glass windows depicting Thai mythological scenes. The *bot*'s principal Buddha image is a replica of the famous Phra Buddha Chinarat of Phitsanulok, whose base contains the ashes of Chulalongkorn.

A gallery behind the *bot* holds 53 original and copied significant Buddha images from all over Asia. Early in the morning merit-makers gather in front of the temple gates to donate food and offerings to monks, who line up here for alms.

Ayutthayan-style Buddha image in the abhaya mudra (reassurance) posture at a gallery in Wat Benjamabophit.

Wat Benjamabophit, the Marble Temple.

CHINATOWN

One of the oldest areas of the city, Bangkok's Chinatown retains narrow lanes of cluttered markets not much changed since its creation. Pungent food stalls, ornate Chinese shrines: loud, boisterous and frenzied, this is Bangkok at its visceral best.

Bangkok's early Chinese inhabitants were brought to Thailand by King Taksin – himself half-Chinese – as labourers to work on his new capital at Thonburi across the river. They lived in what is now Rattanakosin, but were relocated further south by King Rama I when he built the Grand Palace in 1782. The migrants – who arrived, according to an old Chinese saying "with a mat and a pot" – settled on a riverside dirt track called Sampeng Lane. Chinatown was born.

In 1863, after King Mongkut built Bangkok's first paved street, Thanon Charoen Krung (New Road), Chinatown began mushrooming northwards. Later, a third artery, Thanon Yaowarat, appeared between Charoen Krung and Sampeng roads. It became Chinatown's main thoroughfare and the Thai name of the area. Plots of land here were also given to the Indian and Muslim communities.

The Chinese play an important role in Thailand's corridors of power, a position that matured during the Ayutthaya period, when merchants acquired powerful business positions and gained court influence through their daughters becoming royal concubines. In the Rattanakosin period Chinese businessmen gained concessions as tax collectors, and later used the riches they amassed to buy into rice mills, taking advantage of Thailand's greatest export. Modern examples of powerful Chinese include Thaksin Shinawatra, the ex-prime minister and formally Thailand's richest man, Chin Sophonpanich, a one-time labourer who went on to found Bangkok Bank, and Central Group, the country's largest retail chain, which started as a Chinatown magazine stall in the 1920s.

Main Attractions
Sampeng Lane
Wat Chakrawat
Pahurat Market
Wat Mangkon Kamalawat
Soi Itsaranuphap
Talad Kao
Wat Traimit

Map
Page 148

Talad Kao market.

The golden-domed Sri Guru Singh Sabha temple is where Bangkok's Sikh community congregates.

Chinatown's narrow roads and lanes teem with traffic. Luckily it is relatively easy to explore on foot, which allows you to soak up the atmosphere. Away from downtown's plush megamalls, Chinatown is a raw experience of Bangkok past and present: old shophouses, *godowns* (warehouses), temples and shrines, all swelling with activity.

Sampeng Lane ❶

The early Chinese immigrants toiled as labourers, rickshaw runners and dock workers at a time when the river was filled with wooden shops and houses floating on bamboo platforms. They ran two and three lines deep amid a clutter of trading vessels and cross river traffic. Trade with China was at the time Thailand's greatest revenue earner, and goods going both in and out of the country passed through **Sampeng Lane** (Soi Wanit 1). The little dirt lane was rich pickings for anyone with an entrepreneurial spirit, and there were plenty of those arriving by the boatload from southern China. Sampeng Lane was the trading ground for landlubbers, and though today many of the wares will be new, many haven't changed, and neither has the sense of chaos.

By 1900, Sampeng had a reputation as Sin Alley, with opium dens, gambling houses and buildings marked by *khom khiew* (green lanterns). A green-light district was like a Western red-light district, and while the lanterns have disappeared, the term *khom khiew* still signifies a brothel today.

Dodging scooters laden with crates here, you will pass dresses, bags, footwear, toys, party decorations, Thai flags, Chinese dice and scroll paintings, sparkling acrylic bracelets and stones for making your own jewellery. Most of it is available wholesale as well as retail. At the junction of Soi Mangkon (also called Sanjao Mai), on the right is the handsome facade of **Tang Toh Kang**, the oldest goldsmith in Bangkok. It originally opened

Chinatown

Main entrance to Wat Chakrawat.

around 1880, further down Soi Mangkon, and moved to these premises 100 years ago. It has a museum upstairs with gold items and examples of early crafting tools.

Wat Chakrawat ❷

Towards the western end of Sampeng Lane, cross Thanon Chakrawat and turn left to get to **Wat Chakrawat** (daily 8am–4.30pm; free). The temple comprises an odd amalgam of buildings. Dating from the Ayutthaya period, it has a small artificial hill topped by a *mondop* (square-based structure usually topped with a spire) and a small grotto with a statue of a fat, laughing monk. According to legend, the statue was built to honour a devout but very handsome monk who was constantly pestered by women while deep in meditation. His devotion to Buddhism led him to gorge himself to obesity and the women soon lost interest. Also in the grotto is a curious black silhouette on the wall. Adorned with gold leaf, it is supposed to be Buddha's shadow.

Temples will often adopt stranded or unwanted animals, and this *wat* has a star attraction. In the mid-20th

century the monks took in a crocodile nicknamed "One-Eyed Guy" that had been hunted down after terrorising bathers in the surrounding canals. He eventually died, but is preserved in a glass case above a small pond that is home to younger crocs.

Pahurat Market and Sri Guru Singh Sabha

West of Sampeng Lane is Bangkok's Little India at **Pahurat Market** ❸ (daily 9am–6pm), a two-level bazaar of tiny pathways, where Bangkok's main community from the subcontinent converged in the late 19th century. It is filled with Hindus and Sikhs selling all manner of fabrics, saris, Hindu deities and wedding regalia, together with traditional Thai dance costumes and accessories.

Off Thanon Pahurat and Thanon Chakraphet are cheap curry eateries such as the famous **Royal India** (tel: 0-2221 6565; daily 10am–10pm), as well as Indian tea and spice stalls, and confectionery shops.

Close to Pahurat Market, on Thanon Chakraphet, the four-storey, golden-domed Sikh temple of **Sri Guru Singh Sabha** ❹ is a focal

Entrance detail from the Sala Chalerm Krung Theatre.

point for the surrounding Indian–Thai community (daily 8am–5pm; free). It is said to be the second-largest Sikh temple outside India. The main shrine, draped with curtains and garlands of yellow flowers, is found on the top floor in a large open hall covered with rugs. Headscarves must be worn in the temple.

Sala Chalerm Krung Theatre ❺

North of Pahurat Market, at the corner of Thanon Charoen Krung and Thanon Tri Phet, stands **Sala Chalerm Krung Theatre** (box office: tel:

Thanon Yaowarat.

0-2224-4499). The theatre was opened as a gift to the Siamese people from King Rama VII in 1933 to mark the city's 150th anniversary. With its distinct Western Art Deco facade and Thai-style interior, it was once hailed as the biggest and grandest theatre in Asia. Sala Chalerm Krung was also the first Thai movie theatre to screen "talkies". In 1941, because of the scarcity of celluloid during World War II, the theatre was converted into a performance venue for traditional Thai *khon* (drama). Today, the renovated theatre hosts special film screenings, one-off concerts and traditional Thai dance-drama shows every weekend.

Old Siam Plaza

In the same vicinity is the three-floor **Old Siam Plaza** (daily 10am–9pm). Established in 1993 to replace the decaying Ming Muang Market, it is a faux-nostalgic shopping arcade with vendors dressed in traditional garb and wooden carts displaying a variety of handicrafts, including jewellery, silks, *khon* masks and traditional musical instruments. The architecture takes its cue from nearby Rattanakosin rather than Chinatown. It is a sanitised alternative to the market lanes of Chinatown and Pahurat. The ground floor has stalls with delicious traditional glazed fruits and sweets worth sampling.

Thanon Yaowarat and Nakhon Kasem ❻

Parallel to Sampeng Lane is Thanon Yaowarat, where the forest of neon signs makes it look in places much like a Hong Kong street. It is best known for its gold dealers, their shops painted gold and red for good luck, with daily prices scrawled on the windows. The gold is weighed in baht, an ancient unit separate from the Thai currency that is equal to 15 grams (about half an ounce).

At the western end, between Thanon Yaowarat and Thanon Charoen

Krung, and on the corner of Thanon Chakrawat, is **Nakhon Kasem** or Thieves' Market (daily 8am–8pm). A few decades ago, this was a black market for stolen goods. It later developed into an antiques dealers' area, but today you are more likely to find items of a less glamorous description, such as run-of-the-mill household appliances. Nevertheless, it is still possible to find a few shops selling old grandfather clocks, musical instruments and Buddha images.

Wat Mangkon Kamalawat ❼

Address: Thanon Charoen Krung
Tel: 0-2222 3975
Opening Hrs: daily 9am–6pm
Entrance Fee: free
Transport: buses 4, 73

Near Soi Itsaranuphap is the imposing gateway of **Wat Mangkon Kamalawat**, also known as **Leng Noi Yee** (Dragon Flower Temple). The most revered temple in Chinatown, it is a constant swirl of activity and incense smoke from early morning onwards. As with the whole of this district, the temple is overrun at Chinese New Year.

The temple, built in 1871, is one of the most important centres for Mahayana Buddhism (most Thais practice Theravada Buddhism) in all of Thailand. Elements of Taoism and Confucianism are also prevalent. The dragon-crowned roof overlooks a courtyard containing several structures that house altars and images of gilded Buddhas, the Four Heavenly Kings and other Taoist deities.

Soi Itsaranuphap ❽

The most interesting lane in Chinatown is **Soi Itsaranuphap** (Soi 16), which runs south from Thanon Phlab Phla Chai and passes a 19th-century Thai temple called **Wat Kanikaphon**, better known as Wat Mae Yai Fang, after the brothel madam who built it to atone for her sins (daily 6am–4pm; free).

Around the northern entrance to Soi Itsaranuphap are shops selling items made of folded paper that are burnt at the temple in *kong tek* ceremonies. They are offerings thought to provide comfort to deceased relatives, and include hell money, houses, Mercedes cars, mobile phones and furniture. Other shops sell red-and-gold-trimmed shrines for ancestor spirit worship in the home.

Talad Kao and Talad Mai

Soi Itsaranuphap has two of the city's best-known markets. Closer to the corner with Sampeng Lane is the two-century old **Talad Kao** ❾ (Old Market), while a little off Soi Itsaranuphap (closer to Thanon Charoen Krung) is the newer **Talad Mai** (New Market), which has been plying its wares for merely a century. The old market wraps up by late morning, while the newer one keeps trading until sundown. These fresh markets have a reputation for high-quality meat, fish and vegetables, and overflow during Chinese New Year. The raw and dried fish, pungent spices and boiling stoves here can overwhelm the senses.

Bundles of "hell money" found at shops along Soi Itsaranuphap are legal tender only in the afterlife.

The main altar inside Wat Mangkon Kamalawat.

FACT

The Poh Teck Tung Foundation just off Thanon Phlab Phla Chai is a Sino-Thai charity whose workers respond to road accidents, picking up dead bodies and arranging funeral rites if no one claims them.

Wat Pathuma Kongkha

Moving east along Sampeng Lane there are shops with Muslim names and merchants trading gems, and right at the end is **Wat Pathuma Kongkha** ⑩, also called **Wat Sampeng** (daily 8am–5pm; free). One of Bangkok's oldest temples, it dates to the Ayutthayan period, and was where criminals of noble birth were executed for crimes against the state.

Wat Traimit ⑪

Address: 661 Thanon Charoen Krung
Tel: 0-2225 9775
Opening Hrs: daily 8am–5pm
Entrance Fee: charge
Transport: (MRT) Hualamphong

Just east of where Thanon Yaowarat meets Thanon Charoen Krung, close to the Chinatown Gate at Odeon Circle, is **Wat Traimit**. The *wat* itself would be unremarkable except that it is the site of the world's largest solid gold Buddha and is consequently known also as The Temple of the **Golden Buddha**. On the left of the temple is a huge, 600-million-baht marble *mondop*, newly built to hold the 5.5-ton, 3-metre (10ft) Sukhothai-era statue. Believed to date from the reign of King Ramkhamhaeng the Great (*c.*1279–98), the Golden Buddha was probably first moved from Sukhothai to Ayutthaya, but by

Morning scene at Talad Kao.

The solid gold Buddha image at Wat Traimit was found purely by accident.

the time it reached Bangkok it had been covered in stucco, presumably to disguise its worth from Burmese invaders. Its true nature was only revealed in 1955, when an accident while moving it caused the surface to crack off.

The *mondop* is also the location of the **Yaowarat Chinatown Heritage Centre** (daily 8am–4.30pm; charge). The museum layout is preceded by a 3-D hologram show of a grandfather and his grandson discussing the past, which is only interesting for the comically "proper" English translation. The museum itself tells the story of Chinatown's beginnings through old photos, prints of period paintings and tableaux of various life situations, such as the interior of a junk and shops from old Sampeng Lane. The exhibits are well annotated, and it makes an interesting sideshow to the Golden Buddha.

Hualamphong Station

East of Wat Traimit is the city's main railway terminus, **Hualamphong Railway Station**, a fine example of Thai Art Deco style. King Chulalongkorn (Rama V) initiated Thailand's first rail line from here in 1891, carrying passengers the relatively short distance to Paknam. The Italian-designed structure was erected sometime between 1910 and 1916. A renovation in the late 1990s made the station far more comfortable. The MRT metro line terminates here.

The bright neon signs of Chinatown.

Jim Thompson's House, viewed from
the lush gardens.

PATHUMWAN AND PRATUNAM

Fashionable malls make this a great place to shop, but there's plenty to do if your bags are full, including traditional culture at Jim Thompson's House, a fun oceanarium, a puppet theatre and Bangkok's biggest art space.

The commercial heart of downtown Bangkok, **Pathumwan** is a string of shopping malls, all connected by the Skytrain. It's mainly a consumer's paradise, yet there are still plenty of sights more reminiscent of an older and more traditional Bangkok. The man-made canal **Khlong Saen Saep**, cleaved in the early 19th century, enabled the capital to spread east to **Pratunam** and beyond.

PATHUMWAN

Jim Thompson's House Museum ❶

Address: 6 Soi Kasem San 2, Thanon Rama I, www.jimthompsonhouse.com
Tel: 0-2216 7368
Opening Hrs: daily 9am–6pm (last tour 5pm)
Entrance Fee: charge (includes compulsory tour of the museum)
Transport: (BTS) National Stadium

Just a short walk from the National Stadium Skytrain station is one of the finest traditional houses in the city, the **Jim Thompson's House Museum**. Jim Thompson (see page 164) was the American silk entrepreneur responsible for the revival of Thai silk. An architect by training, Thompson arrived in Thailand at the end of World War II, serving as a military officer. After the war he returned to Bangkok, where he became interested in the almost redundant craft of silk weaving and design.

Thompson mysteriously disappeared in the jungles of Malaysia's Cameron Highlands in 1967 but his well-preserved house still stands today near the banks of Khlong Saen Saep. Thompson was an enthusiastic collector of Asian arts and antiquities, many of which adorn his traditional house-turned-museum. The surrounding

Main Attractions
Jim Thompson's House Museum
Bangkok Art and Culture Centre
Siam Square
MBK
Siam Paragon
Erawan Shrine
Snake Farm
Lumphini Park
Suan Pakkad Palace

Map
Page 156

Bustling shoppers at Mahboonkrong shopping centre.

Window displays at Siam Square mainly target the young.

garden is a luxuriant mini tropical jungle and an attraction in itself.

The museum comprises six teak structures, which were transported from Ayutthaya and elsewhere to the silk weaving enclave of Ban Khrua, just across Khlong Saen Saep, before being reassembled at its current spot in 1959. From the windows of the house, it's easy to imagine how scenic the view would have been some 50 years ago, looking across the lush gardens, or "jungle" as Thompson called it, to the canal and its daily life.

Next to the old house is a wooden annexe, housing a pond-side café

with an elegant upstairs bar and restaurant, while opposite is the **Jim Thompson Art Centre**, a contemporary gallery that holds regular exhibitions of local and international art and crafts. Before leaving, be sure to stop by and pick up some silk accessories from the museum gift shop.

Bangkok Art and Culture Centre

Leaving Soi Kasem San 2 and turning left on Thanon Rama I brings you to the **Bangkok Art and Culture Centre** (tel: 0-2214 6630-8; www.bacc. or.th; Tue–Sun 10am–9pm; free).

This 11-storey space stages some of Bangkok's best art and multimedia shows, featuring both local and international artists. The retail outlets on its lower floors have imaginatively been issued to small independent galleries or organisations such as the Thai Film Foundation and Bangkok Opera. Art markets feature regularly on the concourse, and performances in a small auditorium on the ground floor.

Siam Square ❷

Diagonally across the main junction of Thanons Rama I and Phaya Thai is a grid of *sois* called **Siam Square**. The land is owned by Thailand's most prestigious educational institution, Chulalongkorn University, located on the southern edge of the square. Hence, it's packed with students and has a strong youth culture, including its own radio station with blaring street speakers that drown out the noise of the traffic. For many years it's been a hotbed of tyro fashion designers who pop out imaginative threads in boutique shops with eccentric names like It's Happened to Be a Closet. Continual rent hikes by the university and the increasing presence

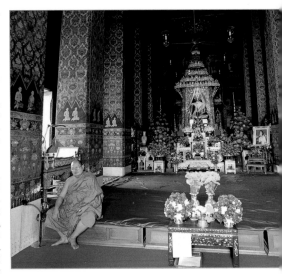

Monk at the main altar of Wat Pathumwanaram.

SILK THREADS

Jim Thompson constructed his house opposite the canal-side Muslim village of Ban Khrua, where the population of specialist weavers were the descendants of 19th-century Cambodian immigrants. There are just two workshops still active, which you can visit by turning left from the Jim Thompson House, then left again along the canal. After 150 metres/yds, take the bridge over the water and walk on for 50 metres/yds to a small lane on the right. Twenty metres/yds along here, a handful of women at looms keep alive a traditional craft that once captivated the world. In the second shop, you may be lucky to catch owner Niphon Manuthas, who as a young boy knew Jim Thompson himself.

of large malls, however, may signal the gradual demise of this creative zone.

Malls along Thanon Rama I

Cross the footbridge over Thanon Phaya Thai from Siam Square and into **Mahboonkrong** (**MBK**) shopping centre. This huge, old-school Thai mall retains a market place ambience, with stalls scattered around the floor space selling goods including cosmetics, cameras, phones, clothes and jewellery. Art lovers head for the ground floor, where teams of painters copy masters from Titian to Klimt.

Leave MBK on the overhead skywalk to the interconnecting malls of **Siam Discovery Centre** and **Siam Centre** on Thanon Rama I. The former, strong on home accessories, also includes Bangkok's own Madame Tussaud's waxworks museum. Siam Centre attracts teens, with local designer, sports and surf clothing.

Siam Paragon

Across the concourse east of Siam Centre is the swanky **Siam Paragon**, full of chi-chi designer labels from Apple to Ferrari, plus restaurants

SHOP

The main shopping areas in downtown Bangkok are linked by the Skywalk – a covered elevated walkway beneath the Skytrain tracks connecting Chidlom, Siam and National Stadium Skytrain stations along Thanon Rama I. This means you can walk from one mall to another under shade and without having to cross the streets.

and an impressive aquarium called **Siam Ocean World** (tel: 0-2687 2000; www.siamoceanworld.com; daily 9am–10pm; charge), filled with over 30,000 marine creatures. Visitors here can ride in a glass-bottomed boat and dive with the sharks.

Wat Pathumwanaram ❸

Hidden to the rear of Siam Centre is **Srapathum Palace**, which is the home of Princess Sirindhorn, and closed to the public. The grounds include **Wat Pathumwanaram** (daily 8.30am–6pm; free), where the ashes of the late king's parents are laid.

Central World

Next door is **Central World**, which at 550,000 sq metres (5.9 million sq ft) is Bangkok's largest mall. It includes the department store **Isetan**, along with a staggering array of shops, restaurants and two enormous cineplexes, **Major Cineplex** and **SF World Cinema**. The adjoining **Centara Grand Hotel** has an open-air restaurant, Red Sky, on the roof. Another department store here, **Zen**, was burnt to the ground during the 2010 Red Shirt protests, but has been rebuilt since.

In 2006, the shrine was destroyed by a mentally disturbed man, but was restored less than three months later.

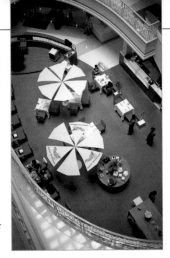

Gaysorn Plaza lobby.

Erawan Shrine ❹

Address: 494 Thanon Ratchadamri
Opening Hrs: daily 6am–6pm
Entrance Fee: free
Transport: (BTS) Chit Lom

After the chaotic junction with Thanon Ratchadamri, Thanon Rama I changes its name to Thanon Ploenchit. At the southeast corner of this junction an aromatic haze of incense hits you before you actually see the **Erawan Shrine**. This, the busiest of all Bangkok shrines, is dedicated to the four-headed Hindu god of creation, Brahma. It was erected in 1956 after an astrologer advised it would ward off bad luck plaguing construction of the Erawan hotel, after which it is named. Because the misfortune subsequently ceased, people believe the shrine has great powers. The hotel has since been replaced by the Grand Hyatt Erawan. Supplicants line up to buy garlands, joss sticks and other gifts as offerings in return for good fortune. Those whose wishes are granted might give thanks by paying the on-site dance troupe to perform. The flower vendors and dancers leave the site at around 6pm, so even though the shrine stays open till 11pm it is best to visit before 6pm to get the full experience.

The site is so revered that when a mentally disturbed man smashed the shrine with a hammer in 2006, he was beaten to death by an angry mob. Photographs of the shrine were displayed so that people could continue to worship until a new one was erected two months later. One thousand people attended the unveiling. Underlining the influence of supernatural belief in Thailand, an opposition leader accused supporters of then Prime Minister Thaksin Shinawatra of being responsible for the destruction, saying they wanted to maintain power over the country through black magic. Adding to the shrine's troubled history, it was the scene of a 2015 bombing which took the lives of 20 people and injuring another 125. The motives behind the attack have never been fully revealed, but the shrine itself remains popular amongst locals and foreign tourists.

Wooden elephants – which represent Brahma's elephant mount, Erawan – sold outside the Erawan Shrine.

Thanon Ploenchit malls

Behind the Erawan Shrine, along Thanon Ploenchit, the boutique mall **Erawan Bangkok** is connected to the Grand Hyatt Erawan hotel and offers a wellness and beauty centre alongside its fashion outlets. Across the street, **Gaysorn Plaza** is an expensive designer mall with tasteful arts and home decor stores and local designers like Stretsis and Fly Now.

North along Thanon Ratchadamri, **Narayana Phand** is a three-floor emporium of Thai arts and crafts, from classical musical instruments and ornate ceremonial headgear to paintings and silk purses.

Chulalongkorn University ❺

South of Siam Square along both sides of Thanon Phaya Thai are the verdant grounds of **Chulalongkorn University**, the country's oldest and most prestigious institution of higher learning. Named in honour of King

Siam Square.

Chulalongkorn (Rama V), it combines Thai and Western architectural styles, and is located on two blocks of the city's most coveted real estate. The university holds regular campus events.

The campus grounds on the same side as MBK host two contemporary galleries. The **Jamjuree Gallery** (tel: 0-2218 3709; Mon–Fri 10–7pm, Sat 12–6pm; free) displays student shows as well as more experimental exhibits by rising artists, whereas the **Art Centre** (tel: 0-2218 2964; Mon–Fri 8am–7pm, Sat 9am–4pm; free), at the Centre of Academic Resources, holds exhibitions by Thailand's internationally recognised artists. The university's **Museum of Imaging Technology** by the lakeside may be of interest to photo buffs; it documents the development of photography in Thailand (tel: 0-2218 5581; Mon–Fri 9am–3pm; charge).

A young volunteer at the Snake Farm gingerly handles a python as he poses for a photograph.

Royal Bangkok Sports Club

East of Chulalongkorn University along Thanon Henri Dunant is the members-only **Royal Bangkok Sports Club** (tel: 0-2255 1420 for race info). Dating from the early 1900s,

Bookstore in Siam Paragon.

the horse-racing club quickly became the favourite recreational spot for the city's upper class. The grounds also served as Bangkok's only airfield before Bangkok International Airport was eventually built. Nonmembers are only allowed through the gates on alternate Sundays for the races, which attract large crowds of feverish gamblers.

Snake Farm ❻

Address: 1871 Thanon Rama IV
Tel: 02-252 0161-4
Opening Hrs: Mon–Fri 8.30am–4.30pm, Sat–Sun 8.30am–noon
Entrance Fee: charge
Transport: (MRT) Silom or Sam Yan

Travellers to the tropics often worry about encounters with dangerous beasts, and a visit to the **Queen Saovabha Memorial Institute**, popularly called the **Snake Farm**, will either enforce or allay such fears. Located south of Chulalongkorn University, it was founded in 1923 as the Pasteur Institute. Now operated by the Thai Red Cross, the institute's principal work lies in the research and treatment of snakebites and the extraction of antivenins. Venom-milking sessions

(Mon–Fri 11am and 2.30pm, Sat–Sun 11am; slide show 30 mins before) are the best times to visit, when various snakes are pulled from the pit and generally goaded for a squealing audience.

Of Thailand's six species of venomous snake, the King Cobra is the largest and most common. A single yield of venom from the King Cobra is deadly enough to send some 50,000 mice to an early grave. Fortunately the King Cobra's basic diet is other snakes. Willing spectators can drape a snake around their necks for a one-of-a-kind photo memento.

Lumphini Park ❼

Green spots are few and far between in Bangkok, but in the heart of Downtown at the intersection of Thanon Rama IV and Thanon Ratchadamri is **Lumphini Park**, Bangkok's biggest outdoor retreat (daily 4.30am–9pm; free). Named after Buddha's birthplace in Nepal, the park was given to the public in 1925 by King Vajiravudh (Rama VI), whose memorial statue stands in front of the main gates.

It has lakes (with pedal boats for hire) and a Chinese-style clock tower.

Lumphini Park.

At sunrise or sunset you see *tai chi* practitioners, joggers, aerobic sessions, bodybuilders lifting weights at the open-air gym and youngsters kicking rattan balls in the sport of *takraw*.

PRATUNAM

North of Pathumwan, as you turn the corner left into Thanon Petchaburi, there are lots of cheap women's fashion items in the five-storey **Platinum Mall**, and in the narrow lanes on the other side of Phetchaburi is **Pratunam Market ❽** (daily 9am–midnight). This bustling warren of stalls is more a lure for residents than tourists, but it

Lumphini Park pedalo fun.

Baiyoke II Tower.

has cheap piles of clothing, fabrics and shoes, and the abundance of African export traders makes for some interesting cafés.

The area is shadowed by Thailand's tallest building, **Baiyoke II Tower**, whose 84th-floor observation deck (daily 10am–10pm; charge) offers eye-popping views of the city and beyond.

If you're hungering for a byte, 200 metres/yds west on the other side of Thanon Petchaburi is **Panthip Plaza**, Bangkok's most famous mall devoted to IT. Frequented by more than just tech-heads, the competitively priced stores stretch over six floors, selling all manner of electronic devices, hard and software and entertainment discs (both genuine and counterfeit).

Suan Pakkad Palace ❾

Address: Thanon Sri Ayutthaya; www.suanpakkad.com
Tel: 0-2245 4934
Opening Hrs: daily 9am–4pm
Entrance Fee: charge, includes guided tour
Transport: (BTS) Phaya Thai

Most tourists make a beeline for Jim Thompson's House, missing out on the equally delightful **Suan Pakkad**

Suan Pakkad Palace.

Palace. Located a short walk along Thanon Sri Ayutthaya from Phaya Thai Skytrain station, the quirkily named Suan Pakkad, or "Cabbage Patch", refers to its previous use as farmland before the palace was constructed in 1952. The former residence of the late Prince and Princess Chumbhot, who were prolific art collectors and gardeners, Suan Pakkad comprises five teak houses sitting amid a lush garden and lotus pond.

Converted into a museum, the wooden houses display an eclectic collection of antiques and artefacts, including Buddha images, Khmer statues, paintings, porcelain, musical instruments and ancient pottery from Ban Chiang. At the rear of the garden stands the mid-17th-century **Lacquer Pavilion**, which Prince Chumbhot discovered in a temple near Ayutthaya and carefully restored as a birthday present for his wife. The pavilion's black and gold leaf panels, considered masterpieces, depict scenes from the life of the Buddha, the *Ramakien* and the lifestyle of the period.

On the same grounds is the **Khon Museum**, a small but interesting exposé on the classic Thai dramatic art form of *khon*.

JIM THOMPSON'S THAI HOUSE

In a city increasingly dominated by Western architecture, this fine museum offers a glimpse of Thailand's rich cultural heritage.

Jim Thompson began his collection shortly after World War II, when Thai antiques were largely under-valued. It includes precious Buddha images, porcelain, traditional paintings, and finely carved furniture and panels collected from old homes and temples throughout Thailand. The traditional Thai houses where his collection is contained are painted with the red-brown hue characteristic of the country. The houses feature dramatic outward-sweeping roofs covered with rare tiles designed and fired in Ayutthaya. Gracefully curving in a *ngo* (peak), they allow the airy rooms to remain open all year long, sheltered from the downpours of the rainy season. The main structure, enveloped by lush tropical greenery, stands elevated a full storey above the ground as protection against flooding. The traditional family lived in several houses around a communal verandah, where they would eat on the floor. This is why people remove shoes before entering.

THE ESSENTIALS

Address: 6 Soi Kasem San 2, Th Rama I, www.jimthompsonhouse.com
Tel: 0-2216 7568
Opening Hrs: daily 9am–6pm (last guided tour 5pm)
Entrance Fee: charge, includes compulsory guided tour
Transport: (BTS) National Stadium

Jim Thompson's House, although not 100 percent authentic in detail, is one of the best examples of a traditional Thai dwelling in Bangkok. Its various elements were brought from around the country and reassembled here.

Traditional houses are built without nails. On marriage, grooms would literally dismantle their bedroom and attach it their bride's family home.

THE KING OF THAI SILK

Jim Thompson.

One Easter day in 1967 Jim Thompson went for a walk in the jungles of the Cameron Highlands in Malaysia and never came back. After years of speculation the mystery of his disappearance is still unsolved. Born in Delaware, USA, in 1906, Thompson worked as an architect before joining the army in 1939. He fought in Europe and Asia during World War II, and when the war ended, he served in Bangkok in the Office of Strategic Service (the forerunner of the CIA). Thompson later returned to Bangkok, where, inspired by swatches of silk he had collected during his trips in Thailand, he decided to track down traditional silk weavers. He found one lone community of Muslim weavers at the canalside Ban Khrua (he eventually built his own house just opposite the canal). Utilising new techniques and dyes that raised the silk's quality, he set up the Thai Silk Company, later exporting his creations around the world. Thompson is one of the most celebrated *farang* (Westerners) in Thailand and his silks remain a treasured part of Thailand's culture.

Jim Thompson inspects a length of Thai silk. On the canal opposite the house there are still a couple of workshops operating today in the original Ban Khrua village where Thompson started his business in the 1950s.

The rooms and verandas in the house are full of antiques, and particularly strong on porcelain and religious art such as these two Buddha statues.

BANGRAK AND SILOM

Bangrak is one of the city's most modern areas, its gleaming glass condos and office blocks a testament to a Bangkok on the move. Yet there are rare glimpses of traditional life, and night-time brings an earthier market trade around "the fleshpots of Patpong".

During the mid-19th-century, Bangkok began to expand on a wave of canal and road construction. Thanon Charoen Krung (New Road), the city's earliest paved thoroughfare, runs parallel to the river, where the earliest communities formed. European traders settled around what is now Bangrak, close to the port entry to the city. Today, the waterside here is dominated by luxury hotels, but the quiet, easily navigable side streets still reveal elements of its history, such as colonial-style buildings that were once home to foreign banks, commercial and diplomatic offices, houses, and the capital's first lodging inns.

Thanon Silom, gravitating eastwards from the Chao Phraya River's premier real estate, is today the principal route that intersects the business district. It ends at Thanon Rama IV, with Lumphini Park beyond. Parallel to Silom are Sathorn, Surawong and Si Phraya roads. These four make up the district of **Bangrak**, with the first two now being full of high-rise glass and steel office blocks, condos and hotels.

But it's not all starchy commerce. After sunset, the upper end of Silom is alive with markets and nightlife, including a thriving gay scene and the infamous (and touristy) girlie bars of Patpong.

Holy Rosary Church ❶

Located behind the River City shopping centre and just off an alley housing a bustling market is the **Holy Rosary Church** or Wat Kalawa (daily 6am–9pm; free). Portuguese Catholics erected the original edifice in 1787 after they moved from the sacked capital of Ayutthaya. After a fire burnt down the wooden church, it was rebuilt around 1890. The neo-Gothic

Main Attractions
Mandarin Oriental Hotel
Assumption Cathedral
State Tower
Maha Uma Devi Temple
Patpong
MR Kukrit Pramoj's
  Heritage Home

Map
Page 169

Thanon Silom flower seller.

The elegant Authors' Lounge at the Oriental.

The Sala Rim Naam restaurant at the Mandarin Oriental Hotel puts on a nightly show of traditional Thai dance-drama accompanied by a Thai set dinner.

sanctuary features some of Thailand's best examples of stained glass.

Continue south past the River City shopping centre, and just next door to the **Royal Orchid Sheraton** hotel is the 1820s **Portuguese Embassy**, the city's oldest. It is best viewed from the riverside.

Mandarin Oriental ②

Further south, the legendary Mandarin Oriental Hotel was founded in the 1870s, and is now consistently rated as one of the world's best. A riverside retreat for the influential and wealthy, the Mandarin Oriental's grandeur has endured despite the boxy exteriors of two newer buildings – the Garden Wing (added 1958) and River Wing (1976) – which detract from the classic look of the original Authors' Wing. To best imbibe the old-world atmosphere, have afternoon tea in the elegant **Authors' Lounge** and muse over the literary greats, such as Somerset Maugham, Noel Coward and Graham Greene, who have passed through its doors. The **Riverside**

Terrace is another charming spot to settle down with a drink.

Assumption Cathedral ③

Address: 23 Charoen Krung Soi 38
Tel: 0-2234 8556
Opening Hrs: daily 6am–9pm
Entrance Fee: free
Transport: Oriental pier

Turn right outside the Oriental Hotel towards the river; a side road on the left leads to a small tree-lined square dominated by the **Assumption Cathedral**. Built in 1910, the red-brick cathedral is surrounded by a Catholic mission. Its rococo interior has stained-glass windows and gilded pillars topped with a domed ceiling. Looming behind it in stark contrast is the unmistakable State Tower.

Oriental Hotel area

Continue to the Tha Oriental ferry point; just to its left is the white-washed and Venetian-inspired **East Asiatic Company ④**. Erected in 1901, it was once the most visible riverside structure in this area; today, it awaits redevelopment. To the left of the Oriental hotel are two early 20th-century buildings, one of which houses the elegant **China House** restaurant (run by the Oriental hotel). A side road to the left leads to the charming **OP Place**. Dating from 1905, this old-world building was one of the city's first department stores. Today, it is mostly filled with shops selling pricey arts and crafts, jewellery and Thai silk. Close by are the home-decor shops of the new **OP Garden** in a beautiful Rama V wooden complex.

Continue past Haroon Mosque to the **French Embassy**, hidden behind high walls and an imposing gate. Then head towards the riverside where the crumbling but wonder-fully atmospheric 19th-century **Old Customs House** stands. It is cur-rently used as a fire station, with the upper floors serving as accommoda-tion for the fire crew's families. Both of these sights are best viewed from the river.

Thanon Silom

Taking its name from irrigation windmills (*si lom*) that used to occupy the area, Thanon Silom and its former parallel canal once transported people and goods from farms and orchards to the river. Today, it is a busy urban commercial district, where shopping and nightlife are the principal attractions. The Skytrain (BTS) and metro (MRT) lines intersect at the top of Thanon Silom (with Thanon Rama IV). The Skytrain's westward line has been extended across the river, and now serves two stations in Thonburi.

Standing tall at the river-end junction of Thanon Silom and Thanon Charoen Krung, the ostentatious, faux-classical **State Tower** ❺ contains the upmarket Lebua hotel and a spectacular 200-metre (656ft) -high drinking and dining complex called **The Dome**. On the 63rd-floor rooftop, **Sirocco**

The imposing gates of the French Embassy. Take a peek from the outside, as entry is forbidden.

(www.lebua.com/sirocco) has some of Bangkok's best panoramas, and claims to be the world's highest outdoor eatery. The Greco-Roman setting – all Doric columns topped by a gold dome – seems incongruous seen from the streets on the edge of Chinatown, but Euro-Asian architecture has a pedigree stretching back over 100 years and is, in fact, very Bangkok.

Heading up Thanon Silom, on the right at corner of Silom Soi 23 is the

Bangrak and Silom

The towering entrance facade of the Maha Uma Devi Temple.

Patpong signs.

three-storey **Bangkok Shell Museum** (daily 10am–9pm; charge), the brain child of a seashell collector who gained small fame as a TV quiz show winner on the subject. It has around 3,000 shells, including a giant clam species that can weigh 200kg (440lbs) and gastropods used as jewellery. Information panels tell how shells were historically used as currency and how some have inspired inventors.

Continuing along Silom, also on the right, at No 919/1, is the soaring **Jewellery Trade Centre**, the heart of Thailand's significant precious-stone market. The connecting **Silom Galleria** houses art galleries and jewellery and antiques shops over several levels.

Further up the road, on the left, is the tourist-oriented **Silom Village**, brimming with shoppers and diners. It has traditional music and dance performed in a couple of its establishments.

Maha Uma Devi Temple ❻

Address: 2 Thanon Pan
Tel: 0-2238 4007
Opening Hrs: daily 6am–8pm
Entrance Fee: free
Transport: (BTS) Chong Nonsi

About a quarter of the way up Thanon Silom on the right, on the corner of Soi Pan, is this vibrantly coloured Hindu temple. Named after Shiva's consort, Uma Devi, **Maha Uma Devi** was established in the 1860s by the Tamil community, whose presence is still strong in the area. Thais know it as Wat Khaek, meaning "guests' temple" (*khaek* is also a less welcoming term used by locals for anyone from the Asian subcontinent).

On holy days, the temple is busy with a lively spectrum of worshippers, including many Indian, Thai and Chinese, who, in addition to the Buddha, find devotional comfort in the images of the Hindu images Vishnu and Uma Devi's son Ganesh. The structure has a prominent 6-metre (20ft) -high facade, adorned with an ornate diorama of religious statuary.

Patpong ❼

Come nightfall, the upper end of Thanon Silom throbs with nightlife,

Patpong in the flesh.

most famously in the go-go bars of **Patpong** (Soi 1 and Soi 2). In the 1960s and 1970s this former banana plantation tempted American GIs from Vietnam, but now, depending on your tolerance levels, there's a surprisingly unsleazy ambience. You still get hustle from touts flashing menu cards with a list of notorious ping-pong acrobatics, but these – along with girls pole-dancing in bikinis – have become prime tourist attractions, enhanced by a busy night market. This type of invitation card has a long history. In 1923, the writer Somerset Maugham recorded a man giving him a card offering the services of "Miss Pretty Girl", who would "put him in dreamland with perfumed soap".

Vendors set up the **night market** in Patpong Soi 1 and Silom Soi 2–8, selling counterfeit watches, fake name-brand bags and clothes, CDs and DVDs, as well as a strong line in binoculars and knives, presumably aimed at wannabe combat heroes.

The adjacent **Patpong 2** is an alley of box-shaped beer and hostess bars that also accommodates the 24-hour supermarket Foodland.

A few lanes east of Patpong, the mainly gay **Silom Soi 4** also attracts straights, mainly for the people-watching opportunities at the outdoor tables. The place becomes a colourful riot of camp and cross-dressing during occasional **soi** parties, such as Gay Pride Week and the Soi 4 Olympics. Nearby **Silom Soi 2** is clubbier and more hard-core gay-oriented. Further towards Thanon Rama IV, the Japanese-friendly **Soi Thaniya** is lined with sushi joints and karaoke bars, where hostesses stand outside greeting tourists with loud choruses of "*Irrashai Mase Dozo!*" (Hello, welcome, please come in). Sometimes on Thaniya, on the left, discreetly placed beyond the entrance to a car park, there's an illicit moonshine stall where you can buy *ya dong* (pickled medicines) and possibly virility drinks such as *phaya chang sarn* (Power of the Great Elephant).

Neilson Hays Library ❽

Address: 195 Thanon Surawong, www.neilsonhayslibrary.com
Tel: 0-2233 1731
Opening Hrs: Tue–Sun 9.30–4pm
Entrance Fee: free
Transport: (BTS) Chong Nonsi

Many of Thanon Silom's even-numbered lanes cut through to parallel **Thanon Surawong**, which

Patpong T-shirt stall.

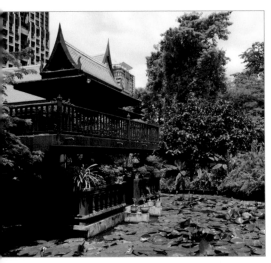

MR Kukrit Pramoj's Heritage Home.

neighbourhood of colonial-style mansions for the city's local and foreign elite. Modern Sathorn evokes little of this historic charm, though the odd period piece still exists – like the stylish **Blue Elephant** Thai restaurant (see margin), which once housed the Thai–Chinese Chamber of Commerce.

Building continues apace, with offices, condos and hotels now lining virtually the whole stretch of Thanon Sathorn, from Thanon Rama IV to the river. Several noteworthy buildings stand out, including the slim **Thai Wah II Tower** with its gaping arch, standing tall between two of the capital's hippest boutique hotels, the **Sukhothai** and **Metropolitan**.

Looking more like a creation of a child's fantasy than a bank headquarters, the **Bank of Asia**, at the corner of Thanon Sathorn and Soi Pikun, was designed by one of the country's foremost modern architects, Dr Sumet Jumsai, and is affectionately dubbed the "robot building".

has seen less of the district's commercial development. Of interest to bookworms is the early 20th-century **Neilson Hays Library**, named after Jennie Neilson Hays, a founder of the Bangkok Ladies Library Association. It is stacked with over 20,000 books, and also exhibits works by contemporary artists in the small **Rotunda Gallery**.

Soi Convent area

Amid the odd numbered **sois** of Silom, and opposite Soi 4, is **Soi Convent**, a busy tree-shaded lane that starts with a barrage of food stalls and continues with several restaurants catering for various tastes – from Irish pub grub to fancy fusion. Just at the corner with Thanon Sathorn is the Anglican **Christ Church** ❾ (daily 8am–5pm; free). Originally built as the English Chapel in the mid-19th-century, the present Gothic-style building was built in 1905.

Thanon Sathorn

Thanon Sathorn grew on either side of a central canal towards the end of the 19th century, and in turn encouraged the growth of an affluent

MR Kukrit Pramoj's Heritage Home ❿

Address: Soi Phra Phinij
Tel: 0-2286 8185
Opening Hrs: Sat–Sun 10am–5pm
Entrance Fee: charge
Transport: (BTS) Chong Nonsi

Tucked away on a lane halfway down Thanon Sathorn is a former residence-turned-museum. Born of royal descent (signified by the title Mom Ratchawong – MR), the late Kukrit Pramoj had a brief stint as prime minister during the disruptive 1970s, but is better remembered as a prolific author and cultural preservationist. This splendid wooden home comprises five stilt buildings that are fine examples of the traditional architecture of the Central Plains. The museum contains antique pottery, memorabilia and photos of the famous statesman, while the ornate garden adds to the sense of serenity.

TIP

If you would like to be a dab hand at Thai cookery, sign up for cookery lessons at the Blue Elephant restaurant. Priced at B5,885 per person, four dishes are taught during the half-day hands-on sessions (tel: 0-2673 9353; www.blue elephant.com/bangkok).

The "robot building".

Benjakitti Park's Lake Ractchada during the Loy Krathong festival.

SUKHUMVIT

The leafy back lanes off Thanon Sukhumvit are flush with condos for expats and the Thai middle class. For food and fun they're spoilt for choice, as the neighbourhood offers the widest range of restaurants and bars in the city.

Bustling, traffic-clogged Thanon Sukhumvit pushes the urban sprawl eastwards, and continues some 400km (250 miles) all the way to Trat, close to the Cambodian border. Once a dirt track surrounded by marshland, the road was built in the 1930s and became Thailand's first proper highway, transporting people beyond the capital. Today it's the efficient Skytrain that provides the fastest means of transport between the upmarket shops, restaurants and entertainment venues that line the Bangkok segment of Thanon Sukhumvit, located mainly around the Nana, Asok, Phrom Phong and Thong Lo stations.

Although thin on key tourist attractions, visitors do come. This is a major residential area, home to many of Bangkok's expanding middle classes and the ever-increasing numbers of European, American and Asian expatriates; plush condo towers line the sometimes quite leafy *sois* that splay either side of the main road, and there are also several top-flight hotels, and seemingly increasing in their number with each passing month. In short, there's a lot of disposable income around, and, consequently, a lot to spend it on. An excellent range of restaurants and

cafés, including Italian, Indian and Middle Eastern, provide early evening fuel stops, and some of Bangkok's best clubs let people party on late into the night.

Sukhumvit's side roads

About 100 metres/yds from the expressway, on the right, is Soi 4, where the raucous go-go bars of the three-storey **Nana Entertainment Plaza ❶** are in full swing every night. Working girls and *katoeys* (ladyboys) solicit customers on the street here, particularly

Main Attractions
Kamthieng House
Benjakitti Park
Thailand Creative and
    Design Centre
Soi Thonglor

Map
Page 176

Outdoor sculpture at Benjakitti Park.

Sukhumvit

after hours, from 1am-ish, and the area is seedier than Patpong, though it is also a good place to try the local delicacy of deep-fried insects from street stalls. There have been recent attempts by authorities to restrict the late-night bars, but with limited success. Opposite is Soi 3, known as "**Soi Arab**" for its lanes of Lebanese cafés and shisha pipes, smoked streetside, like downtown Cairo. Further on Soi 3 is **Bumrungrad Hospital**, the prime beneficiary of Thailand's boom in health tourism. People come here from all over the world for the low-priced, good-quality care in everything from dental work to cosmetics and major surgery. The booming sector has knock-on effects for the country's government hospitals, which are increasingly struggling to find medical staff.

These *sois* mark the beginning of Sukhumvit's profusion of tailors, pool halls, beer bars and hotels. A night market used to crowd the pavements from these early blocks, but the military government enforced a clean-up of the city's streets. The vendors have been moved on, with only a few hardy stall owners daring to ply their trade. However, as with many things in Bangkok and Thailand, the clean-up campaign may only be temporary.

Soi 11 is one of the trendiest streets in Bangkok for eateries and clubs. Current highlights include LEVELS, which markets itself as a lounge bar, but masquerading as more of a late-night dance club, and Sugar Club, which offers the latest hip hop. Both are pick-up spots for all manner of people who like to dance and party until dawn. Close by is **Cheap Charlie's**, a bar that proves Bangkok's variety, with its complete lack of roof or walls (or toilet facilities).

Further along, Soi 21 (Soi Asoke) has another pole-dancing neon strip, **Soi Cowboy**, located on the right, while on the left is the more genteel ambience of the Siam Society.

Siam Society

The headquarters of the **Siam Society** at Sukhumvit Soi 21 (Soi Asoke) is situated in one of Sukhumvit's oldest buildings. It was founded in 1904 to promote the study and preservation of Thai culture (tel: 0-2661 6470-77; www.siam-society.org; Tue–Sat 9am–5pm), and has an excellent library full of rare books on Thai history, plus old manuscripts and maps. For visitors with more than just passing curiosity, look out for the society's regular lectures on regional history and culture. Non-members may attend by paying a nominal fee.

Kamthieng House ❷

Address: 131 Sukhumvit Soi 21, www.siam-society.org
Tel: 0-2661 6470
Opening Hrs: Tue–Sat 9am–5pm
Entrance Fee: charge
Transport: (BTS) Asok, (MRT) Sukhumvit

In the same grounds as the Siam Society is this 150-year-old building, which was a wooden home on the banks of Chiang Mai's Mae Ping river before being transported to Bangkok, carefully reassembled and opened as an ethnological museum. It is reputedly still inhabited by the ghosts of three former residents. Presentations include audio-visual displays on northern folk culture and daily life.

Sukhumvit's parks

Still on Soi Asoke (Soi 21), south of the Sukhumvit intersection is **Queen Sirikit National Convention Centre** (QSNCC), which hosts mainly large-scale business, cultural and entertainment events. The centre looks out over **Benjakitti Park** ❸ (daily 5am–8pm; free), an activity-orientated green space overlooking the artificial **Lake Ratchada**. Part of the park is shaded by trees, including a children's play area, and it's enhanced by large fountains and cascading water displays. In the early morning and evening a crowd of joggers and cyclists circles

TIP

Sukhumvit's odd and even streets *(soi)* are out of synch. For instance Soi 24, beside Emporium mall, is opposite Soi 39, on the other side of the street.

The stylish Indus bar.

Benjasiri Park.

Emporium and Soi Thonglor

On the corner of Soi 24, beside the Phrom Phong Skytrain station, is Sukhumvit's premier shopping mall, **Emporium**, with its six floors of upmarket furniture, clothes and decor shops, bakeries, coffee bars and restaurants. At the top are several cinema screens and the **Thailand Creative and Design Centre**, which is a favourite with art and design enthusiasts for exhibitions ranging from Japanese bamboo crafts to the marketing of Thai street food. There are also occasional film shows in its café.

Soi Thonglor

Further east, just off Thong Lo Skytrain station is **Sukhumvit Soi 55**, or **Soi Thonglor**. Opposite the mouth of the *soi*, Sukhumvit Soi 38 is a great place for street food, as it has lots of different stalls to try, and just down 38 on the left is the classy **Face Bar**. Thonglor itself and the *sois* off it (Thonglor is also the name of the area) have flourished in the last decade and there are now several small enclaves with shopping, clubs, bars and restaurants. It has a boutique, out-of-town-ambience that appeals to both Thais and expats. The clubs and bars are modern and edgy, certainly influenced by the young generation's exposure to international entertainment, but with a stronger local feel than many of their downtown counterparts. Easy Skytrain access means people travel from all over the city to get here. Popular clubs include **Badmotel**, often described as 'crumbling chic' and ultra-hip with Thailand's young high society, and **Demo**, which is a variation on the theme, while shoppers drop by the bijou **H1** mall for coffees and frocks, and the sub *sois* are filling with trendy restaurants, like **Harvey's**, **Red** and **Bo.lan**.

the lake on two designated paths. It's very close to the MRT station and refreshments are available in the QSNCC. The park has recently been expanded, and this addition to Bangkok's greenery has been embraced by Bangkok families who come here to relax and picnic.

Further east, near Soi 24 and Emporium shopping mall, is **Benjasiri Park ❹** (daily 5am–8pm; free). Opened in celebration of the present dowager queen's 60th birthday, the small garden has a large pond, fountains and sculptures by some of the country's most respected artists. There are also basketball courts, a skate park and a swimming pool with Thai pavilions to relax under. The front of the park is often busy with *tai chi* enthusiasts.

BANGKOK'S SUBURBS

Accessible getaways from the big city's relentless pace are sleepy Nonthaburi by the river, delightfully green Rama IX Royal Park, child-friendly Dream World and sprawling Chatuchak Weekend Market – where incurable shopaholics are in seventh heaven.

Main Attractions
Chatuchak Weekend
  Market
Ko Kret
Dream World
Safari World
Prasart Museum

Map
Page 182

There are some surprisingly rural retreats very close to the city centre, where the pace of life is a slow amble. But first there are the strobe lights of Bangkok's biggest dance clubs.

Ratchadaphisek

North along Sukhumvit Soi 21 is Ratchadapisek, an area served by Pra Ram 9 MRT station, and one of the city's designated Nightlife Zones. Most revellers head to the huge clubs of Royal City Avenue (RCA), although a few smaller bars along Thanon Ratchadapisek also draw young Thais. People come here, too, for the cultural shows of **Siam Niramit** (19 Thanon Tiamruammit, Huaykwang; tel: 0-2649 9222; www.siamniramit. com; shows at 8pm; charge) and the **Thailand Cultural Centre**, one of Bangkok's major venues for jazz and classical music concerts.

Chatuchak Weekend Market ❶

Next to Kamphaeng Phet MRT station, and the final stop on the Skytrain's northern line at Mo Chit station, is the sprawling **Chatuchak Weekend Market** (Sat–Sun 7am–6pm). Reputed to be the world's biggest flea market, Chatuchak's sheer scale and variety awes even the least enthusiastic of the estimated 400,000 shoppers that weave through the maze-like alleys every weekend. It's a heady assault on the senses, and an early start (arrive by 9am) is recommended to beat the soaring heat and crowds. Stumbling across gems of kitsch or culture is a great adventure, and you will find anything from crafts, home decor and clothing to flowers, snakes and violins.

Numerous cafés, snack and juice bars are dotted throughout the market

Silk shawls on sale at the Chatuchak Weekend Market.

with many staying busy long after the stalls pack up for the day. After sunset, the edge of the market on Thanon Kamphaengphet comes alive with a string of bars and coffee shops.

If the market overwhelms then retreat to the nearby **Chatuchak Park** (daily 4.30am–9pm; free). Built on land once owned by the State Railway, the park has a small **Hall Of Railway Heritage** museum (Sat–Sun 7am–3pm; free), with displays of old steam locomotives as well as other forms of transport, like London taxis. Alternatively, **Queen Sirikit Park** contains a botanical garden and the **Children's Discovery Museum** (Thanon Kamphaeng Phet 4; tel: 0-2246 6144; charge) with a playground, interactive displays and classes in things like cooking, music and car maintenance.

Nonthaburi ❷

The provincial riverside town of **Nonthaburi**, some 10km (6 miles) north of Bangkok, feels a world away from the hectic city. To get there, take an express boat (around 45 mins) to the end of the line at Tha Nonthaburi pier. The journey passes

Making clay pots in Nonthaburi.

under bridges and weaves past tiny tugboats, gilded temples and communities of stilted houses.

At Nonthaburi, spend some time exploring the streets and markets, or charter a longtail boat to explore the island of Ko Kret (see below) or the scenic canal of Khlong Om. A canal trip along Khlong Om takes you past durian plantations and water-bound communities. Five minutes upriver from Nonthaburi pier brings you to the temple of **Wat Chalerm Phra Kiet**, a beautifully restored 19th-century monastery seemingly set in the middle of nowhere.

Ko Kret ❸

Further upstream from Nonthaburi is the car-free island of **Ko Kret**. Best reached by chartered longtail boat from Nonthaburi to Tha Pa Fai pier on Ko Kret, the island makes for a laid-back half-day tour, allowing tourists to soak up a relaxed pace of life more typical of the rest of Thailand. The island has no roads, and can be walked round in less than two hours. While there are no specific attractions, the island is famous for its earthenware pottery studios. The villagers are

---

MARKET SPREAD

Chatuchak opened in 1982, when the market was moved from Sanam Luang to make room for the Bangkok Bicentennial celebrations, and now its stalls spill onto surrounding streets. On Thanon Pahon Yothin, heading towards Saphan Khwai Skytrain station, traders sell Buddhist amulets; the workshops on the opposite side of Thanon Kamphaengphet 2 have reclaimed teak furniture; and on Thanon Kamphaengphet 1 is Or Tor Kor, possibly Bangkok's best fresh produce market. The streets lining Chatuchak's perimeter fence are busy with stalls selling CDs and DVDs, footwear and clothing. Vendors of food and drink are good places to stock up before you enter the market itself.

TIP

Most people get around Ko Kret either on foot or by bicycle, which are B40-50 a day at various spots en route. In many places, the path is only wide enough for two people abreast, so progress is at a gentle pace. Quicker options are motorbike taxis (there are no cars on the island) or river taxis, which cost about B30 to hop between each pier.

primarily from the ethnic Mon group, a people of Indo-Burmese origin, who migrated to Central Thailand and were a strong regional influence from the 6th to the 11th centuries.

Air Force Museum ❹

Dedicated plane spotters will appreciate the nostalgic **Royal Thai Air Force Museum**, tucked away in several hangars at the Royal Thai Air Force Base behind Bangkok Airport (171 Thanon Phahonyothin; tel: 0-2534 1853; daily 8am–4pm; free).

The rare planes on display include the only Model I Corsaire in existence, one of only two Japanese Tachikawas left, and Thailand's first domestically built aircraft, the 1920s Model II Bomber Boripatr. There are also helicopters and jetfighters on display. The museum is geared more towards organised groups than the occasional wandering tourist, with little English-language signage to guide you around.

Dream World ❺

Those who have visited Disney World or other major US and European theme parks aren't going to be rendered speechless by Bangkok's **Dream World** (Km 7, Thanon Rangsit Nakorn Nayok; tel: 0-2533 1152; www.dream world.co.th; Mon–Fri 10am–5pm, Sat–Sun 10am–7pm; charge).

Nevertheless, the park, located west of Bangkok Airport, is worthwhile if you have a bunch of teenagers with you. The park comprises Dream World Plaza, Dream Garden, Fantasy Land and Adventure Land. A sightseeing train circles Dream Garden, while a cable car and monorail offer nice views of the park and surrounding rural areas.

Thrill seekers should head for Adventure Land, the most stomach-churning section of the park. Along with the two fairly tame rollercoasters, there is a Viking swinging ship, Super Splash log flume and Grand Canyon water ride. In Snow

The main hall at Wat Thammamongkhon.

Bangkok's Suburbs

Town, locals get to experience frosty weather, with sled rides down a slope made of artificial snow.

Safari World ❻

Some 45km (28 miles) northeast of Bangkok near Minburi is **Safari World**, a popular destination for Bangkok families (99 Thanon Ramindra; tel: 0-2914 4100-19; www.safariworld.com; daily 9am–5pm; charge).

The area is laid out as a safari park and a marine park, and you can either drive your car in or take an organised minibus tour with an English-speaking guide. Animals include giraffes, zebras, ostriches, rhinos and camels, while dolphins and sea lions perform acrobatics. Other attractions include water and jungle rides, stunt shows and animal feeding.

Prasart Museum ❼

Little visited, partly because of its rather remote location in Huamak, is the **Prasart Museum** (9 Soi 4A Krungthep Kreetha; tel: 0-2379 3601; visits only by appointment Thur–Sun 10am–3pm; charge). Housed within a garden, the collection of antique Thai arts and crafts on display belong to a private collector, Prasart Vongsakul. The artefacts are contained in several magnificent buildings, all of which are replicas inspired by the region's architectural classics. These elegant structures include a European-style mansion, a Khmer shrine, teak houses from Thailand's North and Central regions, as well as a Thai and a Chinese temple.

Wat Thammamongkhon ❽

At the eastern reaches of Thanon Sukhumvit at Soi 101 is the **Wat Thammamongkhon**, unique for its 95-metre (312ft) -high *chedi*, which at 14 storeys is the tallest in Bangkok and offers commanding views of the low-rise eastern suburbs (daily 6am–6pm; free). Built in 1963, the *chedi* is modern in design, containing study rooms

for novice monks and a lift to the top circular shrine room. At its base is the Will Power Institute, which runs classes in Buddhist meditation. The three-level glass pavilion beside the temple houses a 14-tonne Buddha image and a 10-tonne sculpture of the Chinese goddess Guanyin, both carved from one solid slab of jade.

Rama IX Royal Park ❾

One of the city's largest green spaces, the 81-hectare (200-acre) **Rama IX Royal Park** offers a welcome escape from the city (daily 5.30am–6.30pm; charge). Unfortunately, the park's suburban locale in Sukhumvit 103 means taking a 20-minute taxi ride from the last Skytrain station at On Nut. In a city desperately thin on public greenery, the park's opening in 1987 as a 60th birthday tribute to the king was a welcome addition.

With a dome-covered botanical garden, canals and bridges, and a water lily pond, as well as Chinese and Japanese ornamental gardens, the park is a delight to explore.

An afternoon escapade at the Rama IX Royal Park.

Stacks of crockery in Chatuchak Weekend Market.

The three Khmer-style prang of Prang Sam Yot at Lopburi.

40 miles

40 km

CAMBODIA

BURMA (MYANMAR)

Gulf of Thailand

Bight of Bangkok

Bangkok

Thonburi

Ayuthaya

Kanchanaburi

Ratchaburi

Chonburi

Pattaya

Ko Samet

Ko Chang

Ko Mak, Ko Kut

Tanintharyi (Tenasserim)

Bilauktaung Range

Khao Yai National Park

Kaeng Krachan National Park

BANGKOK'S SURROUNDINGS

When Bangkok becomes overwhelming, an easy three to four hours' drive from the city offers a complete change of scene. Choose from ancient city ruins, sandy beaches dotted with sleepy villages or picturesque national parks and waterfalls.

Bangkok has much to offer, but when you tire of its charms, there is an array of attractions within a few hours' drive, and some, especially beach destinations, can be extended into leisurely week-long stays. Getting around Thailand is relatively easy and cheap. There is a good network of flights to many provincial centres, and a regular, if slow, rail network. Buses are another alternative, although drivers can be reckless. Roads are usually decent, if you want to drive yourself (see page 234 for details on getting there).

Bang Pa-In summer palace.

The nearest and most accessible areas from Bangkok are in the flat, fertile Central Plains, which contain the remnants of former kingdoms and several expansive national parks. To the west are attractions like the Rose Garden cultural shows, the world's largest Buddhist shrine at Nakhon Pathom, and Kanchanaburi, with its legendary Bridge on the River Kwai. The area around Kanchanaburi has river rafting, trekking and waterfalls. South of Bangkok, towards Hua Hin, is where royalty and wealthy Thais have kept holiday homes for over a century.

Fishing boat in Ban Bang Bao, Ko Chang.

The Eastern Seaboard has beach escapades, all the way from scandalous Pattaya, through Ko Samet, to the white sands of Ko Chang. And to the north, the ancient city of Ayutthaya is a grand repository of faded ruins, dating to the 14th century, when it functioned as Thailand's capital. Some say the best part about Ayutthaya is getting there – on a teakwood barge winding up the sinuous Chao Phraya river.

To the northeast of Bangkok, the main attraction is Khao Yai National Park, a favourite spot for Thais seeking picturesque mountains, waterfalls and a break from the city heat.

WEST OF BANGKOK

Home to the world's tallest Buddhist monument, the historic River Kwai Bridge and spectacular waterfalls in rainforest-clad national parks, this region offers attractions for both history and culture enthusiasts as well as nature lovers.

Further afield, in Bangkok's neighbouring provinces are a number of attractions that can be visited on day trips or as pleasant overnight breaks. The western provinces are only a short distance from the capital and share a border with nearby Burma (Myanmar). Most people heading in this direction make a brief stop in Nakhon Pathom province to gawk at the huge *chedi* that dominates the town, before heading to Kanchanaburi province, famous for its so-called "Bridge over the River Kwai" and its tragic wartime associations. However, equally fascinating are the seldom-visited coastal provinces of Samut Sakhon and the lush lowlands of Samut Songkhram.

Trains to Nakhon Pathom and Kanchanaburi leave from Bangkok Noi Railway Station daily. Buses run from Bangkok's southern bus terminal to all destinations in this chapter, and you can hop between them by bus or by hiring taxis or *songthaews*, which will gather at tourist sites and transport terminals. If you plan to make many stops it may be cheaper to hire a car (see page 234).

Rose Garden ❶

Some 32km (20 miles) west from Bangkok on Route 4 towards Nakhon

Pathom is the **Sampran Riverside Resort** (tel: 0-34 322 544; www.sampran riverside.com; daily 8am–6pm; charge). It has well-landscaped gardens with roses and orchids in addition to a resort-style hotel, a cultural centre, restaurants, tennis courts, an artificial lake with paddleboats, a spa and an excellent golf course.

The premier attraction here is the Thai Village Cultural Show held daily in the garden. In a large arena, costumed actors perform folk dances to live traditional music and re-enact

Main Attractions
Rose Garden Riverside Resort
Phra Pathom Chedi
Damnoen Saduak Floating Market
River Kwai Bridge
Prasart Muang Singh
Erawan Falls

Map
Page 186

Bamboo dance demonstration at Rose Garden.

FACT

The Jumbo Queen contest which takes place at Samphran Elephant Ground annually on 1 May seeks a "well-padded" lady who "best exhibits the characteristics of the majestic pachyderm to persuade people to support the cause of elephant conservation in Thailand". Strange but true. More details at www.jumboqueen.com.

a traditional wedding ceremony and a Thai boxing match. Outside, after this, elephants put on their own show, moving huge teak logs as they would in the forests of the north. The elephants then carry tourists around the compound for a small fee. Otherwise, spend time browsing at the Cultural Village, with gift shops and demonstrations by weavers creating thread from silkworm cocoons.

Samphran Elephant Ground and Zoo

Just a stone's throw from the resort is the **Samphran Elephant Ground and Zoo**, another family-oriented attraction that provides a chance to trek on an elephant, feed the crocs and learn about the pachyderm's importance in Thai culture (tel: 0-2284 1873; www.elephantshow.com; daily 8am–5.30pm; charge). Other fauna on view include gibbons, macaques, pythons and a diverse flock of local birds.

At the Crocodile Show, men wrestle with these scaly creatures, while the Elephant Show explains Thailand's historical relationship

The towering Phra Pathom Chedi.

with its national symbol. The war re-enactments are exciting displays, but the elephants' majesty somewhat diminishes when they're made to do silly things, like dance, race and play football in oversized shirts. After the show, you can feed the elephants or go on a 30-minute elephant trek.

Phra Pathom Chedi

Just 56km (35 miles) west of Bangkok, beyond the Rose Garden on Route 4, is the town of **Nakhon Pathom ❷**, known for the colossal **Phra Pathom Chedi** (Thanon Khwa Phra; tel: 0-3424 2143; daily 6am–6pm; charge). Measuring 130 metres (420ft) in height, this golden landmark is claimed as the tallest Buddhist monument in the world, and possibly the oldest Buddhist site in the country.

The original small Sri Lankan-style *chedi* was erected to commemorate the arrival of Indian Buddhist missionaries who supposedly brought Buddhism to Thailand via Burma in 3 BC. The town Nakhon Pathom was settled in the 6th–11th centuries AD by the Dvaravati empire, a Mon civilisation whose culture flourished in Burma and Thailand. In the early 11th century the Khmers invaded

Resident elephant at Samphran Elephant Ground and Zoo.

from Angkor, overrunning the city and replacing the original *chedi* with a Brahman-style *prang*.

Then in 1057, King Anawrahta of Burma besieged the town, leaving the religious edifice in ruins. When King Mongkut (Rama IV) visited the old *chedi* in 1853, he was so impressed by its historical significance that he ordered the restoration of the temple. A new *chedi* was built, covering the older one; the present structure was completed by King Chulalongkorn (Rama V).

Set in a huge square park, the massive *chedi* rests upon a circular terrace and is accented with trees associated with the Buddha's life. Located in the compound is **Phra Pathom Chedi National Museum** (tel: 0-3424 2500; www.finearts.go.th/phrapratomchedi_museum; Wed–Sun 9am–4pm; charge), which is worth seeing for its artefacts, including tools, carvings and statuary from the Dvaravati period.

In former times, a visit to Nakhon Pathom was more than a day's journey, so it's not surprising that a number of palaces and residences were built for visiting royalty. One of them is **Sanam Chan Palace** (www.palaces.thai.net; Thur–Sun 9am–4pm; charge). Located 2km (1 mile) west of Phra Pathom Chedi along Thanon Rajamankha Nai, the palace comprises several buildings, including a Thai-style pavilion that is now used as government offices, and a building in the English Tudor style. The palace was commissioned by King Vajiravudh (Rama VI) in 1907. Be sure to see the **Yaleh Monument**, which honours Yaleh, the pet dog of Vajiravudh. The fierce dog, unpopular with the court, was poisoned by the king's attendants. Even as a statue, Yaleh looks insufferable.

Samut Sakhon ③

A good way to approach the coastal port of **Samut Sakhon** (Ocean City),

28km (17 miles) from Bangkok, is by the Mae Khlong Railway line that connects to Thonburi in Bangkok. The line carries passengers on the 40-minute journey through the capital's suburbs, then through thriving vegetable gardens, groves of coconut and areca palms, and rice fields. A busy fishing port, Samut Sakhon (also called Mahachai) lies at the meeting of the Tachin River, the Mahachai Canal and the Gulf of Thailand. The main landing stage on the riverbank has a clock tower and a seafood restaurant.

At the fish market pier, it's possible to hire a boat for a round-trip to Samut Sakhon's principal temple, **Wat Chong Lom** at the mouth of the Tachin river. Most of the temple structures are modern, except for an old *viharn* (sermon hall) immediately to the right of the temple's river landing. The *viharn* dates back about a century. The extensive grounds overlooking the water are nicely laid out with shrubs and flowering trees. There is also a bronze statue of King Chulalongkorn commemorating his visit to the temple.

Close-up of gold-leaf offerings covering a Buddha image at Phra Pathom Chedi.

Schoolchildren at Phra Pathom Chedi.

Damnoen Saduak Floating Market.

The salt flats of Samut Songkhram.

Samut Songkhram ❹

From Samut Sakhon, cross the river to the railway station on the opposite side. Here, board a second train for another 40-minute trip to the province of **Samut Songkhram**, 74km (46 miles) southwest from Bangkok, on the banks of the Mae Khlong river. The journey goes through broad salt flats, with their picturesque windmills slowly being turned by the sea breezes. Thailand's smallest province, Samut Songkhram has abundant fruit orchards. Pomelo, jackfruit, rose apple, lychee, mango, as well as the more ubiquitous banana and coconuts, are harvested here before being loaded onto the ice-packed vending carts that trundle the streets of Bangkok.

Samut Songkhram itself is just another fishing town; wandering around its wharf is an olfactory and visual experience. Teak barges can be hired for private dinner cruises up the river (ask at riverside restaurants), and the area is known for swarms of fireflies that magically illuminate the shoreline of lamphu trees in the evenings.

King Buddhalertla Naphalai Memorial Park

From Samut Songkhram, you can make a fairly short detour by bus or taxi to the Amphawa District to visit **King Buddhalertla Naphalai Memorial Park**, also known as Rama II Historical Park (park daily 9am–6pm; museum Wed–Sun 9am–4pm; charge), situated at the birthplace of Rama II. This small museum houses displays of art and crafts from the early Rattanakosin period in four beautifully reconstructed teakwood stilted houses, illustrating how Thai people lived during the rule of King Rama II. In the well-maintained gardens around the museum are rare species of trees, some of which are mentioned in classical Thai literature.

Also found in Amphawa is the **Amphawa Floating Market**, which anchors in front of the old Wat Amphawa each Friday, Saturday and Sunday afternoon. About a 10-minute walk from the historical park, the market is smaller and more authentic than Damnoen Saduak.

Don Hoi Lot

Another option, accessible by car or longtail boat from Samut Songkhram, is **Don Hoi Lot**, at the mouth of the Mae Khlong River. Don Hoi Lot is in fact a bank of fossilised shells that has become a popular attraction with locals. It's a great place to enjoy fresh seafood and tube-like clams (*hoi lot* in Thai means straw clams). In the late afternoon when the tide is low, villagers enthusiastically search the muddy estuary for clam burrows. They spread a little bit of lime powder at the entrance of the holes, and when the clams become agitated and come out of the ground, they are eagerly fished out.

Damnoen Saduak Floating Market ❺

From Samut Songkhram, hire a longtail boat for a trip up the Mae Khlong river to **Damnoen Saduak Floating Market** (daily 7am–1pm). An early morning departure is necessary if you want to beat the tour buses from Bangkok, 65km (40 miles) away, that flock to this famous floating market in Ratchaburi province by 10am.

While it is possible to walk along the bankside lined with souvenir stands, it's better to hire a longtail boat to get a better sense of the water-bound commercial bustle. Be prepared though for the worst: this 100-year-old market is little more than a sideshow today, with tourists clambering to snap pictures of the colourful fruit- and vegetable-laden wooden vessels, oared by smiling sun-beaten women wearing wide-brimmed straw hats.

If you've hired your own longtail boat, it might be worthwhile asking the boatman to take you deeper into the canals where you can get a glimpse of the canal communities.

KANCHANABURI

Located around 130km (75 miles) west of Bangkok, the sleepy provincial town of **Kanchanaburi** ❻ is well worth the

two-hour drive it takes to get there. It can be done as a busy day trip but, better yet, plan for a more relaxing overnight, with an evening spent on the banks of the Kwae Yai river.

Kanchanaburi received widespread publicity in the last half-century for its infamous railway, which was built during World War II by Allied POWs and Asian labourers, under the watch of the Japanese occupying army. Thousands of lives were lost as the ill-equipped prisoners struggled in appalling conditions to complete over 400km (249 miles) of railway track, called the "Death Railway", linking Thailand with Burma. Despite its association with the war and the railway, Kanchanaburi remains a laid-back provincial town. Situated close to the Burmese border, it has several interesting temples, as well as nearby caves, waterfalls, forests and the remnants of a 13th-century Khmer palace.

River Kwai Bridge

Spanning the Kwae Yai river (also known as Kwai Yai), the latticed steel **Bridge over the River Kwai** (which takes its name from a movie of the

Selling fresh produce at Damnoen Saduak Floating Market.

The famous bridge spanning the River Kwai.

TIP

Instead of staying at a land-based hotel in Kanchanaburi, opt for a floating guesthouse moored by the riverbank instead. Be warned though: while these are atmospheric, they can also get very noisy during weekends, thanks to discos and karaoke boats packed with drunken young Thais on a night of revelry.

JEATH War Museum.

Only the eight curved sections of the "Bridge over the River Kwai" are original; the rest of it was rebuilt after World War II.

same name) has become a memorial for the fallen. It can be reached by boat or rickshaw from Kanchanaburi town. The bridge has lost some of its significance to tourist commercialisation, but walking across it is a sobering experience. A steam locomotive used shortly after the war is displayed beside the tiny Kanchanaburi station platform, along with an ingenious Japanese supply truck that could run on both road and rail. Floating restaurants and hotels line both banks of the river.

The bridge itself was the second of two bridges, built side by side, crossing the river; the earlier wooden structure was completed in 1942, with the sturdier steel bridge erected by May 1943. Both bridges became a constant target for Allied bombers and were eventually bombed out of action in 1945. Only the eight curved segments on each side of the current structure are original; the rest was rebuilt after the war as part of Japan's war reparations.

The tragic saga of the bridge was represented on celluloid in the 1957 Film *Bridge over the River Kwai*, directed by David Lean and starring Sir Alec Guinness. Winner of seven Academy Awards, this version contains several historic inaccuracies, the most blatant of which was that the bridge

was destroyed by commandos, when in fact it was bombed by allied planes.

Today, most of the old railway tracks have been removed, except for a section that runs from Kanchanaburi west to the terminus at **Nam Tok** near Burma. The 50km (30-mile) journey takes about 90 minutes to complete and the train passes over the reconstructed bridge, the old wooden tracks creaking beneath.

World War II Museum

Located near the bridge is the **World War II Museum** (395–403 River Kwai Road; tel: 034-512 596; daily 7am–6pm; charge), also known as the Art Gallery and War Museum. It contains an odd mixture of exhibits, some of which have nothing to do at all with the war. But if you are into kitsch, there's plenty to interest you. Among life-sized statues of significant war figures like Hitler, Churchill and Hirohito are murals of past winners of the Miss Thailand pageant.

JEATH War Museum

The small but informative **JEATH War Museum** (tel: 034-515 203; daily 8am–6pm; charge), tucked away in the grounds of Wat Chaichumpol on Thanon Pak Phraek in the southern

DEATH RAILWAY

The Japanese began work on a railway between Thailand and Burma in 1942. For most of its 400km (260-mile) length, the railway followed the river valley because this allowed its construction simultaneously in different areas. In the end, nearly 15km (9 miles) of bridges were completed. The Japanese forced some 250,000 Asian labourers and 61,000 Allied POWs to construct 260km (160 miles) of rail on the Thai side, leading to the Three Pagodas Pass on the Thai–Burmese border. An estimated 100,000 Asian labourers and 16,000 Allied POWs lost their lives during 1942–5 from beatings, starvation and disease. It is said that one prisoner died for every sleeper laid.

end of Kanchanaburi town, will give you a better appreciation of the enormous obstacles the prisoners faced. Its peaceful locale on the banks of the Mae Khlong river (the larger river which splits into the two tributaries of Kwae Yai and Kwae Noi), shadowed by a 500-year-old *samrong* tree, provides for a quiet moment of poignant reflection.

The acronym JEATH comes from the first letter of some of the principal countries that were involved in this regional conflict during World War II, namely Japan, England, America, Thailand and Holland. The museum is split into two buildings, the larger of which is a long bamboo hut similar to those that housed the POWs during their construction of the Siam–Burma railway. Inside is a collection of poignant photographs, sketches, paintings, newspaper clippings and other war memorabilia, giving you an idea of the harsh conditions they endured.

Death Railway Museum

Equally fascinating is the **Death Railway Museum** (73 Jaokunnen Road; tel: 034 512 721; www.tbronline.com; daily 9am–5pm; charge) at the

Thailand–Burma Railway Centre, just adjacent to the Allied War Cemetery. The museum has eight galleries that trace the history and recount the sufferings of the people involved, without making biased judgement. It even has a full-scale replica of the original wooden bridge. The museum was founded by Australian Rod Beattie, the local supervisor of the Commonwealth War Graves Commission.

Bomb display at the JEATH War Museum.

Allied War Cemetery

At the **Kanchanaburi Allied War Cemetery** (daily 8am–5pm; free) nearly 7,000 Allied soldiers are buried or commemorated, representing less than half of the 16,000 who lost their lives in the war. Immaculate green lawns planted with colourful flowers add a sense of serenity to the graves of the British, Australian and Dutch soldiers lined row upon row (the US dead were repatriated). Look at the grave markers and you'll notice that most of the young men who died for their countries were under the age of 30. Its location, however, beside noisy

Bomb display and archive photographs at the JEATH War Museum.

Over the years, trees and vegetation have grown and embedded their roots in the ruins of Prasart Muang Singh.

Allied War Cemetery, Kanchanaburi.

Thanon Saengchuto detracts from the solemnity of the place.

Located in a more tranquil setting is the **Chung Kai Allied War Cemetery**, found southwest of Kanchanaburi town across the river (daily 7am–6pm; free). Another 1,750 POWs are buried at this site.

AROUND KANCHANABURI

For those who opt to stay overnight in Kanchanaburi, the surrounding countryside holds plenty of surprises. There are a couple of cave temples found within limestone crags on the southern outskirts of Kanchanaburi, some requiring nimble legwork in order to navigate the claustrophobic passageways that lead to eerily-lit meditation cells filled with Buddha images. While they are generally safe, don't venture into the more remote caves unaccompanied: in 1996 a British female tourist was murdered by a drug-crazed monk at Wat Tham Kao Pun.

One of the frequently visited cave temples is that of **Wat Tham Mangkhon Thong**, primarily known for its "floating nun" (daily 8am–5pm; charge). An old nun, who has since passed away, used to float on her back in a pool of water while in a state of meditation. Today, a young disciple gives her own interpretation of the ritual – in return for a fee – for busloads of gaping Asian tourists.

Prasart Muang Singh 7

Located 43km (27 miles) west of Kanchanaburi, the Khmer ruins of **Prasart Muang Singh** (daily 8am–5pm; charge) are situated in a manicured park. The site makes for a great picnic as it is beside the picturesque Kwae Noi river (a smaller tributary of the Kwae Yai). The central sanctuary of this 13th-century temple complex points east, and is in direct alignment with its more grandiose sister, Angkor Wat in Cambodia. Although nowhere near as impressive or intricate as Angkor Wat, Prasart Muang Singh is still a fascinating testament to just how far west the Khmer empire stretched at the height of its power. On the same site is a small exhibition hall containing duplicates of Khmer sculptures, while near the river is a Neolithic burial site displaying partially uncovered skeletons.

Erawan National Park.

Erawan National Park ⑧

Alternative trips in the vicinity include the spectacular seven-tiered **Erawan Waterfall**, found in **Erawan National Park** (daily 8am–4.30pm; charge). The falls are best visited during and just after the rainy season (May–Nov), when the water is at full flow. Situated some 70km (40 miles) north of Kanchanaburi, Erawan Falls can become quite congested with locals who visit the park at weekends and on public holidays.

The route to the waterfall starts from the national park office. The climb up to level five of the waterfall is manageable; getting up to the slippery sixth and seventh levels is not recommended unless you are fit and have enough derring-do. You can cool off at the inviting natural pools (don't forget your swimsuit) at the base of each of the tiers. The rocks at the highest level are said to resemble the three-headed elephant Erawan, hence its name.

There are several hiking trails in the park, which covers some 550 sq km (212 sq miles) and comprises mainly deciduous forests with limestone hills rising up to 1,000 metres (3,281ft). One of the more popular hiking trails is the 90-minute Khanmak–Mookling trail; the 1,400-metre/yd-long circular trail starts from the national park office. Also taking 90 minutes, the Wangbadan Cave trail takes you through bamboo and evergreen forest along a 1,350-metre/yd-long route.

Sai Yok National Park ⑨

Less visited is **Sai Yok Waterfall** in **Sai Yok National Park** (daily 8am–4.30pm; charge). The waterfall is a little more remote at 100km (62 miles) northwest of Kanchanaburi and best undertaken on an overnight tour. The national park itself covers over 500 sq km (193 sq miles) of mainly teak forests, with one side of it bordering Myanmar (Burma). Apart from the stunning cascade (again best seen in the rainy season, or just after), the park is known as the habitat of the smallest known mammal in the world – Kitti's Hog-Nosed Bat, also known as the Bumblebee Bat. Found in Sai Yok's limestone caves in 1974, the creature, which weighs a mere 2 grams (and hardly larger than a bumblebee), has been declared an endangered species.

More adventurous travellers should enquire in lodges and hotels in these national park areas about organised kayaking, rafting and mountain biking trips.

TIP

There are some 140 gazetted national parks in Thailand, a number of which are easily accessed from Bangkok, like Erawan, Sai Yok, Kaeng Krachan and Khao Sam Roi Yot. For more information on Thai national parks, look up www.thainationalparks.com or www.dnp.go.th/index_eng.asp.

SOUTH OF BANGKOK

A few hours' journey south of the capital brings you to exclusive beach retreats and spa resorts. Meanwhile, large mammals find sanctuary in the mountains and rainforests of Kaeng Krachan, the largest national park in Thailand.

The diverse towns of Cha-am and Hua Hin, south of Bangkok, are popular hangouts for the city's twenty-somethings, for upper class socialites, for expats and holiday-homers in Thailand on spa leave. The trend started with royalty as far back as 1860 when King Mongkut built a summer palace in Phetchaburi. The king also liked to visit the nearby forested areas, now designated national parks. The current royal family has its own summer palace in the region, in Hua Hin.

There are several trains daily from Hualamphong Station to Petchaburi and Hua Hin, and buses from the Southern Bus Terminal to Cha-am, Phetchaburi and Hua Hin.

Phetchaburi ⑩

Historically rich **Phetchaburi**, some 120km (75 miles) south of Bangkok, is one of Thailand's oldest towns and has been an important trade and cultural centre since the 11th century. Lying on the Phetchaburi river, the town has come under the influence of the Mon, Khmers and Thais at various times, and has over 30 temples that reflect the different cultures and architectural styles of its past invaders.

Some of the more important religious sites in Phetchaburi – usually

pronounced "Petburi" – include the laterite Khmer *prang* of **Wat Kamphaeng Laeng**, and **Wat Yai Suwannaram**, thought to have once been a residence of King Suea. It is very evocative of its 17th-century heritage, with many ornately tiled buildings in a low-walled complex. Its fine murals are among the oldest in Thailand, while the stucco work is of a style that predates the symmetric Ayutthayan influences that came to dominate Thai architecture. The old library building on stilts in the

Main Attractions
Wat Yai Suwannaram
Khao Wang
Cha-am
Kaeng Krachan National Park
Hua Hin

Map
Page 186

The distinctive Khmer structures of Wat Kamphaeng Laeng.

Hua Hin is blessed with bountiful seafood and fine restaurants that serve dishes like this grilled squid salad.

Rama VII, the Spanish-style villa is still regularly used by the royal family and is not open to the public.

One of the country's first rail lines linked Bangkok to Hua Hin at the start of the 20th century, transporting the capital's wealthy to the southern shores. Hua Hin thus had the aura of a European spa town, with the royals coming here for the clean air. Today, the coastal town is beginning to reclaim that mantle as several exclusive spa retreats – like the award-winning Chiva Som – cater to the holistic needs of international jetsetters. A string of brand-name resorts like Hilton, Hyatt and Marriott are also represented here, along with local (and equally expensive) concerns like Dusit and Anantara.

After the palace, **Hua Hin Railway Station** is perhaps the second most famous building in town. Although the bucolic lane in which it sits is now busy with 21st-century traffic, the dainty, traditional Thai teak structure maintains enough charm to evoke the 1923 scene of its creation. Five hundred metres/yds towards the beach is another historic landmark, the 1922 colonial-style **Hotel Sofitel Central**, formerly the Railway Hotel, which masqueraded as the Phnom Penh Hotel in the 1984 movie *Killing Fields*.

One of the Hua Hin station staff.

Brown gibbon at the Khao Sam Roi Yot National Park.

Today, the sweeping run of Hua Hin beach is backed by opulent summer homes along with a slew of faceless condo developments. Hua Hin has gained an international reputation as a place to retire, and more and more condos and beach houses are being built to accommodate the upsurge in interest. The beach lacks the character of Thailand's palm-fringed island bays, but is great for long strolls. Pony rides set off from near the main drag. The beaches south of town, **Suan Son** and **Khao Tao**, are rather nicer and more secluded.

Hua Hin activities

Although Hua Hin's nightlife has picked up in the last few years, it is still relatively quiet, with the restaurants and bars clustered mainly in a small area around Thanon Naresdamri and on the parallel Thanon Phunsuk. Soi Bintabaht has the highest concentration of beer bars, and the pier restaurants on Naresdamri grill some of the best seafood in town, in the most atmospheric spot.

Along with this upsurge in nightlife, a number of new restaurants have appeared too. While Hua Hin has always been known as a place for fresh seafood, the diversity of culinary options has expanded beyond just Thai, with Japanese, Korean, Scandinavian, German, French and Italian, reflecting the nationality of tourist arrivals.

Hua Hin sees a lot of activities and events, usually organised at weekends so that the Bangkok crowds can join in. These include the annual **Hua Hin Jazz Festival** in June or July and the **Hua Hin Regatta**, which attracts sailors to the town each July or August.

Outside Hua Hin

Visible a few kilometres south of town is **Khao Takiab** (Chopstick Hill). This rocky outcrop has a steep climb to its summit but the views of the surrounding coast are worth the sweat. Of course, it's incredibly hot, and no one would blame you for taking a tuk-tuk. There's an unremarkable temple at the top with a large Buddha statue standing facing the sea, around which are resident troops of boisterous macaques.

The beaches further south of Hua Hin down towards **Pranburi** are also

starting to see a number of tastefully designed boutique resorts, like the **Evason** and **Aleenta**, making for a stylish, if expensive, escape from Bangkok.

Located around 50km (31 miles) south of Hua Hin, **Khao Sam Roi Yot National Park** ⑭ translates as "Three Hundred Mountain Peaks" and refers to the limestone pinnacles jutting up from the park's mangrove swamps to heights above 600 metres (1,900ft). Carved from the rugged coastline and a haven for kayakers, the park has superb beaches, marshes, forest walks and caves. Wildlife includes a multitude of birdlife, crab-eating macaques and the rare serow – a mountain goat-antelope.

Tham Phraya Nakhon is the most famous attraction here; the huge cave has a large sinkhole that allows shafts of light to shine down and illuminate the grand Thai-style pavilion (*sala*) built in the 1890s for a visit by King Chulalongkorn. Other noteworthy caves are **Tham Sai** and **Tham Kaeo**, the latter meaning "Jewel Cave" and named after its glistening stalactite and rock formations.

The "Three Hundred Mountain Peaks", Khao Sam Roi Yot National Park.

FACT

In 1868, King Mongkut, an astute astronomer, visited Khao Sam Roi Yot National Park to view a total eclipse of the sun, which he had foretold. The king's prediction, to the astonishment of local astrologers, was only four minutes off the mark. Sadly, Mongkut contracted malaria from this trip and died a week after his return to Bangkok.

EASTERN SEABOARD

Southeast of Bangkok there are diverse attractions that include an extraordinary architectural model of the whole country, wildlife parks with tigers, the touristy anything-goes beach town of Pattaya and unspoilt palm-fringed islands such as Ko Samet and Ko Chang.

Main Attractions
Ancient City
Sriracha Tiger Zoo
Pattaya
The Sanctuary of Truth, Pattaya
Ko Samet
Ko Chang

Map
Page 186

In Samut Prakan Province, 30km (20 miles) or about half an hour's drive southeast of Bangkok, are two attractions – Muang Boran, or Ancient City, and the Crocodile Farm and Zoo, which claim to be the world's biggest open air museum and the world's largest crocodile farm, respectively.

Beyond Samut Prakan is Thailand's Eastern Seaboard, which runs from Chonburi province all the way to Trat province, near the Cambodian border, from the ugliness of the country's largest industrial zone, known as "The Detroit of the East", to some beautiful beaches and scenic islands.

Take a bus from Bangkok's Eastern Bus Terminal to reach Samut Prakan, then hire a *songthaew* or take a local bus to the Ancient City. All other destinations in this chapter are on a different route to Samut Prakan, but the quickest access to these is also from the Eastern Bus Terminal.

Ancient City ⓭

One of Bangkok's best-value tourist attractions is the surprisingly under-visited **Ancient City** or Muang Boran (tel: 0-2323 9253; www.ancientcitygroup.net/ancientsiam/en; daily 8am–5pm; charge). The park officially changed its name to Ancient Siam in 2008, although everyone (including the

Sanphet Prasat Palace in the Ancient City.

website) still calls it by the original name. The parkland site is loosely shaped to represent Thailand, with over 100 monuments, palaces and other buildings placed approximately in their correct geographical location. Some are life-size or near life-size reproductions of both existing and long-lost structures, notably royal complexes from the ruins of the former capital, Ayutthaya. Others are completely relocated buildings that would otherwise have been demolished. The result is an educational

TIP

The Erawan Museum is a good stop-off on the way from Bangkok to the Ancient City.

celebration of Thai history and architecture. And, while these may be idealised tableaux, there's not an ounce of Disney about any of it. Its size means it's not practical to tour the Ancient City on foot. You can drive around it (charge), rent bicycles or golf carts at the gate, or take a tram tour, which is available with an English-speaking guide (charge).

It's rewarding to wander around the whole place, which could take around four hours, but for highlights head to the Central region, where the centrepiece is the 15th-century Sanphet Prasat Palace, the main royal residence of the early Ayutthaya period. It was notable at the time because it heralded a new architecture that differed from the earlier Khmer and Sukhothai styles in details such as tapering pillars, pediment doorframes and overlapping roofing. The style became known as the Ayutthaya School and was to dominate the landscape well into the Rattanakosin era four centuries later. The palace was completely destroyed when the Burmese sacked Ayutthaya in 1767. Superb craftsmanship has been allied to painstaking

Buddha statue, Ancient City.

research, using archaeological remains, contemporary accounts and drawings, and details from similar period buildings, to produce an exquisite structure in its own right, even down to interior murals and ornamentation. Close by are other replica monuments of the country's rich "Rice Bowl", such as the beautiful Dusit Maha Prasat Palace and the Phra Kaew Pavilion from the current Grand Palace in Bangkok.

The site also has period houses of various styles, statues depicting famous battles, and mock-ups of regional villages with local crafts for sale. There are small open-air cafés around the grounds serving Thai food, with several near the Floating Market. Aside from the monuments, the park offers a peaceful and secluded environment – particularly if you go mid-week – and one of the charms is that you are left free to wander in and out of buildings at will, with no staff, barriers or stuffy formalities. It's a real treasure.

THE ERAWAN MUSEUM

Lek Viriyaphant, the businessman–philanthropist who built both the Ancient City and The Sanctuary of Truth, left another cultural legacy in the shape of The Erawan Museum (Sukhumvit Soi 119, Samut Prakan; tel: 0-2371 3135; www.erawan-museum.com; daily 8am–3pm; charge). Housed in an extraordinary 43-metre (140ft) -high, three-headed elephant that represents Erawan, the animal ridden by the god Indra in Hindu mythology, the museum is divided into three sections. The basement "Underworld" contains mainly Chinese and Thai pieces from the founder's private antiques collection. The middle section, "Earth", has a stained-glass domed ceiling and examples of Thai art styles from the country's most celebrated craftsmen. These include stucco work from Phetchaburi, hammered tin plating from Nakhon Si Thammarat and ceramics from Ampawa. In the hollow interior of the elephant's belly, "Heaven" is an odd, hippy-esque purple room with abstract murals and antique Buddha statues. Because the museum contains many Buddha images it has assumed the level of religious pilgrimage for many people, who come to a shrine in the gardens to make merit and pray for good luck.

Crocodile Farm and Zoo

Samut Prakan's **Crocodile Farm and Zoo** (www.worldcrocodile.com; daily 8am–6pm; charge) is located a short distance from the Ancient City on the old Sukhumvit Highway (Route 3). The farm has South American caimans and Nile River crocodiles, plus over 60,000 freshwater and saltwater local varieties. It claims to be both the largest crocodile farm in the world, and to have the world's largest captive crocodile, the 6-metre (20ft) -long and 1,114kg (2,456lbs) Chai Yai.

Highlights are the eight daily shows (hourly 9am–4pm, reptile feeding 4–5pm), in which handlers enter a pond teeming with crocodiles to wrestle them and place their heads in their mouths. The farm's shops do a nice line in handbags, belts, shoes and other products made from crocodile and fish skins, which are certified by CITES (Convention on International Trade in Endangered Species). They also sell stewed crocodile meat, purportedly a tonic and aphrodisiac in traditional Chinese medicine.

Other attractions include a Dinosaur Museum, an amusement park and a zoo featuring tigers, ostriches, camels and elephants.

Chonburi

The sprawling town of **Chonburi**, 80km (50 miles) from Bangkok, is the gateway to the Eastern Seaboard, and is usually a brief stop, at most, for visitors on the way to Pattaya and beyond. However, Chonburi has its fair share of attractions. Just outside of town is **Wat Buddhabat Sam Yot** (daily 8am–6pm; free). Built by an Ayutthayan king and renovated during the reign of King Chulalongkorn, this hilltop monastery holds a cast of what is supposedly the Buddha's footprint. The climb to the top of the hill is rewarded with coastal panoramas.

Near the centre of Chonburi, a gold-mosaic image of the Buddha dominates the Chinese **Wat Dhamma**

Nimitr (daily 8am–6pm; free). The largest image along this coastline, and the only one in the country depicting the Buddha in a boat, the 40-metre (135ft) -high statue recalls the story of the Buddha's journey to the cholera-ridden town of Pai Salee.

Bang Saen

Continuing south from Chonburi past the town of Ang Sila, the 2km (1-mile) -long beach at **Bang Saen** springs to life each weekend as hordes of middle-class Bangkok residents descend in cars and buses. The nearest stretch of beach from the capital, it's covered with beach umbrellas and inflatable inner tubes, and the surf is filled with bobbing bodies dressed head-to-toe in clothes to avoid getting a tan (Thais associate tanned skin with poor manual labourers who toil in the sun).

Tucked inland near Bang Phra Reservoir, and operated by Bangkok's Dusit Zoo (see page 144), is **Khao Khieo Open Zoo** (http://kkopenzoo.com/newversion_eng; daily 8am–8pm;

Stained glass in the Earth section of the Erawan Museum.

Wrestling a reptile at Samut Prakan's Crocodile Farm and Zoo.

Family fun on the beach at Ko Si Chang.

little remains of the palace grounds, and the palace itself was dismantled and rebuilt in Bangkok as the Vimanmek Mansion (see page 143). The gardens and ponds are still recognisable. The king used to meditate in the now dilapidated Wat Atsadang.

The island has a couple of reasonably good beaches, though certainly not Thailand's best or cleanest, and it is busy at weekends with Thai day-trippers. Once a transfer point for cargo ships unloading onto smaller vessels to sail up the Chao Phraya river, Ko Si Chang's surrounding seas are still crowded, these days with large freighters.

charge). It exhibits deer, elephants and other animals, and includes a Night Safari (daily 6–8pm; charge).

Si Racha ⑱

The coastal town of **Si Racha** is the original home of one of Thailand's most famous relishes – Si Racha Sauce (*nam prik si racha*), into which diners dip fresh shrimp, crab, oyster and mussels at the town's waterfront restaurants.

The **Sriracha Tiger Zoo**, 9km (6 miles) to the south, claims to be the largest tiger zoo in the world (www.tigerzoo.com; daily 8am–6pm; charge). The zoo has over 100 Bengal tigers in captivity – visitors can attend the nursery to hold and feed the young cubs. In addition, there is a menagerie of other animals, like crocodiles, elephants, ostriches and chimps. While the tigers are the star attraction in the daily circus shows, there is crocodile wrestling, an elephant show and even pig racing.

Ko Si Chang ⑲

A short boat ride from Si Racha's shore is the small island of **Ko Si Chang**, known primarily as a coastal retreat for King Chulalongkorn (Rama V). The king built his summer palace here in the 1890s, although

Pattaya ⑳

Pattaya's reputation as a centre of sex tourism is not undeserved, despite ongoing efforts by hotels and other local businesses to clean up its image. So, it's something of a surprise that this resort is a popular destination for families as well as single men. The reason is that Pattaya has an abundance of accommodation options

Carving in the Sanctuary of Truth at Pattaya.

TIP

If you have time to kill at Si Racha, visit the offshore rock of Ko Loi. It is connected to the mainland by a bridge and supports a picturesque temple with Thai and Chinese elements. A Buddha footprint, cast in bronze, graces the temple along with pictures of the Goddess of Mercy, Kuan Yin, and the Monkey God.

at all prices, plenty of international restaurants and a wide range of attractions and activities for all ages on both land and sea, although its beaches are less pristine than those in the southern islands and are narrow, packed with parasols and too close to the main road for comfort.

The town's notoriety dates back to the Vietnam War when boatloads of American GIs flocked to the then quiet beaches and bars for a spot of R&R. Today, with the Thai Navy still operating from the nearby port at Satthahip, occasional battalions of visiting US Marines still descend on the resort – to the delight of Pattaya's entertainment establishments. And this buzzing, salacious nightlife has become a tourist attraction in itself for many visitors, even if they play no part in the action.

Located 147km (91 miles) from Bangkok, (just over two hours by road), the seaside town has long been popular with Thai youth and families. In recent years, apart from Europeans, visitors from China, Hong Kong and Taiwan are Pattaya's most visible foreign tourists, along with significant numbers of Russians.

It is also a popular spot for condos and beach homes, mainly used as weekend getaways for Bangkok expats, and as winter homes for retirees from Europe. Property prices rise at an astonishing rate, and improvements to infrastructure, especially international schools, are drawing in more respectable residents. But Pattaya's seedy reputation also attracts a strong criminal element, and a browse through the English-language newspaper the *Pattaya Mail* reads like a police alert for Thailand's most wanted. This underworld, however, is rarely visible to the average tourist, and Pattaya feels as safe as anywhere else in Thailand.

The waterfront starts at the fishing village of **Hat Naklua** to the north of town, leading down to the crescent-shaped **Hat Pattaya**, followed by a nicer and slightly wilder 6km (3.5-mile) stretch at **Hat Jomtien**, to the south. Pattaya and Jomtien are good locations for watersports fans, with equipment for windsurfing, sailing, snorkelling and diving available for rent, along with jet skis, water scooters and water-skiing equipment. The brave may try parasailing, strapped into a parachute harness and towed aloft by a speedboat.

Pattaya's land attractions

Pattaya's land-based attractions include everything from golf courses and paintball parks to go-karting, bungee jumping and parachuting. In addition, there are several sights that may be worth seeing.

At the Royal Garden Plaza is a branch of **Ripley's Believe It or Not!**, with its collection of bizarre oddities (www.ripleysthailand.com; daily 11am–11pm; charge). At Thanon Sukhumvit is the **Pattaya Elephant Village** with its elephant shows and rides (www.elephant-village-pattaya.com; daily 8.30am–7pm; charge).

At **Pattaya Park**, the young ones will enjoy the cable car rides as well

TIP

The most popular beach in Ko Si Chang is Hat Tham Phang (Collapsed Cave Beach) on the western part of the island. The privately run website www.ko-sichang.com has more info on where to stay and eat, and tips on what to do on this tiny island.

Parasailing is a popular activity off the beaches at Pattaya.

Pattaya beach is busy even at night.

as the exciting waterslides and whirlpools at this large water amusement facility (www.pattayapark.com; daily 9am–6pm; charge).

The **Sanctuary of Truth** on Naklua Soi 12 (www.sanctuaryoftruth.com; daily 8am–6pm; charge) appears like a fairytale castle right on the edge of the sea. Standing over 100 metres (330ft)

The bright lights of Pattaya.

high, with a central dome of 42 tons, it is made entirely of hardwoods, intricately carved both inside and out with figures of gods and spirits representing Asian religions. Begun in 1981, construction is still ongoing, with surrounding workshops full of carpenters and wood carvers. You can watch them work and take up tools yourself if you want to learn a few moves. The sanctuary also offers horse riding and dolphin shows.

About 18km (11 miles) south of Pattaya is **Nong Nooch Tropical Garden**, a 243-hectare (600-acre) landscaped parkland enclosing two lakes (www.nongnoochtropicalgarden.com; daily 8am–6pm; charge). It offers a variety of activities, including a mini-zoo, with animals such as gibbons, tigers, and ostriches, a butterfly park, a huge orchid garden and cultural shows featuring traditional dances, Thai boxing and elephants.

Pattaya's nightlife

Pattaya's nightlife clusters along or off Beach Road and Walking Street in South Pattaya. There is a staggering range of bars, Irish pubs, German brew houses and nightclubs, as well as an overwhelming saturation of go-go bars and massage parlours (Pattaya heaves with sex workers, both female and male). The international mix here means at least one of the bars now features Eastern European lap dancers. The strip called Boys' Town (Pattayaland Soi 3) is where the gay crowd gathers. Pattaya also has lip-synching Vegas-style cabaret shows which feature a pageant of stunning lady-boys or *katoey* (transsexuals). Tiffany's (tel: 0-3842 1700; www.tiffany-show.co.th) is the most popular.

A more family-oriented option is **Alangkarn Theatre** in Thanon Sukhumvit, which stages a show combining traditional Thai dancers and elephants with lasers and pyrotechnics (tel: 0-3825 6007; www.alang karnthailand.com/theater.htm; Thur–Tue at 6pm; charge). It is kitschy but makes for a fun evening with dinner thrown in.

Ko Larn ㉑

Offshore from Pattaya, **Ko Larn** – identified in brochures as Coral Island but whose name translates as Bald Island – used to be known for its coral reefs. These have long since been destroyed by fishermen using dynamite to stun fish. Yet, glass-bottomed boats still ferry visitors from the mainland to its shore, their passengers peering in vain at the dead grey coral in the hope of seeing something alive and moving. Ko Larn, however, has the wide, soft sand beaches that Pattaya lacks and it's a great place to spend a leisurely day. The shore is filled with good seafood restaurants, and there are watersports facilities for those who want to stir from their beach chairs.

Further south, the coastline continues all the way through **Rayong** and beyond into **Chanthaburi**, with much of it quite undeveloped or with small hotels aimed solely at the domestic market.

Ko Samet ㉒

Located 200km (124 miles) from Bangkok (or over three hours by road) from the capital and a short boat trip across from the fishing harbour of **Ban Phe**, the postcard-perfect island of **Ko Samet** has become a popular weekend getaway for Bangkok residents. The island is famous among Thais as the place where Sunthorn Phu (1786–1855), a flamboyantly romantic court poet, retired to compose some of his works. Born in nearby Klaeng on the mainland, Sunthorn called the island Ko Kaeo Phisadan, or "island with sand like crushed crystal", and it was here that he set his best-known work, *Phra Aphaimani*, a tale about a prince and a mermaid. A weathered statue stands as tribute on the rocky point at the end of the main beach of Hat Sai Kaew.

From a quiet poetic retreat, the island has gained popularity as a superb resort, helped by the fine white sand beaches and turquoise

Spectacular undersea life awaits divers in the waters around Ko Samet.

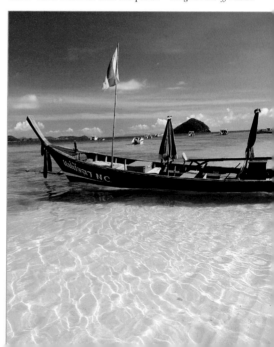

Longtail boat off Phuket.

TIP

While the regular fishing boat ferries are much cheaper, taking a speedboat across to Ko Samet (around B200 per person) from the mainland is much faster, drops you at the bay of your choice, and usually means you escape paying the National Park entry fee of B200 per foreigner, which is pretty steep compared to the B40 that Thais are charged.

Sunset over Ko Chang.

blue waters. Most activity here is relaxed – sunbathing, beach strolls, swimming and snorkelling – though jet skis and inflatable banana boats do occasionally interrupt the peace. The island is part of a national marine park (entry fee upon arrival at the pier), so, technically, most of the resort and bungalow operations are illegal. However, development along the coast has progressed despite the law, though as yet it remains fairly unobtrusive, with simple single-storey huts and bungalows. But as a sign of things to come, a couple of resorts have upgraded their facilities, and the west coast's only beach of **Ao Phrao** has a few upmarket resorts nestled into this small scenic bay.

Almost all the island's sandy beaches run down the east coast, starting near the larger northern tip with **Hat Sai Kaew** (Diamond Sand), and gradually getting less isolated as the island narrows to the southernmost bay of **Ao Karang**. The island is relatively small and can be walked from top to bottom in just a few hours, though the coastal track traverses some rocky headlands. The single

road turns to bumpy dirt track fairly quickly. Hat Sai Kaew is where Thais prefer to stay, having more air-conditioned rooms and seafood restaurants, whereas foreign visitors like the bays of **Ao Phai** and **Ao Hin Khok**.

The island is best avoided on public holidays, when visitors outnumber beds, and tents are pitched on any spare patch of land. Evenings are relatively low-key, with restaurants setting up fresh seafood beach barbeques, and the restaurant-bars at small hotels like **Naga** (Ao Hin Khok) and **Silver Sand** (Ao Phai) the only spots to focus on music, late-night partying and the obligatory fire juggling. The mosquitoes on Ko Samet are known to be monsters, so repellent is a must.

Further down at picturesque **Ao Wong Deuan**, the scene, unfortunately, has become more akin to Pattaya, with European males being pampered by their hired female "guides", raucous bars on the land and noisy jet skis on the waters. **Ao Thian** (Candlelight Beach), the next bay, is a quieter spot and the facilities are more basic.

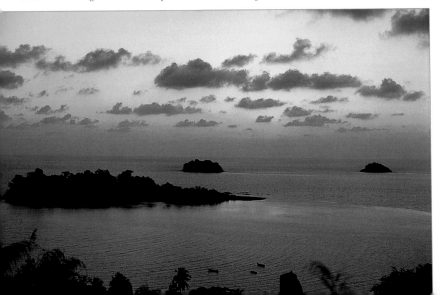

Ko Chang ㉓

Ko Chang (Elephant Island), at 492 sq km (190 sq miles), is Thailand's second-largest island after Phuket. It is part of the Ko Chang Marine National Park which includes some 50 islands. You can drive here in around five hours from Bangkok. Alternatively, the flight to Trat, on the mainland, takes 45 minutes. Either way there is an hour's boat crossing from **Laem Ngop** pier, 20 minutes from the airport.

The verdant island, which is part of Trat province (close to the Cambodian border), has managed to escape the rapid development of Phuket and Ko Samui, despite the government's promotion of Ko Chang as a playground for the rich. There has been a rapid increase in hotel construction and infrastructure in the last two decades (including an upgrade of the road that loops practically the whole island), and the opening of Trat airport. There is now a yachting marina and a greater choice of stylish resorts and spas than there used to be, although still nothing in the luxury class, and the island remains a firm favourite with backpackers.

As the island becomes more popular, the single road is increasingly busy, but despite this it still has a relatively untouched hilly interior, mangroves and some lovely beaches lined up along the west coast. The most developed is **Hat Sai Khao** (White Sand Beach), which is just south of the idyllic stretch of sand at **Hat Khlong Phrao**. Next, you reach **Hat Kai Bae**, and then the last vestige of Ko Chang's hippie traveller scene, **Hat Tha Nam** (Lonely Beach). As more resorts edge in, the last no longer has quite the solitude implied by its name.

Popular activities include snorkelling and diving, including trips to some of the smaller islands, kayaking, and treks to the island's numerous waterfalls. Visit the southern stilted fishing village of **Ban Bang Bao** to get an idea of how local communities

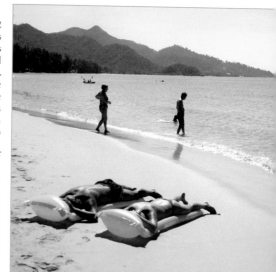

live (and how their lifestyles are changing). The island's nightlife is still relatively subdued, with each beach having its own preferred watering holes. However, Hat Sai Khao is still where the main action is.

Soaking up the rays on Ko Chang.

Islands near Ko Chang

If Ko Chang still feels a little too well trodden, the string of islands off the southern tip are much quieter and worth exploring. The tiny **Ko Wai** has limited and basic accommodation, but the vibe here is very relaxed, the views of the surrounding islands are spectacular, and there is a lovely coral reef just a short swim from the main beach.

An hour by speedboat from the mainland pier of Laem Ngop, the flat island of **Ko Mak** is dense with coconut plantations and has two nice main beaches, where tourists are sparse. The island lies about halfway between Ko Chang and the second-largest island in the archipelago, **Ko Kut**, which attracts a lot of organised tour groups to resorts that mainly cater to all-inclusive packages.

Seashells from the beach at Ko Chang.

The stone Buddha's head embedded in a tree at Ayutthaya.

NORTH OF BANGKOK

The undisputed capital city of the Thai kingdom more than 600 years ago, Ayutthaya is a time capsule that captures the faded grandeur of that violent era. To its west lies Khao Yai National Park, a huge expanse of greenery that's also worth exploring.

Bang Pa-In became a favourite royal retreat from the reign of King Chulalongkorn, over 100 years ago. It is a picturesque stopover before reaching the main event, the ruins of Ayutthaya, the once-powerful old capital of Thailand. Also in this area there are waterfalls and a national park near Nakhon Nayok, wild animal spotting in Khao Yai and more (wildish) animals in the ancient city of Lopburi, where monkeys cause mischief at Prang Sam Yot.

Trains from Hualamphong Station stop at Bang Pa-In, Ayutthaya and Lopburi. Buses to Ayutthaya leave from Bangkok's Northern Bus Terminal, stopping at Bang Pa-In en route. Separate buses leave the same station for Lopburi

Bang Pa-In ❷④

Drive north from Bangkok for about 50km (32 miles) and you reach **Bang Pa-In**, an eclectic collection of palaces and pavilions once used as a royal summer retreat (tel: 0-3526 1673-82; www.palaces.thai.net; daily 8.30am–4.30pm; charge).

The palace buildings one sees today at Bang Pa-in date from the late 19th- and early 20th-century reigns of King Chulalongkorn (Rama

V) and King Vajiravudh (Rama VI), who came here to escape the mid-year rains in Bangkok. Under the instruction of Chulalongkorn, the manicured grounds contain several buildings that feature Italian Baroque, European Gothic, Victorian and Chinese architectural styles. Only parts of the royal quarters are open to public view, providing a glimpse into Chulalongkorn's penchant for European furniture and decor.

The palace buildings of note at Bang Pa-In include the two-storey

Main Attractions
Bang Pa-In
Wat Chai Wattanaram
Wat Phra Sri Sanphet
Wat Ratchaburana
Wat Phra Mahathat
Khao Yai National Park
Lopburi

Maps
Pages 186, 216

Exploring the ruins on an elephant is a novel option.

TIP

Most day trips that visit
Ayutthaya from Bangkok
include Bang Pa-In as a
brief stopover either on
the way there or back.
For more details on tours
to Ayutthaya and Bang
Pa-In, see page 235.

Aisawan Thipphaya-at.

Chinese-style **Wehat Chamrun Palace**
and the nearby islet with the **Withun
Thatsana** observation tower, as well as
the Italianate **Warophat Phiman Hall**.
The 1876 **Aisawan Thipphaya-at**, a
Thai-style pavilion in the middle of
the adjacent lake near the entrance, is
regarded as one of the finest surviving
examples of Thai architecture.

Across the river and slightly south
of the palace, **Wat Niwet Thamma-
prawat** looks more like a Gothic
Christian church than a Buddhist
temple, and is topped by a spire.
Worthy of an hour's stop on the way
to Ayutthaya, the pleasant gardens are
embellished with canals, ponds, fountains, bridges and a topiary of large
elephant-shaped hedges. Coach tours
to Ayutthaya stop off here in the
morning, so to avoid the crowds it's
better to drop by in the afternoon.

AYUTTHAYA ㉕

Even if one were ignorant of the
importance and history of **Ayutthaya**,
one would still be impressed by the
beauty and grandeur of this city –
built by 33 Ayutthayan kings over
400 years. From the ruins, it is easy
to appreciate the genius of the kings
who built it. Located 85km (55 miles)
north of Bangkok, Ayutthaya was laid
out at the junction of three rivers:
Chao Phraya, Pa Sak and Lopburi.

Wat Chai Wattanaram.

Engineers had only to cut a canal across the loop of the Chao Phraya river to create an island. A network of canals – few of which exist today – acted as streets, and palaces and temples were erected alongside. The Europeans dubbed this city "Venice of the East", and even today, chartering a longtail boat for a trip around the natural moat is the most ambient way to see many of the riverbank ruins. As a Unesco World Heritage site, Ayutthaya is a must visit. Several boat operators from Bangkok organise regular trips by river from the capital to the historic city, conveying them in either modern express boats or traditional teakwood barges.

Ayutthaya's foundations

Ayutthaya was founded around 1350 by Prince U-Thong (later known as King Ramathibodi I). Thirty years later, the northern kingdom of Sukhothai was placed under Ayutthayan rule, which then spread its control to Angkor in the east, and to Pegu, in Burma, to the west. It was one of the richest and most cosmopolitan cities in Asia by the 1600s – exporting rice, animal skins and ivory – and had a population of 1 million, greater than that of London at the time. Merchants came from Europe, the Middle East and elsewhere in Asia to trade in its markets, with many eventually settling there. Today, there is a plaque to mark the former Portuguese settlement and a memorial hall and gate to mark the Japanese settlement. Europeans wrote awed accounts of the fabulous wealth of the courts and of the 2,000 temple spires clad in gold.

Thirty-three kings left their mark on the old capital. Although in ruins, very impressive remnants of Ayutthaya's rich architectural and cultural achievements can still be seen today. As fast as it rose to greatness, it collapsed, suffering destruction so complete that it was never rebuilt. Burmese armies had been pounding on its doors for centuries before occupying it for a period in the 16th century. Siamese kings then expelled them and reasserted independence. In 1767, however, the Burmese triumphed again. In a mad rampage, they burned and looted, destroying most of the city's

FACT

In the 1950s, unscrupulous locals plundered Ayutthaya's hidden treasures and Buddha images. The Thai government recently realised that some of Ayutthaya's most important treasures are now housed in overseas museum collections, and they are trying to reclaim these stolen artefacts.

Wat Phanan Choeng.

monuments and enslaving, killing and scattering the population.

Within a year, Ayutthaya was nearly a ghost town, its population reduced to fewer than 10,000 inhabitants as the royal court resettled south near the mouth of the Chao Phraya river in what today is Bangkok. Even after the Burmese garrison was defeated, Ayutthaya was beyond repair, a fabled city left to crumble into dust. Today, the ruins, collectively known as the **Ayutthaya Historical Park** (daily 8am–5pm; charge) stand on the western half of the island, with the modern city of Ayutthaya on the eastern side.

By the riverside

Start close to the junction of the Nam Pa Sak and Chao Phraya rivers, passing by the imposing **Wat Phanan Choeng Ⓐ**. Records suggest that the temple was established 26 years prior to Ayutthaya's foundation in 1350. The temple houses the statue of a giant seated bronze Buddha, so tightly pressed against the roof that the statue appears to be holding it up. With an unmistakably Chinese atmosphere, Wat Phanan Choeng was a favourite with the Chinese traders of the time, who prayed there before setting out on long voyages. The temple also holds the Mae Soi Dok Mak shrine, a tribute to a Chinese princess who supposedly killed herself on this spot after an icy reception from her suitor, an Ayutthayan king.

Ayutthaya was at one time surrounded by fortress walls, only portions of which remain today. One of the best-preserved sections is at **Phom Phet**, across the river from Wat Phanan Choeng. Near Phom Phet is the restored **Wat Suwan Dararam Ⓑ**, built near the close of the Ayutthaya period. Destroyed by the Burmese in 1767, the temple was rebuilt by Rama I, with the wall murals dating from the reign of Rama III; later, a more unconventional (1925–35) mural depicting King Naruesan's famous battle with the Burmese was added. Still used as a temple, the *wat* is magical in the early evening as the monks chant prayers.

Upstream from Wat Phanan Choeng by the river bank is the restored **Wat Phutthaisawan Ⓒ**. Seldom visited, it is quiet, and the landing is an excellent place to enjoy the river's tranquillity in the evenings. Further upstream, the **Cathedral of St Joseph Ⓓ** is a Catholic reminder of the large European population that lived in the city at its prime.

Where the river bends to the north is one of Ayutthaya's most romantic ruins, **Wat Chai Wattanaram Ⓔ**, erected in 1630. Modelled after the Angkor Wat complex in Cambodia, the dramatically placed temple is a photographer's favourite, especially at sunset. Restored in the 1990s, the temple was built by King Prasat Thong, and has a large central Cambodian-style *prang* fringed by several smaller *chedi*. Perched high on a pedestal in front of the ruins, a Buddha keeps solitary watch. This extraordinary temple with rows of headless Buddhas makes a fine contrast to the less impressive white-and-gold **Queen Suriyothai Chedi Ⓕ** on the city side of the river.

The shrine commemorates the life of Ayutthayan Queen Suriyothai, one of the most famous heroines of Thai history. She was the wife of King Maha Chakapat (1548–69), and legend states that when her husband went to engage the invading Burmese armies in the first year of his reign, Queen Suriyothai disguised herself as a man and rode into battle with him. The king, his elephant wounded, was in mortal danger, when the queen rode her elephant between him and his attacker and was herself killed. In 2001, a movie about her called *Suriyothai* was the most expensive film ever made in Thailand and was a huge box office hit. Francis Ford Coppola edited the US release.

Across a river bridge from Wang Luang stands the restored temple of **Wat Na Phra Men** ⓖ. Used as a strategic attack post by the Burmese when they descended on the old city, the temple is one of Ayutthaya's only monasteries not to have been ransacked. Here, a large stone Buddha is seated on a throne, a sharp contrast to the yoga position of most seated Buddhas. Found in the ruins of Wat

Phra Mahathat, the statue is believed to be one of five that originally sat in the recently unearthed Dvaravati-period complex in Nakhon Pathom. The main hall or *bot* contains an Ayutthayan-style seated Buddha in regal attire, which is very unlike the more common monastic dress of Buddha representations.

Royal Palace

The **Wang Luang** ⓗ (Royal Palace) was of substantial size, if the foundations for the stables of some 100 elephants are any indication. Established by King Borommatrailokanat in the 15th century, it was later razed by the Burmese. The bricks were removed to Bangkok to build the city's defensive walls, so only remnants of the foundations survive to mark the site.

A part of the original palace grounds, next door stands the three Ceylonese-style *chedi* of **Wat Phra Sri Sanphet** ⓘ. The royal temple would have held as much importance as the Temple of the Emerald Buddha (Wat Phra Kaew) in Bangkok does today. Two of the *chedi* were built in 1492 by King Borommatrailokanat's son,

Statue of a sitting Buddha at the Wat Yai Chai Monkhon temple in Ayutthaya.

Wat Phra Sri Sanphet.

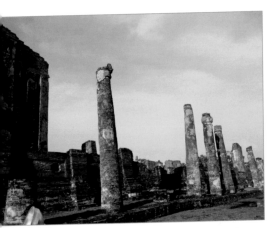

Wat Phra Sri Sanphet.

Ramathibodi II, to hold the ashes of his father and brother. The third was added in 1540 to hold the ashes of Ramathibodi II. The three spires have become the archetypal image of Ayutthaya.

Around the Royal Palace

For two centuries after Ayutthaya's fall, a huge bronze Buddha sat unsheltered near Wat Phra Sri Sanphet. Its flame of knowledge (on the top of its head) and one of its arms had been broken when the roof, set on fire by the Burmese, collapsed. Based on the original, a new building called **Viharn Phra Mongkhon Bophit** ❶ was built in 1956 around the restored statue. Dating back to the 15th century and over 12 metres (39ft) tall, it is one of Thailand's largest bronze images and seems rather cramped in this sanctuary.

In the park just south of Viharn Phra Mongkhon Bophit is **Khun Paen's House** (Thanon Pa Thon; daily 8.30am–4.30pm; charge), which although empty of furnishings is a good example of a traditional Thai "cluster" dwelling. It shows the three separate houses of the extended family arranged around a communal verandah for socialising and dining. People habitually ate on the floor

FACT

Following the defeat of Ayutthaya, King Taksin was desperate for funds to build the new capital in Thonburi. He authorised treasure hunts in the old city, looking for the riches buried by the city's merchants before they fled. Finders were allowed to keep half the loot for themselves.

– the original reason for taking your shoes off when entering a Thai building. It was restored here in 1940, the location of the original city jail.

Across the road to the east, **Wat Phra Ram** ❶ is one of Ayutthaya's oldest temples. Founded in 1369 by the son of Ayutthaya's founding king, Prince U-Thong, its buildings, dating from the 1400s, have been restored twice. Elephant gates punctuate the old walls, and the central terrace is dominated by a crumbling *prang* to which clings a gallery of stucco *naga*, *garuda* and Buddha statues. The reflection of Wat Phra Ram's *prang* shimmers in the pool that surrounds the complex, making it one of Ayutthaya's most tranquil settings.

Ayutthaya's best temples

Two of Ayutthaya's finest temples stand side by side across the lake from Wat Phra Ram. The first is **Wat Ratchaburana** ❶, built in 1424 by the seventh king of Ayutthaya, King Borom Rachathirat II (1424–48) as a

Stupas, Wat Phra Mahathat.

memorial to his brothers who died as a result of a duel for the throne. Excavations during its restoration in 1957 revealed a crypt below the towering central *prang*, containing a stash of gold jewellery, Buddha images and other art objects, among them a magnificent ceremonial sword and an intricately decorated elephant statue – all probably the property of the interred brothers. The narrow, claustrophobic and dimly lit crypt can be accessed through a doorway in the *prang*, leading down steep stairs to some barely visible wall paintings.

The second temple, across the road, is **Wat Phra Mahathat** (Temple of the Great Relic), once one of the most beautiful temple complexes in Ayutthaya, and one of its oldest, dating from the 1380s. It was also one of the most important temples in Ayutthaya's heyday: the seat of the Supreme Patriarch, the focal point for religious ceremonies, and where King Ramesuan (1388–95) resided. Its glory was its huge laterite *prang*, which originally stood 46 metres (150ft) high. The *prang* later collapsed, but its foundations are still there, circled by restored *chedi*. A much revered symbol here is a stone Buddha head that is embedded in the gnarled roots of an old banyan tree. Around the ruins are numerous headless statues, with just the crossed legs of meditation hinting at the positions they once assumed. The souvenir shops at the entrance here mark this as one of the most visited (and most atmospheric) temples, but the Wat Mahathat grounds are large enough to gain serene moments even when accompanied by coach parties.

Next door, the government has built a model of how the royal city may have once looked.

Wat Ratchaburana.

One of the best ways of exploring the widely spread ruins of Ayutthaya is on bicycle. These can be rented for about B50 a day at many guesthouses in Ayutthaya. If you can't be bothered to expend your energy, hire a motorised tuk-tuk with driver for about B200 an hour.

Ayutthaya's museums

While looters quickly made off with a great many of Ayutthaya's glories, the remaining treasures of what was probably Thailand's greatest archaeological discovery are now kept in the **Chao Sam Phraya Museum** just to the south (tel: 0-3524 1587; Wed–Sun 9am–4pm; charge).

Nearby is another museum, the **Ayutthaya Historical Study Centre** (tel: 0-3524 5124; Mon–Fri 9am–4.30pm, Sat–Sun 9am–5pm; charge). Funded by the Japanese government and on land that was once part of Ayutthaya's Japanese quarter, the modern building houses hi-tech exhibits which guide visitors through 400 years of Ayutthaya's development, trade, administration and social changes. There are also models of the city in its glory days, a Chinese junk and small tableaux of village life.

To the northeast is **Chantharakasem National Museum** , formerly known as the Chantharakasem Palace (tel: 0-3525 5124; Wed–Sun 9am–4pm; charge). It was originally constructed outside the city walls, close to the confluence of the rivers and the canal. King Maha Thammaracha built it for his son Prince Naresuan (later king), and it became the residence for future heirs apparent. In 1767, the Burmese destroyed the palace, but King Mongkut (Rama IV) resurrected it in the 19th century as a royal summer retreat for escaping the lowland heat. Today, it looks out on the noisiest part of modern Ayutthaya. The palace's collection isn't that impressive but is still worthy of a perusal.

To its rear is the European-style four-storey **Pisai Sayalak** tower, built by King Mongkut for stargazing. Across the street from the palace is the boat pier for trips around the island, and the night market, with food stalls set up beside the water. It's a good spot to eat cheap local food and unwind at the end of the day.

Ayutthaya's outskirts

Southeast of Ayutthaya is **Wat Yai Chai Mongkhon** , originally established in the mid-1300s. The immense *chedi*, built to match that of Wat Phu Khao Thong, celebrates the victory of King Naresuan, in

Wat Yai Chai Mongkhon.

Seated Buddha images at Wat Yai Chai Mongkhon in Ayutthaya.

single-handed combat on elephant back, over the crown prince of Burma in 1592. Rows of yellow-sashed Buddha images skirt the inner walls. Also of interest is the statue of a huge white reclining Buddha, which, unusually, has its eyes open.

About 2km (1 mile) northwest of Ayutthaya is **Wat Phu Khao Thong Ⓡ**, better known as the **Golden Mount**. Its 80-metre (260ft) -high *chedi* rises amidst the rice fields, its upper terraces commanding a panoramic view of the countryside. While the *wat* dates from 1387, the *chedi* was built by the Burmese after their earlier and less destructive conquest in 1569. In 1957, to mark 2,500 years of Buddhism, a 2,500-gram (5.5lb) gold ball was mounted on top of the *chedi*, only to be stolen almost immediately after.

Nakhon Nayok Ⓩ

The most scenic route to the northeast province is Route 305, which branches off Route 1 (Friendship Highway) just north of Rangsit, 30km (20 miles) north of Bangkok. This wide road runs northeast along a lovely canal,

passing rice paddy fields and small rivers to reach the provincial capital of **Nakhon Nayok**, some 140km (90 miles) from the capital. Nakhon Nayok has long been overshadowed by the more famous tourist destinations in Thailand, but Thai visitors recognise its abundant nearby attractions – natural forests, craggy gorges and tumbling waterfalls – which offer a respite from the chaos of the city.

Other than a glimpse of a typical rural centre, however, the town of Nakhon Nayok itself has little to offer. From the town centre, Route 33 heads northwest and then, after just a few kilometres, a second road leads off to the right towards two waterfalls, one of which is **Sarika Falls**. Surrounded by dense forest, the nine-tier waterfall is in full force towards the end of the rainy season (September to November). But remember to wear sturdy shoes: the stone paths are slippery.

Wang Takrai National Park

Due north of Nakhon Nayok is the **Wang Takrai National Park**,

Countryside around Nakhon Nayok.

TIP

A common end to a day at Khao Yai National Park is a walk to Khoa Luk Chang Bat Cave at dusk to watch thousands of bats fly out as they head off in search of food.

Phra Narai Ratchaniwet ruins.

Harvesting grapes in a Khao Yai vineyard.

Most of Khao Yai is located 400 metres (1,300ft) above sea level, making it a pleasant escape from the hot, humid lowlands of Central Thailand. Most people visit during the dry season from November to February; be sure to bring warm clothes during this period as temperatures can plummet to as low as 10°C (50°F) at night. Alternatively, the rainy season is one of the best times for animal spotting and waterfalls, although you'll need to cover up bare legs and arms, as leeches are common then.

Often clad in mist, Khao Yai's highest peaks lie in the east along a landform known as the Korat Plateau. **Khao Laem** (Shadow Mountain) is 1,350 metres (4,430ft) high while **Khao Khiew** (Green Mountain) rises to a height of 1,020 metres (3,350ft). Evergreen and deciduous trees, palms and bamboo blanket the park, and unlike much of Thailand, patches of indigenous rainforest can still be seen here. Khao Yai is home to some 200 elephants, while monkeys, gibbons, deer, langurs, boar and gaurs are also commonly spotted. Bears are less often seen, and big cats such as leopards and tigers are rare. In addition, over 300 species of migrant birds have been identified, with regular sightings of great hornbills.

established by Prince Chumbhot (of Suan Pakkad Palace fame in Bangkok, see page 162) in the 1950s (daily 6am–6pm; charge). His wife, Princess Chumbhot, a keen horti-culturalist, planted many varieties of flowers and trees, including some imported species. Cultivated gardens sit among tall trees, which line both banks of the main stream flowing through the 2km (1-mile) stretch of the 80-hectare (195-acre) park. For those wishing to stay overnight in the area, bungalows are available for rent.

Just outside the park entrance, the road on the left crosses a river and continues 5km (3 miles) to **Nang Rong Falls**, an inviting three-tiered cascade located in a steep valley.

Khao Yai National Park ㉗

Khao Yai National Park, one of Thailand's oldest and most popular nature reserves, lies 200km (125 miles) northeast of the capital (daily 6am–6pm; charge). It is Thailand's second-largest national park at 2,168 sq km (837 sq miles) and cuts across four different provinces.

WINE COUNTRY

Wines from local vineyards are beginning to grow in both popularity and quality. Khao Yai region's favourable climate is supposed to be ideal for grape cultivation, with vineyards such as PB Valley Khao Yai (tel: 0-2562 0858), GranMonte Family Vineyard (tel: 0-2653 1522) and Village Farm & Winery (tel: 0-4422 8407) getting into the act. The word from connoisseurs is that while these wines are eminently palatable, they still need considerable refinement before they will be ready to compete with international wines. Tours, tastings and, in some places, accommodation can be arranged.

The macaques in Lopburi's Prang Sam Yot are honoured (or pacified) in late November with a feast of fruit, veggies and other foods in a spectacle known as the Monkey Buffet.

More than 50km (30 miles) of marked trails criss-cross the park, most of them originally forged and still used by elephants. In several clearings, there are observation towers where you can watch animals feed. Park rangers have information about the area, but few speak English, so it might be worth getting a guide, (try **Jungle Planet**; tel: 88 9282 2280; www.khaoyai-jungle-planet.com) from the nearest town, Pak Chong, or from one of the surrounding resorts. The guides are handy because the better ones carry spotting scopes for you to use, and they can explain what you're looking at. They may even have guidebooks on wildlife, flora and fauna for more in-depth information. On longer overnight treks you may sleep in a tent close to ranger stations.

Other attractions in the park include the three-level **Heaw Narok** waterfall, southeast of the park headquarters, which rises to a height of 150 metres (492ft) of, and, further north, the 20-metre (66ft) -high **Heaw Suwat** waterfall, which Leonardo di Caprio jumped off in the film *The Beach*.

Near the entrance to the park are numerous lodges and bungalows, including the luxury Kirimaya, a boutique resort in the vein of African safari camps with tented villas. Other pursuits include teeing off at internationally designed golf courses and jungle rides on ATVs (all-terrain vehicles).

Lopburi ㉘

Lopburi lies 150km (100 miles) north of Bangkok, a two- to three-hour drive through the fertile rice bowl of Thailand. Centuries before Lopburi became the favoured summer residence for Ayutthayan King Narai, the town was known as Lavo and had been a part of the Mon Dvaravati kingdom (6th–10th centuries). From the 10th to 13th centuries, the strategic town became a Khmer outpost for the Angkor empire; later it came under the influence of the Sukhothai kingdom to the north. Lopburi had its heyday in the mid-1600s when Ayutthaya flourished as a bustling capital city of more than 1 million people. It was where King Narai retreated each summer to escape from Ayutthaya's heat. When

Headless Buddha image at Prang Sam Yot.

Phiman Mongkut Pavilion.

The massive walls of Phra Narai Ratchaniwet.

the Dutch imposed a naval blockade on Ayutthaya from the Gulf of Siam, King Narai decided to install Lopburi as a second capital, running his court from there. It was said that, while his throne was in Ayutthaya, his heart belonged to Lopburi; indeed, after his new palace was completed he began spending more and more time there.

Wat Phra Si Rattana Mahathat

Just across from Lopburi's main train station is **Wat Phra Si Rattana Mahathat** (daily 8am–6pm; charge). Originally a Khmer temple with a tall stucco-decorated laterite *prang*, around the 12th century King Narai added a large *viharn* (sermon hall) that infused elements of European and Persian architecture, the latter influence coming from the strong Persian presence at the Ayutthayan court. On the grounds are several smaller *chedi*.

Phra Narai Ratchaniwet

Just northwest, the grounds of **Phra Narai Ratchaniwet** (or Lopburi Palace), built between 1665 and 1677, are enclosed by massive walls, which still dominate the centre of

the modern town (daily 8am–6pm; charge). Built in a mélange of Thai, Khmer and European styles, the palace grounds have a complex of official, ceremonial and residential buildings in three sections.

The outer grounds contained facilities for utilities and maintenance. The middle section enclosed the **Chanthara Phisan Pavilion**, the first structure built by King Narai, later restored by King Mongkut. On its south side is the **Dusit Maha Prasat Hall**, built for the audience granted by King Narai in 1685 to the French ambassador of Louis XIV.

Narai National Museum

To the left is the **Phiman Mongkut Pavilion**, a three-storey colonial-style mansion. It was built in the mid-19th century by King Mongkut, who wanted to restore the entire palace. The immensely thick walls and high ceilings averted the summer heat. The mansion, small but full of character, now functions as the **Narai National Museum** (tel: 0-3641 1458; Wed–Sun 9am–4pm; charge). It has a display of bronze statues, Chinese and Sukhothai porcelain, coins,

Buddhist fans and shadow-play puppets. Some of the pieces, particularly the Ayutthaya bronze heads and Bencharong porcelain, are superb. The inner courtyard housed the private chambers of King Narai, but not much is left except the foundations and the **Suttha Sawan Pavilion**, nestled amid gardens and ponds.

Baan Vichayen

North of Phra Narai Ratchaniwet are the remains of **Baan Vichayen** palace, said to have belonged to Constantine Phaulkon (daily 8am–6pm; charge). Phaulkon was a Greek adventurer who arrived in Siam in 1678 to work for the English East India Company. He settled in quickly, becoming fluent in Siamese and gaining favour with King Narai, who promoted him to be his most senior minister. However, he antagonised many of the other foreign settlers in Ayutthaya, as well as Thai nobles who felt threatened by a foreigner wielding so much influence. Phaulkon forged strong ties with the French, but when more Catholic missionary priests started arriving in Siam, local Buddhists believed the Greek was conspiring with King Louis XIV to convert Siam to Christianity. As King Narai lay on his deathbed, his successors had Phaulkon arrested and later executed for treason. The following period saw the Siamese court become more wary of foreign influence.

The palace buildings show strong European influences, with straight-sided walls and decorations over Western-style windows.

Prang Sam Yot

To the east are the three laterite towers of **Prang Sam Yot** (daily 8am–6pm; charge). This much-photographed sight is of interest as the towers were originally built by the Khmers as a Hindu shrine honouring the gods Brahma, Vishnu and Shiva. It was later converted into a Buddhist shrine, incorporating a hodge-podge fusion of Brahman, Khmer and Buddhist elements that is often dubbed the Lopburi style. Beware of the annoying monkeys at this site.

Riding past the Narai National Museum.

Baan Vichayen.

Bangkok's Skytrain.

TRAVEL TIPS
BANGKOK

TRANSPORT

GETTING THERE AND GETTING AROUND

GETTING THERE

By Air

Bangkok is not only a key gateway between Asia and the West, but also a major transportation hub for the rest of Southeast Asia.

Suvarnabhumi Airport

Bangkok International Airport, Suvarnabhumi (pronounced "su-wa-na-poom") Airport (www.airportthai.co.th) is located about 30km (19 miles) east of Bangkok in Samut Prakan province. It takes about 45 minutes to get to the airport from the city by taxi, depending on traffic conditions. The airport handles all international flights to Bangkok as well as many domestic connections.

Suvarnabhumi has one main passenger terminal with seven concourses, easily capable of handling 76 flights per hour, according to the Airport Authority of Thailand (AOT). The airport has its fair share of complaints, usually sparse toilet facilities, a congested arrival hall and long walks between gates. But the experience is pretty hassle-free, the main bugbear being rogue taxis (see below).

The airport has a good range of facilities, including foreign exchange outlets, ATMs, a Tourism Authority of Thailand (TAT) office, medical centre, Internet facilities and a wide array of shops and restaurants.

For more details check the airport website or call any of the following:
Airport Call Centre: tel: 0-2132 1888
Arrivals: tel: 0-2132 9328–9
Departures: tel: 0-2132 9324–7

In line with the practice of major airports the world over, the airport tax for international flights out of Suvarnabhumi is now incorporated into the price of your air ticket.

Don Muang Airport

Don Muang Airport (tel: 0-2535 1111; www.airportthai.co.th) services a growing number of budget carriers, both domestic and international. The airport has undergone a recent refurbishment and is now regarded as Bangkok's second airport (after Survarnabhumi). Air Asia is the major stakeholder, but other airlines include Nok Air, Lion Air and Thai Smile. There are two terminals, one serving domestic arrivals and departures, the other international.

Don Muang is about 30km (19 miles) north of the city centre. It takes about 40–45 minutes by taxi, depending on traffic, to get to or from the airport.

Note: if making a flight connection between Suvarnabhumi and Don Muang airports, be sure to allow for sufficient time as taxi travel time between the two airports could take up to 1.5 hours. There is a bus operating between both airports (No. 555), which takes only fractionally longer than a taxi.

Flying from UK and US

Even if you don't plan to spend any time in Thailand, Bangkok is the most convenient (and sometimes the only) way to transfer to neighbouring countries like Laos, Cambodia and Burma. Low-cost airlines mean that domestic and regional flights to nearby destinations like Malaysia and Singapore and even destinations in southern China have become incredibly cheap – if booked in advance.

Passengers from UK and Europe can fly direct to Bangkok in about 12 hours, though it is considerably cheaper to take an airline that makes a stopover in Europe, the Middle East or Asia. Airlines that fly non-stop include British Airways, Qantas, Thai and EVA Airways. Many travellers to Australia and New Zealand choose Bangkok as a transit point on their journey.

Travel time from the US is considerably longer. Flying from

the West Coast usually takes around 18 hours (not including transit time) and often involves a connection in North Asia – Japan, Korea or Taiwan; the East Coast route via Europe takes about 19 hours in the air.

By Rail

The **State Railway of Thailand** (tel: 0-2222 0175, hotline: 1690; www.railway.co.th) operates trains that are generally clean, cheap and reliable, if a little slow. There are three entry points by rail into Thailand. Two are from Malaysia, the most popular of which is the daily train that leaves Butterworth near Penang at 1.15pm for Hat Yai (south Thailand) and arrives in Bangkok's Hualamphong Station at 10.50am the next morning. Trains leave Hualamphong daily at 2.45pm for Malaysia. In 2009, a short line opened from Nong Khai in northeastern Thailand to Thanaleng, in Laos. It will eventually run to Vientiane.

If you like to travel in style and prefer not to fly, then plump for the **Eastern and Oriental Express** (www.belmond.com/eastern-and-oriental-express). Travelling several times a month between Singapore, Kuala Lumpur and Bangkok, the 22-carriage train is a very expensive but very elegant way to travel.

By Road

Malaysia provides the main road access into Thailand, with crossings near Betong and Sungai Kolok. From Laos, it is possible to cross from Vientiane into Nong Khai in northeast Thailand by using the Friendship Bridge across the Mekong River. From Cambodia, the most commonly used border crossing is from Poipet, which connects to Aranyaprathet, east of Bangkok. One other option is overland from Kompong Cham in Cambodia, crossing over to Hat Lek in Thailand.

GETTING AROUND

From the Airport

The journey from Suvarnabhumi Airport to the city centre takes about 45 minutes, depending on traffic conditions (the worst period is between 4 and 9pm). Negotiating an exit from the Arrival Hall, however, can be more daunting. If you are on a business trip, you'll understand why it is the norm for Bangkok hosts to deploy a personal greeter and escort. Emerging in the Arrival Hall, you may be harangued by taxi (and hotel) touts both inside and outside the barriers. Never volunteer your name or destination to these people. If you already have a reservation at a hotel, a representative will have your name written on a sign, or at least a sign bearing the name of your hotel. If you haven't made prior arrangements, use one of the following modes to get to the city.

By Taxi

Operating 24 hours daily, all taxis officially serving the airport are air-conditioned and metered. When you exit the Arrival Hall, there is an official taxi booth outside on the fourth-floor concourse. Join the queue and tell the person at the desk where you want to go. A receipt will be issued, with the licence plate number of the taxi and your destination in Thai written on it. Make sure the driver turns on the meter. At the end of your trip, you need to pay what is on the meter plus a B50 airport surcharge. If the driver uses the expressway to speed up the journey, he will ask for your approval first. If you agree, you will have to pay the toll fees, which will be around B70 in total. Depending on traffic, an average fare from the airport to the city centre is around B300 (excluding toll fees and airport surcharge).

By Limousine

There are two limousine operators stationed at the Arrival Hall.

Airports of Thailand Limousines (tel: 0-2134 2323-6) operates a variety of standard vehicles that can take you to the city centre for B950–B1,100. Luxury cars include Mercedes E Class at B1,600 and 7-series BMW at B2,200. Rates to Pattaya start at around B2,600, depending on the vehicle used. **Thai Airways Limousines** (mobile tel: 081-652 4444; www.thaiairways.com) also operates a premium car service. Prices are similar to that charged by AOT.

By Airport Bus

The Airport Bus passes the main hotels in downtown Bangkok. You must first get on the free airport shuttle to the Public Transportation Centre, which is separate from the main terminal building. Buses depart every 15 minutes from 5.30am to 12.30am, and the cost is B150 per person.

Airport Bus Routes:

AE-1 – to Silom via Pratunam, Thanon Phetchaburi, Thanon Ratchadamri, Thanon Silom and Thanon Surawong.

AE-2 – to Banglamphu via Thanon Phetchaburi, Thanon Lan Luang and Thanon Khao San.

AE-3 – to Sukhumvit (Nana) via Bangna, Thanon Phrakhanong, Ekkamai, Asok, Thanon Ratchadamri, Thanon Phetchaburi and Thanon Sukhumvit.

AE-4 – to Hualamphong Railway Station via Victory Monument, Thanon Ploenchit, Thanon Rama, Thanon Phaya Thai and Thanon Rama IV.

By Rail

The 28km (17-mile) Suvarnabhumi Airport Rail Link (SARL) connects the airport to the city. The high-speed system has two services. The 24-hour City Line to Phaya Thai calls at eight stations en route – Lat Krabang, Ban Thap Chang, Hua Mak, Ramkhamhaeng, Asoke, Makkasan, Ratchaprarop and Phaya Thai – and takes 30 minutes for the full journey. It links to the Skytrain system at Phaya Thai. The Express Line

(6am–1am) runs direct to Bangkok City Air Terminal, at Makkasan (a 15-minute journey), where passengers can check in and drop their luggage. Makkasan will eventually link to Phetchaburi Metro station. Tickets: B15–40 (City Line), B150 (Express Line).

Orientation

Bangkok is a flat, low-lying city that sprawls over 1,565 sq km (602 sq miles) in the heart of Thailand's fertile Central Plains delta. It sits almost in the middle of the country's north–south length, at the mouth of Thailand's longest river, the Chao Phraya, which separates Thonburi to its west from Bangkok to its east.

The modern city has no definitive centre, with major business and shopping areas now occupying Pathumwan, Silom and Sukhumvit. Rattanakosin, the Old City and Chinatown hold most of the city's historic architecture. Dusit mixes the palatial grandeur of European-influenced royal buildings with tiny lanes of the homes of immigrant Vietnamese and Cambodian refugees. Across the river, Thonburi, despite its urban sprawl, offers trips through countryside canals.

Walking is hot work, but the colourful streets give an insightful peek into everyday life as you pick your way through hawker stalls. Ease your progress with water or

chopped fresh fruit, served in a bag with a cocktail stick, so it makes it easy to eat on the move.

Public Transport

Skytrain (BTS)
BTS Tourist Information Centre: tel: 0-2617 7340; hotline: tel: 0-2617 6000; www.bts.co.th.

The Bangkok Transit System's (BTS) elevated train service, better known as Skytrain, is the perfect way of beating the city's traffic-congested streets. It consists of two lines. The **Sukhumvit Line** runs from Mo Chit station in the north to Bearing station in the southeast. The **Silom Line** runs from National Stadium, near Siam Square, south to Bang Wa station, across the river in Thonburi. The lines intersect at Siam station.

The Skytrain is fast, frequent and clean, but suffers from overcrowding during peak hours. Accessibility is a problem for the disabled and aged as there aren't enough escalators or lifts, compounded by the surrounding streets often being unsuitable for wheelchairs or mobility impaired customers to get to the stations.

Trains operate from 6am to midnight (3 minutes peak; 5 minutes off-peak). Single-trip fares vary according to distance, starting at B15 and rising to B40. Self-service ticket machines are found at all station concourses.

Tourists may find it more useful to buy the unlimited ride 1-Day Pass (B120) or the 30-Day Adult Pass (which comes in three types: B440 for 20 rides, B600 for 30 and B800 for 40) – all available at station counters.

BTS Tourist Information Centres are found on the concourse levels of Siam, Nana and Saphan Taksin stations (daily 8am–8pm).

Metro (MRT or Subway)
Customer Relations Centre: tel: 0-2624 5200; www.bangkok metro.co.th.

Bangkok's metro line is operated by the Mass Rapid Transit Authority (MRT). The line has 18 stations, stretching 20km (12 miles) between Bang Sue in the northern suburbs of Bangkok and the city's main railway station, Hualamphong, at the edge of Chinatown. Three of its stations – Silom, Sukhumvit and Chatuchak Park – are interchanges, where passengers can transfer to the BTS network, though you need to pay separately for each service.

Operating from 6am to midnight, the air-conditioned trains are frequent, with never more than a few minutes' wait (2–4 minutes peak, 4–6 minutes off-peak). Fares start at B16, increasing by B2–3 every station, with a maximum fare of B42.

Unlike the BTS, coin-sized plastic tokens are used instead of cards, with self-service ticket machines at all stations. Also available at station counters are passes with unlimited rides: the 1-Day Pass (B120), 3-Day Pass (B230), 15-Day Pass (B600) and the stored-value Adult Card (B200, which includes a B50 deposit).

Taxis
Taxis are in Bangkok are metered, air-conditioned, inexpensive and comfortably seat 3–4 persons. It's best to hail them on the streets, as those parked outside hotels often hustle for a no-meter

STREET NAME CONFUSION

Note that *Wireless Road* (a street full of embassies and hotels) is more commonly known by its Thai name, *Thanon Withayu*. Similarly, *Sathorn Road*, a main thoroughfare divided into north and south which runs between Lumphini Park and the river, is often referred to as *Sathorn Nua* (north) and *Sathorn Tai* (south). With no standard translated English spellings for the Thai language, it is common to find a

street or area spelt with several variants and broken or joined syllables. Even more confusing, some streets have as many as four names, based on old and new official names and landmarks. Skytrain station names often differ from the street sign spelling, so Chidlom district becomes Chit Lom station, Thanon Asoke becomes Asok station, and Soi Thonglor becomes Thong Lo.

fare. Metered taxis are recognisable by the sign on their roof, and they have an illuminated red light above the dashboard indicating whether it's available for hire or not.

The flag-fall is B35 for the first kilometre, then B5–8.50 per kilometre, depending on distance travelled. If stuck in traffic, a small per-minute surcharge kicks in. If your journey crosses town, ask the driver to take the expressway. The network of elevated multi-lane roads can cut the journey time by more than half. The toll fare of B10–60 is given to the driver at the payment booth, not at the end of the trip.

Before starting, check that the meter has been reset and turned on. Generally, drivers are far better than their reputation in this regard, but will try it on occasionally. This happens particularly if there is heavy rain, when it is sometimes wise to negotiate, otherwise you may be stuck for some time but the meter will keep ticking. Fares, however, are negotiated for longer distances outside Bangkok: for instance, to Pattaya (B1,500), Koh Samet (B2,000) or Hua Hin (B1,800–2,300). Often, drivers don't speak much English, but should know the locations of major hotels. It is a good idea to have a destination written in Thai.

The following taxi companies take bookings (there's a B20 surcharge):
Siam Taxi, hotline: 1661
Nakhornthai Transportation, tel: 02-878 9000

Tuk-Tuks

Tuk-tuks are the brightly coloured three-wheeled taxis, whose name comes from the incessant noise their two-stroke engines make. Few tuk-tuk drivers speak English, so make sure your destination is written down in Thai. Negotiate the fare before you set off. Expect to pay B30–50 for short journeys of a few blocks or around 15 minutes or less, and B50–100 for longer journeys. A B100 ride should get you a half-hour ride across most parts of downtown. Be sure to negotiate the fare beforehand. Although they can be a fun experience, unless you bargain hard, tuk-tuk fares are rarely lower than metered taxi fares and you are surrounded by traffic fumes.

Motorcycle Taxis

Motorcycle taxi stands are noticeable by their drivers – a gathering of men in fluorescent numbered vests found at the mouth of many sois, at busy intersections, buildings and markets. Hire only a driver who provides a passenger helmet, and negotiate fares beforehand. For longer journeys motorcycle taxis are rarely cheaper than taxi fares for the same distance travelled, but they are a great way to beat the traffic and economical for short journeys, such as the length of a street, which will cost B20–30. Longer rides (B100–150 should get you a half-hour trip across most parts of downtown) are more expensive during rush hour (8–10am,

4–6pm). Hold on tight and keep your knees tucked in (Thai women usually ride side-saddle, with their hands clasped between their knees for modesty). If the driver is going too fast, ask him to slow down in Thai: "*cha-cha*".

Buses

Buses are very cheap but with little English either spoken by staff or on signage, finding the right bus can be frustrating. They come in air-conditioned or non-air-conditioned varieties and the Bangkok Metropolitan Authority (BMA) have made attempts to clean up the surrounding air by banning buses with heavy exhaust fumes. Municipal and private operators all come under the charge of the Bangkok Mass Transit Authority (tel: 0-2246 0973; www.bmta.co.th). Free maps found at the airport and tourist centres often have bus routes marked.

Boats

The most common waterborne transport is The **Chao Phraya Express Boat Company** (tel: 0-2623 6143; www.chaophraya boat.co.th), which runs several services between Nonthaburi pier in the north to Ratburana in the south. Boats run every 15 minutes from 6am to 9pm, and stop at different piers according to the coloured flag on top of the boat. Yellow and green flags are fastest, but stop at only 12 piers, while orange flags are slowest but stop at every pier. Sat and Sun have only orange flags. Tickets cost B14–34 and are purchased from the conductor on board or at some pier counters.

The **Chao Phraya Tourist Boat** (tel: 0-2623 6143; www.chao phrayaboat.co.th) operates daily from 9.30am to 3pm and a trip costs B120. After 3.30pm, you can use the ticket on regular express boats. A useful commentary is provided on board, plus a small guidebook and a bottle of water. The route begins at the Sathorn pier and travels

A – Z

LANGUAGE

TRANSPORT ETIQUETTE

While it is quite normal to let an elderly person stand up on a crowded bus or train, legions of locals are quick to vacate their seats if a young child steps aboard. On buses, the two seats nearest the door must be vacated for monks; female passengers should not sit next to a monk on any kind of transport. Queuing is still a novel concept to most Thais, so don't expect any orderly behaviour at bus stops or boat piers. At rush hours on the Skytrain and metro, you often see commuters standing in front of train doors blocking passengers from getting off while squeezing to get in.

upriver to the Phra Athit pier, stopping at 10 major piers along the way. Boats leave every 30 minutes and you can get off at any pier and pick up another boat later on this hop-on-hop-off service.

River **ferries** are used for getting from one side of the river to the other. They can be boarded close to the jetties that service the Chao Phraya River Express Boats; cost from B3 per journey; and operate from 5am to 10pm or later.

Longtail boat taxis ply the narrow inner canals, carrying passengers from the centre of town to the outlying districts. Many of the piers are located near road bridges. Be sure to tell the conductor your destination, as boats do not stop otherwise. Tickets cost B5–10, depending on distance, with services operating roughly every 10 minutes until 6–7pm. While there are routes serving Thonburi's canals and Bangkok's outskirts, tourists will probably only use the main downtown artery of Khlong Saen Saep, which starts from the Saphan Phan Fah pier near Wat Saket, into the heart of downtown and beyond to Bang Kapi. It's useful if going to the Old City, Jim Thompson's House, Siam Paragon and the Thanon Ploenchit malls or all the way to Thonglor and Ekkamai.

If you wish to explore the canals of Thonburi or Nonthaburi,

private longtail boats can be hired from most of the river's main piers. A 90-minute to two-hour tour will take you into the quieter canal communities. Negotiate rates beforehand and get an agreement on what sites will be included and which route the boat will take. On the journey ask to pull up and get out if anything interests you. An hour-long trip should cost B700–800, rising to B1,000 and more for two hours. The price is for the entire boat, which seats up to 16 people, not per person.

Rental Cars

Driving in Bangkok has some frustrations, but with a few adjustments and *jai yen* (a cool heart), the experience is generally comfortable. The problems include: drivers will often cut in front of you with little warning, side streets are very narrow and busy, signalling is rarely used, motorbikes are everywhere, and again have little road discipline, so use of wing mirrors needs to be constant. It might sound scary, but drivers generally stick to their lane, at least, and if you're used to city driving there should be little to worry about. If you park on the street at night, someone may approach you for a parking fee (usually B40) to watch your car. This is unofficial, but it is better to

pay, otherwise your car will be keyed. An international driver's licence is necessary to drive a car; these are available for hire from around B1,000 a day, including insurance.

Avis: 2/12 Thanon Withayu; tel: 0-2255 5300-4; and Bangkok International Airport Building 2; tel: 0 84 700 8157-9; www.avis thailand.com.

Hertz: Soi 71, Thanon Sukhumvit; tel: 0-2266 4666; www.hertz.com.

Sathorn Car Rent: 6/8–9 Thanon Sathorn; tel: 0-2633 8888.

TRIPS OUT OF BANGKOK

By Road

Thailand has a good road system with over 50,000km (31,000 miles) of motorways and more being built every year. Road signs are in both Thai and English and you should have no difficulty following a map. An international driver's licence is required.

Driving on a narrow but busy road can be a terrifying experience, with right-of-way determined by size. It is not unusual for a bus to overtake a truck despite the fact that the oncoming lane is filled with vehicles. A safer option is to hire a car or a van with driver for trips outside of Bangkok. A reliable option is www.thaicarhire.com, with rates from around B1,400 per day.

You can get to several places outside Bangkok, like Pattaya and Hua Hin, by simply flagging a taxi on the street or booking one beforehand. Be sure to negotiate a flat rate before boarding; don't use the meter.

By Air

Thai Airways International (THAI) services a domestic network, with as many as 14 daily flights to the more popular destinations such as Chiang Mai and Phuket. **Bangkok Airways** is the second-largest domestic

The busy and colourful streets of Bangkok.

operator. In recent years, a slew of low-cost airlines – like **Air Asia** and **Nok Airways** – have entered the market, flying to the main tourism centres in Thailand.

Air Asia: Bangkok International Airport, tel: 0-2215 9999; www.airasia.com.

Bangkok Airways: 99 Moo 14 Thanon Vibhavadi Rangsit; tel: 1771; www.bangkokair.com.

Nok Air: Bangkok International Airport, tel: 1318 (Call Centre); www.nokair.com.

Orient Thai Airlines: 222 Thanon Vibhavadi Rangsit; tel: 0-2229 4260; www.orient-thai.com.

Thai Airways International: Bangkok International Airport; tel: 0-2134 5483; www.thaiair.com.

By Bus

Air-conditioned buses service many destinations in Thailand. VIP coaches with extra leg room are the best for overnight journeys. All buses are operated by the **Transport Company Ltd** (www.transport.co.th), with terminals at the following locations:

Eastern (Ekamai) Bus Terminal: Thanon Sukhumvit opposite Soi 63, tel: 0-2391 8097.

Northern and Northeastern Bus Terminal: Thanon Khampaengphet 2, Northern: tel: 0-2936 2841–48; Northeastern: tel: 0-2936 2852–66 ext. 611.

Southern Bus Terminal: Thanon Boromrat Chonnani, Thonburi, tel: 0-2435 1200.

By Train

State Railway of Thailand (tel: 0-2222 0175, hotline 1690; www.railway.co.th) operates three principal routes – north, northeast and south – from **Hualamphong Railway Station** (Thanon Rama 4; tel: 0-2225 0300). Express and rapid services on the main lines offer first-class air-conditioned or second-class fan-cooled carriages with sleeping cabins or berths. In addition, some trains depart from **Bangkok Noi Station** (tel: 0-2411 3102) in Thonburi.

West

Kanchanaburi

By Train: Take the Southern line from Bangkok Noi Station to Kanchanaburi or to the Kwai River Bridge (via Nakhon Pathom). Two departures daily (7.45am and 1.55pm) for the 2.5-hour journey.

By Bus: Although Kanchanaburi is west of Bangkok, buses leave from the Southern Bus Terminal every 20 minutes from 5am to 10.30pm. Journey time: 2.5 hours.

South

Hua Hin

By Taxi: A taxi ride from Bangkok to Hua Hin, taking 3 hours, can be negotiated for a flat rate of B1,500–2,000.

By Train: There are 12 daily departures between 8.05am to 10.50pm for Petchaburi and Hua Hin from Hualamphong Station. The journey takes around 4 hours.

By Bus: Buses leave from the Southern Bus Terminal every 30 minutes between 6.30am and 5.30pm, stopping at Petchaburi and Cha-am before arriving at Hua Hin. The journey takes around 3.5 hours.

Eastern Seaboard

Pattaya

By Taxi: A taxi ride from Bangkok to Pattaya can be negotiated for a flat rate of B1,500. The ride will take 90 minutes.

By Bus: Buses leave every 40 minutes from 5am to 11pm from the Eastern Bus Terminal. The journey takes around 2 hours.

Ko Samet

By Taxi: A Bangkok taxi will make the 3-hour ride to Ban Phe pier in Rayong province for a flat rate of B2,000.

By Bus: Buses leave every hour from 5am to 9pm from Eastern Bus Terminal to Ban Phe pier. Travel time is 3.5 hours.

By Boat: Once in Ban Phe pier, fishing boats leave every 30 minutes to an hour (or when there

are enough passengers) for the short ride to Na Dan pier on Ko Samet. If there are a few of you, hiring a speedboat is much faster (B1,000–B1,500).

Ko Chang

By Bus: Buses leave from Eastern Bus Terminal to Trat every 90 minutes between 6am to 11.30pm. The journey takes around 5 to 6 hours. From Trat bus station take a *songthaew* (van with bench seats) to Laem Ngop pier.

By Air: Bangkok Airways has three 50-minute flights a day to Trat airport. From the airport take a 20-minute taxi ride to Laem Ngop pier.

By Boat: From Laem Ngop pier, ferries leave nine times a day between 7am and 5pm for Tha Dan Kao pier in Ko Chang.

North

Ayutthaya

By Train: There are 11 daily departures from Hualamphong from 7am to 10pm. The journey takes around 2 hours.

By Bus: Buses leave every 30 minutes from the Northern Bus Terminal between 5am and 8pm. The journey takes 90 minutes.

By Boat: Several companies operate canal cruises to Ayutthaya; some return the same day, while others take a leisurely 2 to 3 days. The **Chao Phraya Express Boat** (tel: 0-2623 6001) operates a day trip every Sunday at 8am. The **River Sun Cruise** travels one way by coach and returns by boat (tel: 2266 9125; www.riversuncruise.co.th). More expensive is the overnight trip on board a restored teakwood barge by **Manohra Cruises** (tel: 0-2477 0770; www.manohracruises.com).

Lopburi

By Train: 11 daily departures from Hualamphong from 7am to 10pm. Journey time: 3 hours.

By Bus: Buses leave every 30 minutes from the Northern Bus Terminal between 5am and 8pm daily. The journey to Lopburi takes about 3 hours.

A – Z

AN ALPHABETICAL SUMMARY OF PRACTICAL INFORMATION

A

Addresses

Given the size of the city and its many twisting alleyways, finding your way around Bangkok can be a bit confusing. The city is mostly laid out with main roads having smaller streets – called soi – leading off, each having the main road's name followed by a number. For example, Sukhumvit Road (or Thanon Sukhumvit) has side streets called Sukhumvit Soi 1, Sukhumvit Soi 3, etc, running in sequence, odd and even numbers on opposite sides of the road. Soi may be sub-divided using a slash after the number followed by another number. The same system is used for shop and house addresses, a slash separating the block or building number from the shop. So an address might read 36/1 Sukhumvit 33/1. Street names are usually written in Thai and English and most hotels provide business cards with the address written in Thai to show taxi drivers.

B

Budgeting for your Trip

By Western standards, many things in Bangkok are a bargain. Budget accommodation can be as cheap as B300 a night, with a delicious streetside meal and beer around B150. Five-star hotels cost from B6,000, and a three-course meal may be had for B1,000 without drinks (although wine is expensive and one bottle will at least double that price). In bars, refreshments start around B70, and even in posh clubs they may be as little as B200. Bus fares cost B7 to B22, a Skytrain or Metro ride from B16 to B40 and taxi meters start at B35. If you live frugally, you can get by on B700 a day.

Business Travellers

As Thailand strives to become a regional business hub, the capital hosts an increasing number of business travellers. Most hotels have business centres with communications and secretarial services in several languages. Elsewhere in Bangkok, it is possible to lease small offices with shared clerical staff. Interpreter services are also available.

A good starting point for overseas business people wanting to start a company in Thailand is the **Board of Investment** (BOI), tel: 0-2537 8111; www.boi.go.th. They are authorised to grant tax holidays and other incentives to promote certain key industries.

CLIMATE CHART

Bangkok

- Maximum temperature
- Minimum temperature
- — Rainfall

C

Children

Travelling with children is not especially difficult in Thailand, although Bangkok footpaths are often in disrepair and invariably obstructed by something or someone. Leave the baby stroller at home and bring back- or chest-mounted baby carriers. Many department stores and malls have play areas and baby-changing facilities and some upmarket hotels have baby-sitting services. The tropical heat is intense, so sun block and hats are important, while clean hands help ward off possible stomach bugs.

Climate

There are three official seasons in Thailand: hot, rainy and cool. But to the tourist winging in from more temperate regions, Bangkok has only one temperature: hot, with humidity above 70 percent. There is little wind and the mercury drops only a few degrees during the night. Evenings during the cool season, however, can be very pleasant. Air-conditioning of course makes Bangkok tolerable indoors, at least. These temperature ranges give you an idea of what to expect:
Hot season (Mar to mid-June): 27–35°C (80–95°F)
Rainy season (June to Oct): 24–32°C (75–90°F)
Cool season (Nov to Feb): 18–32°C (65–90°F), but with less humidity.

What to Wear

Clothes should be light and loose and preferably of natural fibres, which "breathe" better. A shirt and tie are expected for business appointments. A hat will offer protection from the sun, and it's best to carry an umbrella during the rainy season. Convenience stores sell them if you get caught out. Temples and places of Buddhist worship require visitors to dress modestly. Covering shoulders and wearing long trousers or dresses is usually the minimum requirement for such religious sites.

When to Visit

The cool season is overwhelmingly the best time to visit for most people. The temperature is not only lower, but there is also significantly less humidity. This means walking the city sights is more comfortable, hence you can see more. In addition there is hardly any rain then. When it rains in Bangkok, it happens suddenly and ferociously, which hampers many

a plan. That said, even in the rainy season, parts of most days will be sunny. Waterfalls in national parks such as Khao Yai will be at their fullest in the rainy season or in the early cool season.

Crime and Safety

Bangkok, like all cities, has an underbelly of violent crime, but tourists rarely encounter it and the streets are generally very safe. The biggest risk to travellers is from scams and con artists. If you do run into trouble in Bangkok, there are Tourist Police specially assigned to assist travellers, though much of the time there is little they are able to do but record the details of the crime and provide a report for insurance purposes.
Tourist Police: Tourist Service Centre, TAT headquarters, 4 Thanon Rachadamneon Nok, tel: 0-2281 5051; hotline: 1155.

Most members of the force speak some English. Tourist Police booths can also be found in tourist areas including Lumphini Park (near the intersection of Rama IV and Silom) and Patpong (at the Surawong intersection).

Common Scams

Touts on Patpong offering live sex shows upstairs. Once inside, you are sometimes handed an exorbitant bill and threatened if you protest. Pay, take the receipt, and go immediately to the Tourist Police, who will usually take you back and demand a refund.

Don't take free or very cheap boat rides into the canals. Once you are well into the canal, you are given the choice of paying a high fee or being stranded.

Don't follow touts who offer to take you to a gem factory for a "special deal". The gems are usually synthetic or of substandard quality and there is no way to get your money back.

There are no tuk-tuk rides for B10. If a driver takes you on one, you will end up stopping at every

gem, silver and tailor shop in the city, where he will collect commission for wasting your day.

Bear in mind that in Thai culture, strangers rarely approach and engage foreigners in conversation, so if you find yourself on the receiving end, be on guard no matter how polite and innocent they appear to be. Feel free to be rude and walk away, even if it goes against the rules of polite behaviour.

Customs Regulations

In Thailand the import or export of drugs, dangerous chemicals, pornography, firearms and goods displaying the Thai flag are prohibited. Attempting to smuggle heroin or other hard drugs in or out may be punishable by death. Scores of foreigners are serving very long prison terms for this offence.

Foreign currency exceeding US$20,000 either entering or leaving the country should be declared. Thai currency leaving the country is restricted to B50,000. Foreign guests are allowed to bring in 200 cigarettes and one litre of wine or spirits tax free.

Buddha images, antiques and art objects can only leave the country with a Department of Fine Arts permit. For more information contact the National Museum, Bangkok (tel: 0-2224 1333).

For more details check the Thai **Customs Department** website at www.customs.go.th, or call the hotline: 1164.

D

Disabled Travellers

Bangkok falls short on accommodating the disabled. The uneven pavements are studded with obstructions and few buildings have wheelchair ramps. Traffic is relentless and drivers generally unsympathetic to pedestrians. However, there have been signs of improvement in

TRANSPORT
A – Z
LANGUAGE

Thai Royal Family.

recent years. Although only a few Skytrain stations have lifts, the Metro has them at every station, and pricier hotels and shopping malls will often have disabled access and modified toilets. Taxi drivers, if arranged beforehand, can be quite cooperative. As it is a challenge for a lone disabled traveller, a companion may be preferable.

E

Electricity

Electrical outlets are rated at 220 volts, 50 cycles and accept flat-pronged or round-pronged plugs. Adaptors can be purchased at department or hardware stores.

Embassies and Consulates

Bangkok

Australia: 37 Thanon Sathorn Tai, tel: 0-2344 6300. Visas: Mon–Fri 8.15am–12.15pm.
Canada: 15/F, Abdulrahim Place, Thanon Rama IV, tel: 0-2636 0540, 2254 2530.
New Zealand: M Thai Tower, 14th Fl, All Seasons Place, 87 Thanon Withayu, tel: 0-2254 2530.
Singapore: 129 Thanon Sathorn Tai, tel: 0-2286 1434.

UK: 1031 Thanon Ploenchit, tel: 0-2305 8333. Visas: now handled by post via Hong Kong.
US: 120-122 Thanon Withayu, tel: 0-2205 4000. Visas: Mon–Fri 7.30–10am.

Overseas

UK: Royal Thai Embassy, 29–30 Queen's Gate, London SW7 5JB tel : 020 7589 2944; www.thaiembassyuk.org.uk. Visas: Mon–Fri 9.30am–12.30pm.
US: Royal Thai Embassy, 1024 Wisconsin Ave, N.W. Washington D.C. 20007; tel: (202) 944 3600, www.thaiembdc.org. Visas: Mon–Fri 9am–1pm.

Etiquette

Thais are remarkably tolerant and forgiving of foreigners' eccentricities, but there are a few things that upset them.

Buddhism

In general, it is impolite to point your feet at Buddha images or to have bare legs or shoulders when visiting temples. Monks have taken vows of celibacy, and women should avoid physical contact with them, including passing items directly to them. Instead, place the object somewhere to be picked up.

Head and Feet

The Hindu religion, which has had a strong influence on Thai Buddhism, regards the head as the wellspring of wisdom and the feet as unclean. For this reason, it is insulting to touch another person on the head (children are an exception), to point one's feet at anything or to step over another person. In formal situations, when wishing to pass someone who is seated on the floor, bow slightly while walking and point an arm down to indicate the path to be taken, and a path will be cleared.

Public Behaviour

Two decades ago, Thai couples showed no intimacy in public.

That has changed due to modernisation and foreign influence on the young, but even these days, intimacy rarely extends beyond holding hands. As in many traditional societies, displaying open affection in public, such as kissing, is a sign of bad manners.

The Royal Family

Thais have a great reverence for the monarchy, and disapprove of any disrespect directed towards members of the royal family. Thailand also has lese-majesty laws that, although usually invoked to settle business or political rivalries, may result in jail terms for people convicted of defaming, insulting or threatening royalty. Standing for the National Anthem is expected in cinemas and in public offices and parks (8am and 6pm).

Temple Dress Code

Shorts are taboo for women and men who wish to enter some of the more highly revered temples. Women wearing sleeveless dresses and short skirts may also be barred from certain temples. Improperly dressed and unkempt visitors will be turned away from Wat Phra Kaew and the Grand Palace (though some clothing can be borrowed at the entrance).

Terms of Address

Thais are addressed by their first names, usually preceded by the word *khun*, the equivalent of Mr or Ms. For example, Silpachai Krishnamra would be addressed as Khun Silpachai.

Thai Greetings

The common greeting and farewell in Thailand is *sawadee* (followed by *khrap* when spoken by men and *kha* by women). In more formal settings this is accompanied by a *wai* – raising the hands in a prayer-like gesture, the fingertips touching the nose, and bowing the head slightly. In business meetings, the *wai* is often followed by a handshake. Foreigners are not expected to *wai*.

F

Festivals

The dates for the traditional festivals listed here change from year to year. Check dates on the Tourism Authority of Thailand's website at www.tourismthailand. org. Also see box for a list of public holidays. In addition to these traditional festivals, the calendar is jam-packed with secular events of all sorts, with many new ones added every year. These range from the high-brow (the International Festival of Dance and Music) to the glitzy (Bangkok International Motor Show) and the sexually-liberating, on-off Bangkok Pride Festival.

January/February

Chinese New Year (late Jan/early Feb): The full moon of Chinatown comes alive as the capital's large Thai–Chinese community celebrates with typical mayhem – expect firecrackers, lion and dragon dances, and feasting galore.

February/March

Makha Puja (late Feb/early Mar): The full moon of the third lunar month marks the gathering of 1,250 disciples to hear the Buddha preach before he entered Nirvana. In the evening, Thais gather at temples for a candle-lit procession with offerings of incense and flowers.

April

Chakri Day (6 Apr): Celebrates the founding of the Chakri dynasty (which presently rules

Thailand) in 1782. The festivities are confined to the palace. Most Thais celebrate it as a day off from work.

Songkran (13–15 Apr): Thailand's official New Year. In days gone by people would celebrate by visiting temples and sprinkling water on each other's heads. Nowadays it's a different story, as people get wet and wild on the streets with water pistols the size of machine guns. No one is exempt as revellers career around the streets in open trucks with barrels of water, drenching everyone in sight. Sanam Luang is one of the best places to witness the festivities. Nearby Thanon Khao San is a relentless party zone where both Thais and Westerners dance and douse each other with gallons of water.

May/June

Royal Ploughing Ceremony (early May): Held at Sanam Luang in early May, this Brahman ritual is presided over by King Bhumibol and marks the official start of the rice-planting season. Crimson-clad attendants lead buffaloes drawing a plough over specially consecrated ground.

Visakha Puja (late May/early June): The most important Buddhist day, marking the birth, enlightenment and death of Lord Buddha. Thai people visit temples to listen to sermons by the monks. In the evenings candle-lit processions are held at temples.

July/August

Asanha Puja and Khao Phansa (late July/early Aug): Asanha Puja marks the day when the Buddha preached to his first five disciples. It is celebrated on the full-moon night in similar manner to Magha Puja and Visakha Puja. Immediately afterwards, the three-month Buddhist Lent (Khao Pansa) begins, when monks start a season of prayers and meditation known as the Rains Retreat. Most Thai men

will at some time in their lives enter a monastery, even for a brief time, and this is the most common period.

HM **The Queen's Birthday (12 Aug):** Often dubbed "Mother's Day", this celebration is in honour of Her Majesty Queen Sirikit's birthday. Thais decorate their houses and public buildings with flags and pictures of the Queen. At the time of writing, the country is in mourning after King Bhumibol's passing and it is not known if this will still be marked in the future.

October

Ok Phansa: October full moon marks the end of the three-month Buddhist Lent, and the beginning of the *kathin* season when Buddhists visit temples to present monks with new robes.

Chulalongkorn Day (23 Oct): Honours King Rama V (1868–1910), who led Thailand into the modern era.

November

Loy Krathong: On the full-moon night of November, Thais everywhere launch small floats with candles, incense and flowers into rivers, canals and ponds, asking for blessings from the water spirits.

December

Trooping of the Colour (3 Dec): Presided over in the past by the king and queen, this annual event is a brilliant spectacle. Amid pomp and ceremony, the Royal Guards swear allegiance to the Royal family.

King's Birthday Celebrations (5 Dec): Dubbed "Father's Day" in honour of King Bhumibol's birthday. Thai people all over the country decorate homes and buildings with flags and lights, and there are firework displays at night. At the time of writing, it is not known if this will continue to be celebrated after the king's passing.

G

Gay and Lesbian

Foreign gays quickly discover that Thailand is one of the most tolerant countries in the world. The gay nightlife scene is a thriving one. See **Bangkok After Dark** (see page 83).

Utopia at www.utopia-asia.com is Bangkok's major online gay resource. It's a good place to make contacts and to find out what's happening on the gay scene in Thailand and Asia.

Purple Dragon is a travel agency that caters exclusively for gay travellers, located at Tarntawan Place Hotel, 119/5-10 Thanon Surawong, tel: 0-2634 3186, www.purpledrag.com.

H

Health and Medical Care

Visitors entering Thailand are not required to show evidence of vaccination for smallpox or cholera. Check that your tetanus boosters are up-to-date. Immunisation against cholera is a good idea as are hepatitis A and B inoculations. Malaria and dengue persist in rural areas but generally not in Bangkok. When in the countryside, especially in the monsoon season, apply mosquito repellent on exposed skin at all times – dengue mosquitoes are at their most active in the day.

Many first-time visitors take a while to adjust to the heat. It is important to drink plenty of water, especially if you've drunk alcohol. Avoid too much sun when out and about and use sunblock – the sun is far more powerful at this latitude than in temperate regions. Tap water in Bangkok has been certified as potable, but bottled water is still safer and is available widely. Within Bangkok, ice is clean and presents no health problems.

Buy travel insurance before travelling to Bangkok.

Dental Clinics

Apart from the dental clinics at the BNH and Bumrungrad hospitals above, the **Dental Hospital** at 88/88 Soi 49 Thanon Sukhumvit, tel: 0-2260 5000-15, with its long-standing good reputation, is recommended. It looks more like a hotel than a dental hospital and has the latest equipment.

Hospitals

The level of medical care can be excellent in Bangkok, particularly at the following hospitals, all of which have specialised clinics as well as general medical services and are of international standard. In fact, there has been a growing business in "medical tourism" over the past 10 years, with people coming to Thailand to have procedures performed (including cosmetic surgery and sex changes) that would cost many times more at home or require waiting in a months-long queue. Equipment is up-to-date and the doctors are usually trained overseas and speak English. By Thai standards, these are considered expensive, but the fees are a fraction of what they are in most Western countries. The hospitals listed also have dental clinics.

Bangkok Christian Hospital, 124 Thanon Silom, tel: 0-2233 6981-9, www.bch.in.th/en/. A medium-sized hospital, a bit less luxurious than the others listed here but with high standards.

BNH Hospital, 9/1 Thanon Convent, Silom, tel: 0-2686 2700; www.bnhhospital.com. This squeaky-clean hospital offers comfortable rooms, top-notch equipment and a large team of specialists. Service is efficient and English is widely spoken.

Bumrungrad Hospital, 33 Soi 3, Thanon Sukhumvit, tel: 0-2667 1000; www.bumrungrad.com. This one is the top of the heap, and looks more like a five-star hotel than a hospital. Offers a huge

range of specialised clinics, excellent staff, and a selection of rooms from basic four-bed to luxury suites, the latter at only slightly more than the cost of a similar hotel room.

Medical Clinics

For minor problems, the **British Dispensary**, 109 Thanon Sukhumvit (between Soi 3 and 5), tel: 0-2252 8056, has British doctors on its staff. All the major hotels also have an on-premises clinic, or a doctor on call.

Pharmacies

These are found everywhere in downtown Bangkok. In recent years, official control on prescription drugs has been more strongly applied and requires the presence of a licensed pharmacist on the premises. Nonetheless, most antibiotics and many other drugs that would require a prescription in the West are available without a prescription.

Check the expiry date on all drugs you buy, and, wherever possible, purchase them from an air-conditioned pharmacy. There are several branches of **Boots** and **Watson's** pharmacies in central Bangkok.

I

Internet

There are wi-fi zones at the airport, and access is available in some hotels and most coffee shops. Major hotels usually include in-room internet, and public internet cafés mainly have reasonable speed broadband at around B20 per hour. There are some located around Thanon Khao San. Otherwise, ask in your hotel.

L

Left Luggage

There are two left-luggage facilities at Bangkok International

Airport. One is on the 1st floor of the Arrivals Hall, and the second is on the 3rd floor of the Departures Hall near the currency-exchange counter. The fee is B20 per bag per day. All hotels and guesthouses offer a left-luggage service, usually for a small daily fee.

Lost Property

If you lose any valuable property, report it as soon as possible to the **Tourist Police** either in person (see page 237) or on their hotline: 1155, to get an insurance statement.

Airport: For property lost at the airport, contact tel: 0-2535 1254.

Public Transit: BMTA city bus service, tel: 0-2246 0973; **BTS Skytrain**, tel: 0-2617 6000; **MRTA subway**, tel: 0-2624 5200, **Hualamphong Railway Station**, tel: 0-2225 6964, hotline 1690.

Taxis: Taxi drivers frequently listen to **JS100 Radio 100FM**, hotline: 1137, which has set up a lost-property hotline, and it is surprising how often forgetful passengers get their lost items back.

M

Maps

Basic maps of Bangkok are available free at the Tourism Authority of Thailand (TAT) offices (see page 244) and at big hotels. More detailed ones can be found at bookshops. The *Insight Fleximap* of Bangkok is probably the best. Other more funky insights into Bangkok's attractions can be found in Nancy Chandler's *Map of Bangkok* and Groovy Map's *Bangkok by Day* and *Bangkok by Night*.

Media

Magazines

There are several what's on and listings publications in English

that cover events, nightlife, art galleries, restaurants, and more, although most are sparsely filled, unreliable and often consist of advertising copy disguised as editorial. The best free sheet is *BK*, which also has a regularly updated website. The small format glossy *Bangkok 101* costs B100, and usually leads with a Bangkok photo feature. It also has a good run-down of art shows and venues, along with events and restaurant and nightlife reviews. See page 244 for website addresses.

Newspapers

Thailand has two longstanding English-language dailies, the *Bangkok Post* and *The Nation*. The *Bangkok Post* is more conservative than *The Nation*, which is more maverick and has had several run-ins with the government. Many big hotels furnish one or the other for free with the room, or they can be purchased at newsstands for B30.

Radio

AM radio is devoted entirely to Thai-language programmes. FM frequencies include several English-language stations with the latest pop hits. Some frequencies have bilingual DJs and play a mixture of Thai and English songs in the same programme.

97 MHz: Radio Thailand has 4 hours of English-language broadcasts each day.

105.5 MHz: Tourism Authority of Thailand offers useful tips to tourists every hour.

Fat FM 104.5: Has the latest on Thailand's thriving indie music.

Eazy FM 105.5 FM: As the name suggests, mostly easy-listening, middle-of-the-road music.

FMX 95.5 FM: Contemporary dance and pop hits.

Television

Bangkok has six Thai-language television channels. ITV or Independent Television

specialises in news and documentaries. The rest mainly air soaps, songs and game shows with a sprinkling of mostly domestically-orientated news. There is also TRUEVISION, a cable television network that provides subscribers with a wide choice of international channels, including BBC News, HBO, ESPN and MTV Thailand.

Money

The baht is the principal Thai monetary unit. Though it is divided into 100 units called satang, this is becoming outdated; only 50- and 25-satang pieces are used.

Banknotes are of different colours and denominations, and include 1,000 (light brown), 500 (purple), 100 (red), 50 (blue) and 20 (green). There is a 10-baht coin (brass centre with silver rim), a 5-baht coin (silver with copper edge), a 2-baht coin, a 1-baht coin (silver) and two small coins of 50 and 25 satang (both brass-coloured).

ATMs

ATMs are available 24 hours a day at banks, malls, major train and bus stations, and airports. Many accept credit cards and MasterCard and Visa debit cards.

Changing Money

Banking hours are Mon–Fri 9.30am–3.30pm, but nearly every bank maintains money-changing kiosks in tourist areas. Better hotels almost always have exchange kiosks, but generally give poor exchange rates compared to banks.

Credit Cards

American Express, Diner's Club, MasterCard, JCB and Visa are widely accepted throughout Bangkok. Credit cards can be used to draw emergency cash at most banks. If you lose your credit card, call one of the numbers below:

TRANSPORT

A – Z

LANGUAGE

American Express: tel: 0-2273 5222
Diner's Club: tel: 0-2238 3660
Visa: tel: 001-800-441-3485
Mastercard: tel: 001-800-11-887-0663

Warning: Credit-card fraud is a major problem in Thailand. Don't leave your credit card in a safe-deposit box. When making a purchase, make sure that you get the carbon-copies and dispose of them.

Travellers' Cheques

Travellers' cheques can be cashed at all exchange kiosks and banks, and generally receive better exchange rates than cash. There is a nominal charge of B25 for each travellers' cheque cashed.

Tipping

Tipping is not a custom in Thailand, although it is becoming more common in upper-end establishments. However, people will generally leave any change left from their bill, in both cafés and taxis. A service charge of 10 percent is included in the more expensive restaurants and is usually, though not always, divided among the staff.

O

Opening Hours

Government offices operate Mon–Fri 8.30am–4.30pm. Most businesses are open Mon–Fri 8am–5.30pm, while some are open 8.30am–noon on Sat. Banks are open Mon–Fri 9.30am–3.30pm. Money-changing kiosks in the city are open until 8pm daily.

Department stores are open 10.30am–9pm daily, though larger stores are open as late as 10pm. Ordinary shops open at 8.30am or 9am and close between 6pm and 8pm, depending on location and type of business.

Small open-air coffee shops and restaurants open at 7am and

close at 8.30pm, though some stay open past midnight. Large restaurants generally close by 10pm, though some in Bangkok stay open later on Friday and Saturday. Most hotel coffee shops close at midnight; some stay open 24 hours, and the city has several outdoor restaurants that are open as late as 4am for post-bar-hopping suppers. Clubs and bars are subject to loosely applied licensing laws and may close anywhere between midnight and 5am, depending on location and political and policing climate.

P

Postal Services

The Thai postal service is reasonably reliable, though mail seems to go more astray upcountry and at Christmas time. The odds for domestic mail can be improved by registering or sending items by **EMS** for a fee of B20 for a business-sized letter. EMS is supposed to guarantee that a letter reaches a domestic destination in one day, and it generally does, particularly in Bangkok. If you wish to send valuable parcels or bulky documents overseas, it is better to use a courier service.

The **General Post Office** at Thanon Charoen Krung, tel: 0-2233 1050, is open from Mon to Fri 8am to 8pm, and Sat, Sun and holidays 8am to 1pm.

Post offices elsewhere in Bangkok usually open at 8am and close at 4pm on weekdays. The GPO and many larger offices sell packing boxes and materials.

You can find mini post offices in some office buildings and hotels. Look for a red sign in English. These outlets offer basic mail services and accept small packages, but have no telecommunications services. Kiosks along some of the city's busier streets sell stamps and also ship small parcels.

PUBLIC HOLIDAYS

Note that these are subject to change due to the passing of the king. At the time of writing, the government were yet to announce the new calendar.
1 Jan: New Year's Day
Jan/Feb: (full moon) Magha Puja. Note: Chinese New Year is not an official holiday but many businesses close for several days.
6 Apr: Chakri Day
13–15 Apr: Songkran
1 May: Labour Day
5 May: Coronation Day
Late May/June: (full moon) Visakha Puja
Late July/Aug: (full moon) Asanha Puja and Khao Pansa
12 Aug: Queen's Birthday
23 Oct: Chulalongkorn Day
5 Dec: Father's Day
10 Dec: Constitution Day

Courier Services

The usual global courier services are available in Bangkok. You can call direct or book online.
DHL: tel: 0-2345 5000; www.dhl.co.th.
FedEx: tel: 0-2229 8800, or hotline: 1782; www.fedex.com/th.
UPS: tel: 0-2712 3300; www.ups.com/th.

R

Religious Services

Buddhists will find no lack of temples to worship at. There are also several mosques, one major Hindu temple, the Maha Uma Devi, a few churches and at least one synagogue.

Anglican

Christ Church Bangkok, 11 Convent Rd; tel: 0-2234 3634. Sunday services at 7.30am, 10am and 5pm.
International Church of Bangkok, 67 Soi 19, Thanon Sukhumvit, tel: 0-2258 5821. Services at 8am.

Catholic

Holy Redeemer Church, 123/19 Soi Ruam Rudi, Thanon Withayu, tel: 0-2256 6305. Sunday Mass at 8.30am, 9.45am, 11am and 5.30pm.
St Louis Church, 215/2 Thanon Sathorn Tai, tel: 0-2211 0220. Sunday Mass at 6am, 8am, 10am and 5.30pm.

Jewish

Even Chen Synagogue, Chao Phraya Office Tower, Shangri-La Hotel, Charoen Krung Soi 42/1; tel: 0-2236 7777. Services: Mon–Thur 8am, Fri 8am and 6.15pm, Sat 9am–noon, Sun 8.30am–9.30am.

Muslim

Assalafiyah Mosque, 2827 Thanon Charoen Krung; tel: 0-2688 1481. Service times vary.

T

Tax

Thailand has a Value-Added Tax (VAT) of 7 percent. This is added on to most goods and services (but not goods sold by street vendors and markets). It is possible to get the 7 percent VAT refunded from your shopping if you purchase goods from stores displaying the "VAT Refund for Tourists" sign. Refunds can only be claimed on single purchases of B2,000 or more, with a minimum overall expenditure of B5,000. At the time of purchase, present your passport and ask the sales assistant to complete the VAT refund form. Before departure at the airport, present

TIME ZONE

Thailand is 7 hours ahead of GMT. Since it gets dark between 6 and 7pm, uniformly throughout the year, Thailand does not observe daylight savings time.

your goods together with the VAT refund form and sales invoice to the Customs officers for inspection. After approval, present your claim to the Revenue officers at the airport's VAT Refund Counter.

Refunds under B30,000 will be made in cash (in baht) or by bank draft or credit to your credit-card account. Those over B30,000 cannot be made in cash. There is an administrative fee of B100 for cash refunds; bank drafts and card refunds will incur extra charges. See www.rd.go.th for more details.

All major hotels add 10 percent tax plus service charge to the room rate. At top-class restaurants, 10 percent service charge is added to the bill on top of VAT.

Telephones

International Calls

The country code for Thailand is 66. When calling Thailand from overseas, dial your local international access code, followed by 66 and the 8-digit number (without the preceding 0) in Thailand.

To make an international call from Thailand, dial 001 or 009 before the country and area codes followed by the telephone number (again, without the preceding 0). If you need international call assistance, call the local operator at tel: 100.

Peak-hour calls made 7am–9pm cost the most; non-peak rates are charged 5–7am and 9pm–midnight. The lowest call rates are midnight–5am.

Prepaid international phone cards (called Thaicard) with values of B300, B500 and B1,000 can be used to make international calls. These can be bought at post offices, certain shops that carry the Thaicard sign or the office of the **Communications Authority of Thailand**, tel: 0-2950 3712, www.cat.or.th.

Local Calls

Area codes in Thailand have been merged with phone numbers and in theory don't exist anymore.

The prefix 0 must be dialled for all calls made within Thailand, even when calling local numbers in Bangkok. Services such as bus companies and airlines increasingly have four-digit hotline numbers that link directly to customer services. If you need local directory assistance, dial 1133.

Any local number that begins with the prefix 08 denotes a mobile number.

Mobile Phones

Only users of **GSM 900** or **GSM 1800** mobile phones with international roaming facility can hook up automatically to the local Thai network. Check with your service provider if you're not sure, especially if coming from US, Korea or Japan. Your phone will automatically select a local service provider, and this enables you to make calls within Thailand at local rates. However if someone calls your number, international call rates will apply. Charges will be billed to your account in your home country.

If you're planning to travel in Thailand for any length of time, it's more economical to buy a local SIM card with a stored value from a mobile-phone shop. You will be assigned a local number and local calls to and from the phone will be at local rates. International rates will apply if you make overseas calls.

Public Phones

Public telephones accept B1, B5 and B10 coins. Phone cards for local calls in denominations of B50, B100, B200 and B400 can be purchased at convenience shops throughout the city.

Toilets

There are few public toilets in Bangkok, though the city is beginning to address this in

Essential Thai vocab.

tourist areas. Restrooms are usually very dirty and often of the squat-toilet variety, a tricky experience for the uninitiated. Your best bet is usually to sneak into fast-food outlets, which are very easy to find. Shopping malls usually have clean toilets as well, particularly near the food courts. Sometimes a small fee of a few baht applies.

Tourist Information

The **Tourism Authority of Thailand** (TAT) have information outlets in several countries and service kiosks within Thailand that offer maps and other promotional materials as well as advice on things to do and places to see.

Bangkok

TAT Call Centre: tel: 1672. Open daily 8am–8pm.
Airport Information Counter: Arrival Hall, Suvarnabhumi Airport; tel: 0-2132 1888. Open: daily 24 hrs.
Tourism Authority of Thailand Main Office: 1600 Thanon Phetchaburi, Makkasan, Bangkok 10400; tel: 0-2250 5500. Open daily 8.30am–4.30pm.
TAT Tourist Information Counter (Ratchadamnoen): 4 Thanon Ratchadamnoen Nok; tel: 0-2283

1500, ext. 1620. Open daily 8.30am–4.30pm.

Overseas Offices

Australia and New Zealand: Suite 20.02, Level 20, 56 Pitt Street, Sydney, NSW 2000; tel: 61-2 9247 7549.
UK: 3rd Floor, Brook House, 98–99 Jermyn Street, London SW1 6EE; tel: 44-20 7925 2511.
US: 61 Broadway, Suite 2810, New York, NY 10006; tel: 1-212 432 0433; and 611 North Larchmont Blvd, 1st Floor, Los Angeles, CA 90004; tel: 1-323 461 9814.

Visas and Passports

Visa regulations vary for different nationalities. For updated information, check with a Thai embassy or consulate or on the Thai Ministry of Foreign Affairs website (www.mfa.go.th).

All foreign nationals entering Thailand must have passports with at least six month's validity. You can get 60-day tourist visas at the Thai embassy in your home country prior to arrival, or at the airport. Nationals from most countries can get a visa on arrival, valid for 15–90 days, depending on the country. Visas can be extended for 30 days at a time for B1,000 or you can leave the country (even for half an hour) and return to receive another visa on entry.

In total, tourists are allowed to stay in Thailand for a cumulative period not exceeding 90 days within any six-month period from the date of first entry. Overstaying can carry a fine of B500 daily, up to a maximum of B20,000, on leaving the country, but if the police catch you before you leave you may face imprisonment.
Thai Immigration Bureau Government Centre

Chaengwattana, 120 Moo 3, Chaengwattana Road; tel: 0-2141 9889; www.imm.police.go.th; Mon–Fri 8.30am–4.30pm.

Websites

www.tourismthailand.org
The official website of the Tourism Authority of Thailand.
www.bangkokpost.com
Daily news from the *Bangkok Post* daily newspaper.
www.nationmultimedia.com
Daily news clips from *The Nation* newspaper.
www.bangkoktourist.com
Information on Bangkok from the Bangkok Tourist Bureau.
www.langhub.com/en-th
Audio and video files to help foreigners learn Thai, and vice versa.
www.bkmagazine.com
Website of weekly free listings mag with features, events and restaurant reviews.
www.khaosanroad.com
Backpackers resource with accommodation, work advice, upcountry travel, forums etc.

Weights and Measures

Thailand uses the metric system, except for their traditional system of land measurement (1 rai = 1,600 sq metres) and gold (1 baht = 15.2 grams).

Women Travellers

Thailand is generally safe for women travellers, even those travelling alone. Thais tend to be non-confrontational, and the country is generally safe in terms of both casual harassment and serious assault. That said, there have been sporadic cases of rape, particularly when walking alone at night on island beaches.

LANGUAGE

UNDERSTANDING THE LANGUAGE

ORIGINS AND INTONATION

For centuries the Thai language, rather than tripping from foreigners' tongues, has been tripping them up. Its roots go back to the place Thais originated from in the hills of southern China, but these are overlaid by Indian influences. From the original settlers come the five tones that seem designed to frustrate visitors. One sound can have five different tones: high (h), low (l), mid (m), rising (r) and falling (f), and each of these means a different thing from the other (see box).

Therefore, when you mispronounce a word, you don't simply say a word incorrectly, you

THE FIVE TONES

Mid tone (m)**:** Voiced at the speaker's normal, even pitch.
High tone (h)**:** Pitched slightly higher than the mid tone.
Low tone (l)**:** Pitched slightly lower than the mid tone.
Rising tone ®**:** Sounds like a questioning pitch, starting low and rising.
Falling tone (f)**:** Sounds like an English speaker suddenly understanding something: "Oh, I see!"

say another word entirely. It is not unusual to see a semi-fluent foreigner standing before a Thai and running through the scale of tones until suddenly a light of recognition dawns on his companion's face. There are misinformed visitors who will tell you that tones are not important. These people do not communicate with Thais – they communicate at them in a one-sided exchange that frustrates both parties.

PHONOLOGY

The way Thai consonants are written in English often confuses foreigners. An "*h*" following a letter like "*p*" and "*t*" gives the letter a soft sound; without the "*h*", the sound is more explosive. Thus, "*ph*" is not pronounced "*f*" but as a soft "*p*"; without the "*h*", the "*p*" has the sound of a very hard "*b*". The word *thanon* (street) is pronounced "*tanon*" in the same way as "Thailand" is not meant to sound like "*Thighland*". Similarly, final letters are often not pronounced as they look. A "*j*" on the end of a word is pronounced "*t*"; "*l*" is pronounced as an "*n*". To complicate matters further, many words end with "*se*" or "*r*", which are not pronounced.

Vowels are pronounced as follows: **i** as in *sip*, **ii** as in *seep*, **e** as in *bet*, **a** as in *pan*, **aa** as in *car*,

u as in *pool*, **o** as in *so*, **ai** as in *pie*, **ow** as in *cow*, **aw** as in *paw*, **iw** as in *you*, **oy** as in *toy*.

In Thai, the pronouns "*I*" and "*me*" are the same word, but it is different for males and females. Men use the word *phom* when referring to themselves, while women say *chan* or *diichan*. Men use *khrap* at the end of a sentence when addressing either a male or a female to add politeness, or in a similar manner as "please" (the word for "please", *karuna*, is seldom used directly), ie *Pai* (f) *nai*, *khrap* (h) (eg Where are you going, Sir?). Women add the word *kha* to their statements, as in *Pai* (f) *nai*, *kha* (h).

To ask a question, add a high tone *mai* to the end of the phrase ie *rao pai* (we go) or *rao pai mai* (h) (shall we go?). To negate a statement, insert a falling tone *mai* between the subject and the verb ie *rao pai* (we go), *rao mai pai* (we don't go). "Very" or "much" are indicated by adding *maak* to the end of a phrase ie *ron* (hot), *ron maak* (very hot), or *phaeng* (expensive), *phaeng maak* (very expensive), and the opposite *mai phaeng* (not expensive).

THAI NAMES

From the languages of India have come polysyllabic names and words, the lexicon of literature.

Thai names are among the longest in the world. Every Thai person's first and surname has a meaning. Thus, by learning the meaning of the name of everyone you meet, you would acquire a formal, but quite extensive vocabulary.

There is no universal transliteration system from Thai into English, which is why names (and street names) can be spelled in three different ways. For example, the surname Chumsai is written Chumsai, Jumsai and Xoomsai depending on the family. This confuses even the Thais. If you ask a Thai how they spell something, they may well reply, "how do you want to spell it?" So, Bangkok's thoroughfare of Ratchadamnoen is also spelled Ratchadamnern. Ko Samui can be spelled Koh Samui. The spellings will differ from map to map, and from book to book.

To address a person one has never met, the title khun is used for both male and female. Having long and complicated surnames, Thais typically address one another by their first name only and preceded by the title khun for formality, ie Hataichanok Phrommayon becomes Khun Hataichanok. Thais usually adopt nicknames from birth, often accorded to their physical or behavioural attributes as a baby, eg Lek (small), Yai (big), Daeng (red), Moo (pig) etc. If the person is familiar – a friend, relative, or close colleague – then according to the senior age relationship between both persons, they are addressed Pii (if older) or Nong (if younger). So an older friend would be addressed Pii Lek, or if younger Nong Lek.

NUMBERS

0 soon (m)
1 nung (m)
2 song ®
3 sam ®
4 sii (m)
5 haa (f)
6 hok (m)
7 jet (m)
8 bet (m)
9 kow (f)

10 sip (m)
11 sip et (m, m)
12 sip song (m, r)
13 sip sam (m, r) and so on
20 yii sip (m, m)
30 sam sip (f, m) and so on
100 nung roi (m, m)
1,000 nung phan (m, m)

USEFUL WORDS AND PHRASES

Days of the Week

Monday wan jan
Tuesday wan angkan
Wednesday wan phoot
Thursday wan pharuhat
Friday wan sook
Saturday wan sao
Sunday wan athit
today wan nii (h)
yesterday meua wan nii (h)
tomorrow prung nii (h)

Colours

white sii kao
black sii dum
red sii daeng
yellow sii leuang
blue sii num ngern
green sii keeow
orange sii som
pink sii chompoo

Short Phrases

Hello/goodbye Sawadee (a man then says khrap; a woman says kha: thus sawadee khrap or sawadee kha)
How are you? Khun sabai dii, mai (h)
Well, thank you Sabai dii, khopkhun
Thank you very much Khopkhun maak
May I take a photo? Thai roop (f) noi, dai (f) mai (h)
Never mind Mai (f) pen rai
I cannot speak Thai Phuut Thai mai (f) dai (f)
Where do you live? Khun yoo thii (f) nai (r)
What is this called in Thai? An nii (h), kaw riak aray phasa Thai
How much? Thao (f) rai

Directions and Travel

go pai
come maa
where thii (f) nai (r)
right khwaa (r)
left sai (h)
turn leo
straight ahead trong pai
Please slow down Cha cha noi
Stop here Yawt thii (f) nii (f)
fast raew
slow cha
hotel rong raem
street thanon
lane soi
bridge saphan
police station sathanii dtam ruat
ferry reua
longtail boat reua haang yao
train rot fai
bus rot may
skytrain rot fai faa
metro/subway rot fai tai din
pier tha reua
bus stop pai rot may
station sathanii (rot may, rot fai, rot fai faa)

Other Handy Phrases

yes chai (f)
no mai (f) chai (f)
Where's the toilet? Horng narm yoo tee nai
Do you have…? Mii…mai (h)
expensive phaeng
Do you have something cheaper? Mii arai thii thook (l) kwa, mai (h)
Can you lower the price a bit? Kaw lot noi dai (f) mai (h)
Do you have another colour? Mii sii uhn mai (h)
too big yai kern pai
too small lek kern pai
Do you have any in a bigger size? Mii arai thii yai kwa mai (h)
Do you have any in a smaller size? Mii arai thii lek kwa mai (h)
I don't want it Mai ao
hot (heat hot) rawn (h)
hot (spicy) phet
cold yen
sweet waan (r)
sour prio (f)
delicious aroy
I do not feel well Mai (f) sabaiw

FURTHER READING

GENERAL

Mai Pen Rai Means Never Mind by Carol Hollinger. Amusing book describing hilarious experiences in Thailand half a century ago.
Travellers' Tales Thailand edited by James O'Reilly and Larry Habegger. A stimulating collection of observations and true stories.

FICTION

Bangkok Haunts by John Burdett. More hard-boiled capers with the half-Thai, half-American Buddhist policeman of Bangkok 8 fame.
The Beach by Alex Garland. The beach read that inspired the movie starring Leonardo di Caprio about a group of backpackers trying to find their own paradise.
The Big Mango by Jake Needham. An action-adventure story about a search for millions of dollars in cash that went missing during the fall of Saigon in 1975.
Evil in the Land Without by Colin Cotterill. A gripping novel about Detective John Jessel being threatened by a serial killer called "The Paw".
A Killing Smile by Christopher G. Moore. A gripping thriller set in the capital city of Thailand.
Sleepless in Bangkok by Ian Quartermaine. A tough and funny erotic thriller, based on actual events, about an ex-SAS security consultant on a covert assignment to Siam.

HISTORY & SOCIETY

The King Never Smiles: A Biography of Thailand's Bhumibol Adulyadej by Paul M. Handley. An unauthorised portrait of the late King Bhumibol. The book is banned in the kingdom and throughout Southeast Asia.
A History of Thailand by Dr Pasuk Phongpaichit and Chris Baker. Concise and well-informed history, mainly of the Rattanakosin period.
A History of Southeast Asia by D.G.E. Hall. The classic history text.
Jim Thompson: The Legendary American by William Warren. The intriguing story of the American Thai silk magnate, Jim Thompson.
The Revolutionary King: The True-Life Sequel to The King and I by William Stevenson. An intimate portrait of the late King Bhumibol Adulyadej. As monarchy matters are taken very seriously here, the book is unavailable in the kingdom.
Bangkok Then and Now by Steve Van Beek. A hardcover book with many photos both old and new showing how the city has changed in many ways, but also remained the same in others.
The Balancing Act: A History of Modern Thailand by Joseph Wright. Accessible and detailed history of modern Thailand from 1932 to 1991.

ART AND CULTURE

Thai Folk Wisdom: Contemporary Takes on Traditional Proverbs by Tulaya Pornpiriyakulchai and Jane Vejjajiva. Dual-language coffee table book that looks at society through 50 proverbs. Illustrated with paintings by leading Thai artists.
Very Thai: Everyday Popular Culture by Philip Cornwel-Smith. If you've ever wondered why every compound in Thailand has a spirit house or why insect treats are such a hit, this book is for you. A must-read for tourists and residents.

Flavours: Thai Contemporary Art by Steven Pettifor. Brimming with colourful illustrations, this is the only book that offers insights into Thailand's burgeoning contemporary visual arts scene.
The Arts of Thailand by Steve Van Beek and Luca Tettoni. Beautifully illustrated and includes the minor arts.
Things Thai by Tanistha Dansilp and Michael Freeman. Coffee-table book that presents quintessential Thai objects and artefacts.
The Grand Palace by Nngnoi Saksi, Naengnoi Suksri and Michael Freeman. Beautifully illustrated and detailed account of Bangkok's Grand Palace and its surroundings.

RELIGION

A History of Buddhism in Siam by Prince Dhani Nivat. Written by one of Thailand's most respected scholars.
What the Buddha Taught by Walpola Rahula. Comprehensive account of Buddhist doctrine.

COOKERY

Thai Food by David Thompson. Almost 700 pages of traditional recipes and food background from the chef at Europe's only Michelin-starred Thai restaurant.

OTHER INSIGHT GUIDES

The Insight Guides series includes several titles on Thailand, including *Thailand, Thailand's Beaches and Islands, Explore Bangkok*, and *Fleximap Bangkok*.

TRANSPORT

A – Z

LANGUAGE

INSIGHT ◉ GUIDES
OFF THE SHELF

Since 1970, INSIGHT GUIDES has provided a unique perspective on the world's best travel destinations by using specially commissioned photography and illuminating text written by local authors.

Whether you're planning a city break, a walking tour or the journey of a lifetime, our superb range of guidebooks and phrasebooks will inspire you to discover more about your chosen destination.

INSIGHT GUIDES

offer a unique combination of stunning photos, absorbing narrative and detailed maps, providing all the inspiration and information you need.

PHRASEBOOKS & DICTIONARIES

help users to feel at home, when away. Pocket-sized with a free app to download, they go where you do.

CITY GUIDES

pack hundreds of great photos into a smaller format with detailed practical information, so you can navigate the world's top cities with confidence.

EXPLORE GUIDES

feature easy-to-follow walks and itineraries in the world's most exciting destinations, with our choice of the best places to eat and drink along the way.

POCKET GUIDES

combine concise information on where to go and what to do in a handy compact format, ideal on the ground. Includes a full-colour, fold-out map.

EXPERIENCE GUIDES

feature offbeat perspectives and secret gems for experienced travellers, with a collection of over 100 ideas for a memorable stay in a city.

BANGKOK STREET ATLAS

The key map shows the area of Bangkok covered by the atlas section. An index of street names and places of interest shown on the maps can be found on the following pages. For each entry there is a page number and grid reference

Map Legend

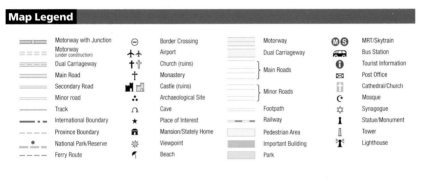

Motorway with Junction	⊖	Border Crossing		Motorway	ⓜⓢ MRT/Skytrain
Motorway (under construction)	✈✈	Airport		Dual Carriageway	🚌 Bus Station
Dual Carriageway	†✝	Church (ruins)	} Main Roads		❶ Tourist Information
Main Road	†	Monastery			✉ Post Office
Secondary Road	🏰	Castle (ruins)	} Minor Roads		✝ Cathedral/Church
Minor road	∴	Archaeological Site			☾ Mosque
Track	∩	Cave		Footpath	✡ Synagogue
International Boundary	★	Place of Interest		Railway	🛉 Statue/Monument
Province Boundary	⌂	Mansion/Stately Home		Pedestrian Area	∏ Tower
National Park/Reserve	※	Viewpoint		Important Building	⌇ Lighthouse
Ferry Route	⌁	Beach		Park	

Rattanakosin, Old City & Dusit

Pathumwan & Pratunam

Chinatown & Thonburi

Bangrak & Silom, Sukhumvit

A | B

PHAYA THAI

1

Chitralada Palace

Th. Sukothai
Soi Suandusit
Soi Sukothai 1
Soi Sukothai 2
Soi Sukothai 3
Soi Sukothai 4
Soi Sukothai 5
Thanon
Thanon Sawankhalok
Rama VI
Soi 4
Soi 5
Soi Bun Chuai
Soi Phai
S Phahon

Thanon Ratchawithi
Thanon
SawanKhalok
2nd State Expressway
Khlong Samsen
Soi Suan Ngen

Prasat Neurological Hospital
Phramongkhut Medical College
Phramongkhutklao Hospital

National Cancer Institute
School for the Blind
Research Institute of Medical Science
Wat Aphai Thayaram
Soi Wat Makog
S. Bandit

Health Hygiene Centre
Ramathibodi Hospital
Mahidol University
War Veterans Organization
Thanon Ratchawithi

Robin

2

Mahidol University
Ministry of Sciences, Technology & Energy
Ratchawithi Hospital
Children's Hospital
Anutsawari Chaisamoraphum (Victory Monument)
Thanon
Soi Loet Panya
S. Wattana

Thanon Sri
2nd State Expressway
Ayutthaya
Mineral Research Museum
Provost Marshal General Dept
Soi Senarak
Yothi
Victory Monument
Thai
S

Buddhist Monk's Hospital
Soi Loet Panya

Mahidol University
Thanon
Soi Loet Panya

RATCHA THEWI
Phaya
Akara Theatre
Soi Polalit
Soi Sombunsuk

Thanon SawanKhalok
Metropolitan Police Headquarters
Thanon
Phaya Thai
S
Sri
Suan Pakkad Palace

3

Petchaburi 1
Soi Man Sin 4
S. Chawakul
S. Wiraya
Decha Hospital
Soi Kolit
PRATUN

Yommarat Market
Soi Man Sin 3
Soi Man Sin 2
Soi Man Sin 1
Soi Phetchaburi 5
Soi Phetchaburi 7
S.Daeng Bunga
Soi Chamsai
S.Aram Si
Thanon
Soi 11
Soi 13

Rama VI
Soi 2
S. Uruphong 1
S. Uruphong 2
S. Uruphong 3
Thanon
Soi 4
Soi 6
Soi 3
Soi 10
Soi 14
Soi 16
Darun Aman Mosque
S.Nom Chit
Soi Senakit
Soi 9
Soi Phetchaburi 13
Church of Christ
Juldis Tower
Soi 15
Center Point
Soi 17
Soi 19
Ba

Phetchaburi
Phetchaburi Market
Wongwian Ratchathewi

4

Wat Phaya Yang
S. D. Coliseum Dept. Store
Thanon Phaya Nak
S. Rongrian Sudarak
S. Rongrian King Phet
Soi Phetchaburi 12
Asia Bldg
S. Phaya Nak
Ratchathewi
S
Soi Phetchaburi 18
S.20
Soi Phetchaburi 13
Panthip Plaza
Soi 22
Soi 24
Soi 26
N

S.Worarit
Student Christian Centre

0 ___ 400 m
0 ___ 400 yards

Khlong Saen Saep
Jim Thompson House Museum
Srapathum Palace

A | B

D
E

Yothin

$ Sanam Pao

TV Channel 5

Thanon Sa Nam Phrao

Thanon Wiphawadirangsit

31

Veterans
General Hospital

Soi Din Daeng

Soi Athiawimon

Soi Santisuk

Soi Phra Nang

Soi Bun Chu Si

Soi Bun Chu

Soi Amnonarumit

Soi Ruamit

Thanon Mit Maitri

Thanon Mit Maitri 2

Thanon Mit Maitri 3

Prachakhom
Church

S. Phen Lae Phuen

1

Din Daeng
Sports Complex &
Auditorium

HUAY KHWANG

S. Rongrian Chamnong

Uthawon
Market

Thanon Prachasongkhro

d State Expressway

Asoke Din Daeng

Thanon

Thanon Mit Maitri 1

Thanon

Asoke

Din

Daeng

S. Rongrian
Ratprasong

Uthai Thip

Soi Uthai Thip

Soi Phrasan Saraban

Soi Pracha Santi

Thanon Din Daeng 1

Ratchanukun
Hospital

Phayathai
Market

Soi Sutthiphon

Trakulnut

Soi Sutthiphon 1

Soi Thatsuwan 1

Soi Sutthiphon 2

Soi Mahawong Nua

Soi Khwanphattana 1

Khwan
Patthana
Market

2

S. Taksiwanich

Soi Wat
Taphan

Ratchaprarop

S. Maphanomsapha

Soi Bun Prarop

Soi Ratchaprarop

S. Ratchadaphan

Soi Morleng

Bangkok
Doll Factory
& Museum

Si Din
Daeng
Market

Soi Tukkhupa

Soi Thimakon

Soi Mae Phra Fatima

Fatima
Church

S. Hemawong

S. Thabsuwan

S. Chumchon

S. Maha-
wong Tai

Soi Mahawong Tai

3

Makkasan
Market

Thanon

Wongwian
Makkasan

Chalerm

Makha

Khlong Samsen

2nd State Expressway

Bung Makkasan

Ratchaprarop

Soi Watthanawong

Soi
Watthanasin

nam
ket

Makkasan
Market

Makkasan
Railway Station

Thanon

Nikhom

Makkasan

Mahanakhon

Railway
Hospital

Soi Hasadin

Chalermlap
Market

Soi 23
Soi 25
Soi 27
S. 29

Soi Chaurat

Soi 33

Soi Phetchaburi 35

Soi 37

Metro
D.S.

31

Expressway

New

Phetchaburi

Soi 39

Soi
41

Hope of
Bangkok Church

TAT

4

Soi 30

Soi 32

Soi Chitlom

Thanon

Petchaburi Hospital

Khlong Saen Saep

Soi Nana Nua

Soi 36

D
E

A   B

S. Wat
Phibye
Tham

**RATTANA-
KOSIN**

SANAM

Thanon   Charoen   Krung   Cha

Thanon Thai Wang

LUANG

Long
Krasuang
Market

Old S
Pla

0   400 m

Tha Tien

Wat Po
(Reclining
Buddha)

Th.Chettuphon

S. Tha
Tien

Th

HiFi

Siri
Singh S

S.
Sanam

Th. Phra
Phiphit

Market

0   400 yards

S. Phatu
Nokyung

Th. Phra Phitak

Pahu
Mar

N

Soi Isaraphap

S. Thanee,
thaphisek

42

Thanon
Chaeng

Khlong Wat

Soi 40

Soi Prok Wat Arun 3

Wat Arun
(Temple of Dawn)

Maharat

Pak Khlong Talad
(Flower Market)

Chai

S. Setthakan

PAHU

Thanon Chakka-

Wat Ratc
burana

1

Thanon Itsaraphap

S. Pr. Wat Arun 1

S. Pr. Wat Arun 2

S. Yuthia
Saksa

S. Prok
Wat Arun 1

Vichaiprasit
(Old Fort)

Rajinee

Thanon Ban Mo

Asadang

Phet

**Phra
Buddha Yo
Monument**

Phak
Khlong
Talad

Yot Phimai
Market

Thanon Saphan

S. Wat Hong

Thanon Wang Doem

Thanon Arun Amarin

Phosamton
Market

Soi 38

**Wat
Kalayanamit**

S. Wat Kanlaya

Memorial
Bridge

Phut

Saphan Phra

Pok Kiao

Soi 36

**Santa Cruz
Church**

S. Kudi Chain

Saphan Phra Buddha Yodfa
[Memorial Bridge]

Wangw
Lek Ma

Soi 34

Santa Cruz
Convent

2

Thanon Itsaraphap

Soi Itsaraphap 28

Soi 23

Soi 32

Soi 30

Th. Thetsaban Sai 1

Soi Pho

**Wat Prayun-
wongsawat**

S. Khlong Thom

Th. Phra Mai

Somdet Chao Praya

Soi Somdet Chao Praya

S. Somdet Phaya

Soi Uthai

Soi Isaraphap 21

Thanon

Thetsaban Sai 2

Soi 26

Thanon Thetsaban Sai 2

**Thonburi
Christian
Hall**

Th. Thetsaban Sai 3

Thanon

THONBURI

Soi 19

Soi 17/1

Soi 15

S. 22

Soi 24

S. Montri

Prachathipok

Soi 16

Soi 14

Thanon

Soi 10

Khlong Bangkok Yai

Thanon Itsaraphap

Soi 20

Soi 18

Soi 12

3

Soi Phet Kasem 4

Khlong Bang Sakai

Soi 13

Soi 11

Soi 9

S. Khang Rong Rap
Chamnam

Thanon

Soi 5

Soi 3

Soi 8

Soi 6

Itsara

Soi 7/1

Soi 9

**Wat Yai
Si Suphan**

S. Saraphi 2
S. Saraphi

S. Khiao
Chinda

Mittraphab
Hospital

Central D. S.

Thanon

Lad

Ya

Soi 11

Th. Phetkasem

Naowachamnian
Bridge

Th. Intharaphithak

**Taksin
Circle Wongwian Yai**
(King Taksin Mon.)

S.Saeng-
muang

Soi Wiset San

Soi 2

Rat

Soi 12

Charoen
Rat Market

Charoen

Soi Suthisuk

4

Th. Thoet Thai

**Wongwian Yai
Railway Station**

Thanon

Soi 4

Soi Ratruam
Charoen

Soi Ratying
Charoen

Tr. Yenchit

**Wat Th
Phl**

Tr.
Ratchawadi

Soi 5

Soi 1

Soi Saksin

Tr. Nai
Thorigbai

Tr. Manawitthaya

S. Sanchao Arnew

A   B

Wat Sa Bua

State Railway of Thailand

Chongchin Hospital

Wat Thepsirin

Central Hospital

Wat Phiapphla Chai

Nakhon Kasem Market

San Chao Dtai Hong Kong

Wat Chai Chana Songkram

CHINATOWN

Wat Mangkon Kamalawat

Wat Kanikaphon Li Thi Miew

Railway Police Station

Sampeng Market

Wat Chakrawat

Yaowarat

Kwongsew Hospital

Cathay D.S.

Phutalet Market

Ga Buang Kim

Huai Choi Kanh Temple

Hualamphong Railway Station

Talad Kao Market

San Chao Kao

1 Soi Wiwat Wiang
2 Th. Bamrung Rat
3 Th. Soem Sinkha
4 Th. Plaeng Nam

Wat Traimit (Temple of the Golden Buddha)

Rachawongse

Mae

Nam

Chao

Wat Pathuma Kongkha

Hualamphong

Th. Rama IV

Th. Kao Lan

Swat Market

Chakkawat Market

Wat Thong Thammachat

Wat Thong Nopphakhun

Marine Dept.

Phraya

Kalawa (Rosary Church)

River City Shopping Centre

Chao

Praya

Somdet Chao Praya Hospital

Taksin Hospital

Thanon Si Phraya

St Joseph Hospital

Morphetch Morphloy Market

Si Phraya

Thanon

Lad

Ya

Rat

BANGRAK

General Post Office (G.P.O.)

Wat Muang Kae

KHLONG SAN

Haroon Mosque

Khlong Wat Thong Phleng

Wat Suwan Ubasikaram

Mahesak Hospital

Oriental

Assumption Convent

Assumption Cathedral

Wat Suan Phlu

State Tower

Soi Charoen Nakhon 14

SIAM

Charoenphol Market

Thanon Rama I

Bangkok Art & Culture Centre

Siam Discovery Centre

Srapathum Palace

Siam Paragon

Siam Centre

Wat Pathumwanaram

Muang 5

National Stadium

National Stadium

S. Siam Square

Siam

Th.

Rama I

Thong

Soi 6

Soi 8

Soi 10

Mahboonkrong Shopping Centre (MBK)

S. Siam Square

Siam Square

Soi Chulalongkorn 64

SQUARE

PATHUMWAN

Th. Charat Muang

Banthat

Soi Chulalongkorn 7

Soi 14

Soi 16

Soi 18

Soi Chulalongkorn 12

Soi Chulalongkorn 62

Uthenthawai Technological School

Prathumwan Sinaicha Rintharawirot University

Royal Bangkok Sports Club (R.B.S.C.)

Batchada

Suan Luang Market

Soi 20

Chulalongkorn Property Office

Chulalongkorn Health Dept.

Triem Udom Suksa School

Thai

Phaya

Dunant

Soi 24

Soi 26

Soi 28

S. Chulalongkorn 22

Chulalongkorn 9

Stadium Charusathian

National History Museum

Imaging Technology Museum

Chulalongkorn University

Henri

Thanon

Prathumwan

Soi Chulalongkorn

Soi 32

Soi 34

Thanon

Soi 38

Soi 40

Soi Chulalongkorn 42

Soi 44

Soi 48

Soi 50

S. 11

S.15

Soi 52

Prathumwan D.O.

Soi 36

Thanon Rama IV

Saphan Luang Chinese Church

S.54

Sam Yan

S.Chulalongkorn 60

Soi 58

Chulai 56

The Thai Red Cross Society

Queen Saovabha Memorial Institute (Snake Farm)

Prathumwan Waterworks

Chulalongkorn Hospital

S. Phra Nakharet

Th. Kit Phanit

Tr. Morsun

Soi Song Phra

S. Chom Sombun

S. Saphan Tia

S. Chinda Thawin

S. Somtan Panya

Tr. Lang Wat Hua Lamphong

Sap

Maiwat Hua

Thanon

Charn Issara Tower

Si Lom

Rama VI Stat (King Monkhu

Thanon Si Phraya

Thanon

Surawong

Wallstreet Tower

Ram

BANGRAK

Soi Santi Phap 1

Soi Santi Phap

Naret

Thanon

Soi Thian Thawin

Soi Pradit

Bangkok Christ. Hosp

Foodland D.S.

Silom Sala Daeng

Soi Phuttha-Osot

Neilson Hays Library

American International Tower

Anuman

Rajchon

ITF Silom Palace Bldg

Boonmitr Bldg.

CP Tower

St Joseph Convent

Sathorn Hospital

Th. Surawong

S. Prasan

S. Prachun

S. Pradit

Decho

Soi 14

Soi 16

Xavier Church

Silom Plaza

Thanon

Narathiwat Ratchanakharin (Chong Nonsi)

Soi 7

Soi 5

Soi Silom 3

Soi Phiphat 2

S. Chongrahoras

Soi Sala Daeng 2

Thanon Sala Daeng

Soi Sala Dae

Soi Sala 1

Christ Church

Soi Pramot 1

Soi Pramot 2

Silom Village

Soi 20

S. Prachum

Soi 22

Soi 24

Silom

Soi Silom 9

Soi Silom 13

Suksa

Soi Silom 11

Witharak

Soi Phiphat 1

Soi Phiphat

City Plaza

Sathorn

Sathorn

Frenc Associatio

Central Dept Store

Maha Uma Devi Temple (Wat Khaek)

Soi 17

Th. Pramuan

Th. Pan

Chong Nonsi

Bangkok Bible College

Sathorn Thani Bldg

Thanon

Soi Suanphu

S.Suan phu 2 S. Thana-slip

Soi 19

Thanon

Soi Phra Phimj

400 m

400 yards

N

D

Robinson D.S.
hadamri
Thai Daimaru D.S.
Siam Pen House IV
rana 1 S.C. (icr. Cent.)
Soi Chitlom
Soi Tonson
Thanon Withayu
Loet
31

Bank of America Building

Central D.S.

Ploenchit Arcade S.C.

Chit Lom Thanon
Erawan
Maneeya Center D.S.
a S.C.
Ploenchit
Soi Nai
Phloen Chit
Mahatun Plaza S.C.

Tourist Shopping Plaza

Soi Ruen Rudi 1
Soi Sukhumvit 1
Soi Sukhumvit 3
Bumrungrad Hospital

SUKHUMVIT

Soi 5
Soi 7

Seth Insaf Tower

Shiva Tower

1

Thanon
Sukhumvit
SUKHUMVIT
Soi Sukhumvit 4
Soi Sukhumvit 11
Soi Sukhumvit 13
Soi Sukhumvit 15

Soi 2
Nana
Shopping
Thanon Sukhumvit
Area Sukhumvit

ntlek Luang 1

Suan
Soi Tonson (Wireless Road)

ntlek Luang 2

Soi Lang Suan 1
Soi Lang Suan 2
Soi Ruam Rudi
Soi 1
Jai Smarn Church
SNC Tower
Soi 17

ntlek Luang 3

Lang
Soi Lang Suan 3
Soi Lang Suan 4
Soi Lang Suan 5
Soi Lang Suan 6
Soi Lang Suan 7

Soi 3
Soi Ruam Rudi 2
Soi 4
Soi 5

Sunstar Complex
Omni Complex

Orchid Tower
Golden Tower
Asok

Soi Sukhumvit 8

Soi 12

2

Calvary Baptist Church
Soi Ulit
Soi Sama Han

S.Ruam Rudi
Holy Redeemer Church

hanon Sarasin

Chalerm
Mahanakhon
Khlong Phai Singto
Evangelical Church

Withayu

S. Polo

JAN

MPHINI
(MPHINI PARK)

S. Phra Chen

S. Sanam Khli

Thanon

Expressway

3

Ratchada

BENJAKITTI PARK

ang
ation
ng
Cathay Trust Bldg

YWCA
College
JUSMAG

Nua
Tai
Soi Atthakan

Goethe Institute

Goethegasse

Thai-Belgium Bridge
Lumphini
Thanon Rama IV

Queen Sirikit National Convention Centre

4

Prasit
Soi Ngam Duphli
S. Saphankhu
S. Sawatsawat
Thai-Belgium Br.
Khlong Toel
Thanon Rama IV

Soi Nantha
Bhirasri Institute of Modern Art

D

E

STREET INDEX

ART AND PHOTO CREDITS

INDEX

INSIGHT ⊙ GUIDES
BANGKOK

Editor: Carine Tracanelli
Updater: Simon Stewart
Head of Production: Rebeka Davies
Pictures: Tom Smyth
Cartography: original cartography
Berndtson & Berndtson, updated by
Carte

Distribution

UK, Ireland and Europe
Apa Publications (UK) Ltd
sales@insightguides.com

United States and Canada
Ingram Publisher Services
ips@ingramcontent.com

Australia and New Zealand
Woodslane
info@woodslane.com.au

Southeast Asia
Apa Publications (SN) Pte
singaporeoffice@insightguides.com

Hong Kong, Taiwan and China
Apa Publications (HK) Ltd
hongkongoffice@insightguides.com

Worldwide
Apa Publications (UK) Ltd
sales@insightguides.com

Special Sales, Content
Licensing and CoPublishing

Insight Guides can be purchased in
bulk quantities at discounted prices.
We can create special editions,
personalised jackets and corporate
imprints tailored to your needs.
sales@insightguides.com;
www.insightguides.biz

Printing

CTPS-China

First Edition 1988
Sixth Edition 2017

ABOUT THIS BOOK

This new edition of *City Guide Bangkok* was commissioned by Managing Editor **Carine Tracanelli** and was thoroughly updated by **Simon Stewart**, who has lived in Thailand since 2003. As a travel writer, Stewart has contributed to other Insight Guides, magazines and books about Southeast Asia and has also written for online media publications.

This edition builds on the success of an earlier edition produced by the late **Howard Richardson**. An award-winning feature writer, he contributed a monthly column to the Thai Airways inflight magazine *Sawasdee* for six years

and wrote for publications such as *GQ* and the BBC's food magazine *Olive*. He was also the editor of *Bangkok Metro*, when it was Thailand's biggest selling English-language magazine. Richardson worked on numerous Insight Guides to Bangkok and Thailand.

Past contributors also include **Francis Dorai** and **Steven Pettifor** as well as authors **Sarah Rooney**, **Chami Jotisalikorn** and **Dr Andrew Forbes**.

Among the talented photographers whose images bring Bangkok to life are Jason Lang (whose work has been featured in *Wallpaper* and *Travel and Leisure*), Peter Stuckings and Marcus Wilson-Smith.

SEND US YOUR THOUGHTS

We do our best to ensure the information in our books is as accurate and up-to-date as possible. The books are updated on a regular basis using local contacts, who painstakingly add, amend, and correct as required. However, some details (such as telephone numbers and opening times) are liable to change, and we are ultimately reliant on our readers to put us in the picture.

We welcome your feedback, especially your experience of using the book "on the road". Maybe we

recommended a hotel that you liked (or another that you didn't), or you came across a great bar or new attraction that we missed.

We will acknowledge all contributions, and we'll offer an Insight Guide to the best letters received.

Please write to us at:
Insight Guides
PO Box 7910, London SE1 1WE
Or email us at:
hello@insightguides.com